The American Institute of Architects Guide to Dallas Architecture

With Regional Highlights

Larry Paul Fuller
Editor

D1550690

American Institute of Architects
Dallas Chapter

McGraw·Hill Construction Information Group

First edition, May 1999. Printed in the United States of America.

Guidebook Committee
Larry Good, FAIA, Chairman
Nestor Infanzon, AIA; Dennis Stacy, FAIA; Willis Winters, AIA

Editor
Larry Paul Fuller

Writing Team
Foreword, Guide to the Guide: Larry Good, FAIA
Overview: Larry Paul Fuller
Chapter Introductions: Lisa Germany, Larry Good
Project Entries: Willis Winters, Jim Steely, Ray Don Tilley, Mark Denton
Index: Jim Steely

Design
FD&S (Fuller Dyal & Stamper), Austin, Texas
Herman Ellis Dyal, AIA, with Jill Wittnebel, Andrea Castañeda, Christopher Muñiz

Guidebook Photographer
Craig Blackmon, AIA

Cover Photograph
The Flying Red Horse atop the 1921 Magnolia building was the signature element of the Dallas skyline for decades. Photo by Craig Blackmon, AIA.

Production
Paul Herrmannsfeldt, McGraw-Hill Construction Information Group, John Foschino and Wayne L. Peiser, McGraw-Hill Corporate Manufacturing

Library of Congress Cataloging-in-Publication Data
The American Institute of Architects guide to Dallas Architecture:
  with regional highlights / Larry Paul Fuller, editor; American
Institute of Architects, Dallas Chapter. — 1st ed.
      p. cm.
  Includes bibliographical references and index.
  ISBN 0-07-982381-5
    1. Architecture — Texas — Dallas Metropolitan Area Guidebooks.
  2. Architecture — Texas — Fort Worth Metropolitan Area Guidebooks.
  3. Dallas Metropolitan Area (Texas) Guidebooks. 4. Fort Worth
Metropolitan Area (Texas) Guidebooks. I. Fuller, Larry Paul.
II. American Institute of Architects. Dallas Chapter. III. Title:
Guide to Dallas Architecture.
NA735.D2A43 1999
720'.9764'2812 — dc21   99-26176
                                                                CIP

Contents

Acknowledgements

The design and production of this comprehensive guide would not have been possible without the dedication of an elite volunteer committee of the Dallas Chapter AIA. Nestor Infanzon, Dennis Stacy, FAIA, and Willis Winters covered miles of Dallas streets; combed books, magazines and newspaper articles for facts; and provided valued advice and welcomed criticism at every decision point along the way. These architects know our region like few others. They are talented and special friends.

I want to thank my firm, Good Fulton & Farrell Architects, for tolerating my divided attention for two years, and for being a major financial investor with the Dallas Chapter AIA to design, write, and secure photography for the Guide. Although more than 350 photographs in the book are the fine work of Dallas photographer Craig Blackmon, AIA, many architects and their photographers, local and beyond, unselfishly lent images to us for publication, and I extend our gratitude.

The Austin-based design and communication firm, FD&S, was selected over two other highly qualified teams to design the Guide and to write the text. Herman Dyal's graphic touch and Larry Paul Fuller's editorial leadership have been exemplary. I also want to recognize Jill Wittnebel and Andrea Castañeda (layout) and Christopher Muñiz (maps) of FD&S for their contributions to the book. Mapsco, Inc., of Dallas, was a valued and supportive resource for our maps.

The writing team deserves special thanks. Mark Denton, Lisa Germany, Jim Steely, Ray Don Tilley, and Willis Winters each skillfully wrote building descriptions or chapter introductions – sometimes with precious little to work from. Willis took on the inner city chapters, which required a mountain of research and invaluable attention to detail.

For assistance with research we want to recognize the following: Carol Roark, manager of the Texas/Dallas History and Archives Division, Dallas Public Library; "Historic Preservation Council for Tarrant County, Texas" and its Historic Resources Survey, cosponsored with the Texas Historical Commission; Texas Historical Commission Library, Austin, and its designation files for the National Register of Historic Places and Recorded Texas Historic Landmarks.

Finally, we want to thank McGraw Hill Construction Information Group, who agreed to publish the Guide under such favorable terms that the project reached feasibility. And a generous stipend from the A.H. Belo Foundation closed the final gap, allowing us to move forward confidently with a book from which we hope many will benefit. – *Larry Good, FAIA, Chairman, Dallas Chapter AIA Guidebook Committee*

Foreword

This is the third guide to Dallas architecture, after *The Prairie's Yield* (1962), and *Dallasights* (1978), but the first to attempt a comprehensive survey of historic and contemporary buildings, gardens, parks and outdoor sculpture in a topographic format to facilitate touring. Like the earlier guides, this one is produced under the auspices of the Dallas Chapter of the American Institute of Architects (AIA), a regional professional association of approximately 1,400 architects and affiliate members, and one of the nation's largest and most active AIA chapters. The chapter is committed to excellence in architecture, service to the public, and the continuing education of its membership.

The Guide is offered with several objectives. It will introduce professional and lay visitors to the richness of the region's architecture and will also be a resource to area residents, serving to increase their knowledge of the architects and architecture that have shaped the urban fabric of greater Dallas. The *AIA Guide to Dallas Architecture* arrives at a time when growth and development threaten earlier generations of buildings. It is hoped that our inclusion and documentation of meritorious buildings will increase appreciation of our architectural heritage and encourage its preservation.

The geographic area covered by the book includes those areas within roughly a 50-mile radius of downtown Dallas. Although selections are admittedly weighted toward Dallas, we have also attempted to include the best "Regional Highlights" from Fort Worth and the Hinterlands. The time span covered begins with the rare remaining pioneer houses and courthouses of the mid-to-late nineteenth century and ends with projects to be completed in 1999.

To be selected for the guide a project had to meet at least one of the following criteria: (1)Excellence in design. (2)Representative of the work of an influential architect (local or otherwise). (3)Representative of a characteristic period in the region's architectural history. (4)Contributing to the physical character of an important neighborhood or district. (5)Part of a significant ensemble of buildings. (6)A building attracting keen public attention and discussion. (7)A noteworthy eccentricity.

Selections were made by our committee of four, uninfluenced by any sponsor or higher AIA authority. We could not resist looking at Dallas architecture with a discerning eye. The brief text for each entry may contain opinions as well as more factual observations and descriptions. The opinions expressed are those of the authors, not of the Dallas Chapter AIA. Efforts have been made to ensure the accuracy of the documentation in the Guide. However, we invite readers who are aware of any inaccuracies to report these to the Dallas Chapter AIA office, so that we may correct them in our next edition. – *Larry Good, FAIA*

Guide to the Guide

This is a guide to the man-made structures, gardens, parks, outdoor sculpture and other features that make up the physical environment of the greater Dallas metropolitan region. Utilizing a topographic format, each chapter presents a geographic sector of the region, introduced by a short essay on the history, development and current character of that district, and a map that locates the building sites.

Of necessity, these maps are drawn to different scales, as indicated by the gridded border around the edge of each map, which is drawn at four segments per mile to give the reader a sense of changing scale. And regardless of scale, in order to communicate the texture of the city, all streets are shown on each map, although not all streets are labeled. In smaller districts, such as the two Downtowns, Uptown, and the Park Cities, a supplementary map may not be required, but for the avid architectural tourist, we suggest the purchase of a Mapsco Guide to assist in navigation of vast areas and to find those entries which fall "off map."

With rare exception, vehicular rather than pedestrian travel will be necessary to tour the work featured. The chapters are sequenced to begin in Downtown Dallas and move in an outward spiral, first to urban neighborhoods, then to the suburbs, on to Fort Worth, and finally to the outlying counties with their world class late-nineteenth century courthouses.

The entries section and photographs comprise the bulk of each chapter. Each entry identifies the building, its address, date of completion, name of architect or designer (if known), and provides a brief description. More than half of the entries are accompanied by photographs. Occasionally, where a district contains a significant cluster of buildings by a single important architect, a highlighted page or pages includes a brief biographical sidebar.

Also, in order to broaden the scope of the Guide in minimum space, we frequently mention a nearby building of merit, a noteworthy interior, or public art within the text of a related entry. These "mentions" are typically highlighted in boldfaced type.

Entities are identified by the building name current as of time of publication and in some cases, secondarily, by a well-known popular or historic name. Residences are identified solely by address; owners' names are listed on rare occasion when the house has become widely known to the public by that name (Aldredge House, Rachofsky House, Elbert Williams Residence).

In some cases, buildings obscured or not visible from public thoroughfare are included as a duty to record works of particular significance. This being said, we emphasize that the inclusion of a building in this guide does not mean the owners have given permission to enter the grounds or the building. Please respect the privacy of the occupants of these buildings and avoid trespassing.

Overview

Dallas architecture is not great." So observed the authors of *The Prairie's Yield*, the first significant guide to the city's architecture, published by the Dallas Chapter of the American Institute of Architects (AIA) as hosts of the 1962 AIA national convention. Their cautious assessment remains somewhat valid today after almost four subsequent decades of building, if only as a sweeping generalization.

Dallas architecture is *not* great, as a whole – certainly not on an international level, nor as compared to the fabric of archetypal American cities such as New York, Chicago, and Philadelphia. But if Dallas architecture is not great, it does indeed have its great *moments*.

Many of the works included in this book are of interest primarily as refreshing departures from local norms – a successful flourish here, a modest innovation there. Some are notable as museum-piece examples of period styles, or as components of local traditions or of a fondly regarded body of work. Some are exceptional for their illumination of regional sensibilities, or perhaps for their ambitious scale and prominence. But some works, a rare few, are truly distinguished and legitimately should make Dallas proud.

In the Beginning. The quick-read account of Dallas' origin and continued prosperity, disseminated like gospel through the years, is conveniently tidy but essentially true: the emergence of what is now the eighth-largest city in America from an improbable setting of dismal prairie is due to the sheer force of will and a prevailing entrepreneurial spirit first manifested in 1841 when a Tennessee lawyer named John Neely Bryan set up a trading post near the three forks of the Trinity River for the purpose of trading with the Indians. Several years later, Bryan filed a claim for 640 acres of adjoining land. Without the benefit of European influences that helped shape America's northeastern cities, he pragmatically laid out a uniform grid oriented toward the bluff of the river and called it a city. Bryan did set aside one block for a courthouse. But, rather like inheriting a bad set of teeth, Dallas was thus born with an imperfect spatial configuration that – through various forms of corrective effort and compensation through the years – it has tried to overcome.

The one obvious topographical asset of the new town, which Neely called "Dallas" in honor of a friend by that name, was the Trinity River. But this fickle waterway proved unsuitable for its envisioned role as a steamboat link to the Gulf (and, indeed, the question of how to capitalize on the Trinity as an urban amenity remains among the city's top planning priorities).

With little economic benefit to be had from the river, the establishment of railroad connections became an objective that was pursued with legendary can-do spirit and deal-making acumen. In 1872, city leaders used cash and right-of-way offers to attract the north-south Houston and Texas Central Railroad, which had planned to bypass Dallas to the east. After the later arrival of the east-west Texas and Pacific, Dallas became a commercial crossroads. Goods such as hides, garments, farm implements, and agricultural products fueled commerce in Dallas, which had grown to a population of 20,000 by 1885. These mercantile activities spawned an enclave of factories and warehouses that lives on as the West End Historic District. Here is ample evidence of the then-popular Chicago School commercial style, with its flat roofs, overhanging cornices, and broad rectangular windows. Efforts to restore and revitalize the 20-block area as an enclave of offices, restaurants, clubs, and shops have yielded what is essentially a commercially successful tourist zone.

Commerce Takes Off. With the city's commercial machinery running smoothly by the turn of the century, as the population moved toward 100,000, one industry built upon another, evolving toward today's economy of diversified interests: food, fiber, banking, insurance, electronics, petroleum, retailing, and fashion. The latter category, an ongoing source of cachet for this style-conscious city, can be traced back to 1907 when Neiman Marcus opened downtown as an exclusive clothing store for women. Some 50 years later, Dallas' preoccupation with style became institutionalized when young developers Trammell Crow and John Stemmons began what is now the Dallas Market Center. As the world's largest wholesale trading complex, these monumentally-scaled buildings range architecturally from the relatively modest, fifties-era Decorative Center to the Infomart, an overt reference to London's Crystal Palace.

If it was the railroad that led to Dallas' first waves of commercial development, it was the new regional airport that opened up whole new realms of economic promise, resulting in explosive growth. Situated roughly half-way between Dallas and Fort Worth, and as large as the island of Manhattan, the D/FW Regional Airport opened in 1973 to serve a vast territory now numbering almost five million people. D/FW became even more than the focal point of a new megamarket known as the Metroplex. It became a new gateway to the world. The sky, in a metaphor by visionary Dallas mayor Eric Jonsson, became Dallas' ocean.

Sizing up the Skyline. Approaching the city by freeway from virtually any direction, one is struck by the contrast in terrain as the cluster of tall buildings that is downtown Dallas erupts from endless prairie as if by some mysterious force. **[Special Moment: Viewing the skyline from the Trinity levees at sunset.]** Of course "tall" is a relative term, and Dallas hasn't pushed for big-league status when it comes to world rankings of building height. The 1986 NationsBank Plaza, by JPJ Architects, the city's tallest building at 921 feet, ranks only about 35th worldwide and barely makes the U.S. top 20.

Despite its height, and its two miles of green argon lighting, NationsBank Plaza is not the main visual cue to one of America's most readily identifiable skylines. Since its opening in 1978, Welton Becket's Hyatt Regency Hotel and Reunion Tower has been the primary signature element – the only modern-day Dallas icon that rivals the giant Flying Red Horse atop the city's first skyscraper, the 1922 Magnolia Building. The Hyatt's sculpted, stepped forms with their glitzy, dazzling sheen – punctuated so boldly by the adjacent tower and sphere – create an unforgettable ensemble that captures the spirit of Dallas like no other single element of the cityscape.

Out of a very respectable line-up of post-70s Dallas office towers, one of the best shares the Hyatt's role as a defining skyline element. The Wells Fargo Bank at Fountain Place (1987), designed by Henry Cobb of I.M. Pei's office, is a bold exercise in abstract minimalism employing shimmering expanses of smooth, cool-green glass in colliding trapezoids and triangles. The impact of the huge tower base is softened at ground level by landscape architect Dan Kiley's spectacular public plaza – a "fountain place" of cascading and falling water complemented by orderly ranks of cypress trees.

Three nearby skyscrapers, all credited to Richard Keating (then of Skidmore, Owings & Merrill), stand in contrast to the Modernist sensibilities of Fountain Place. The 1984 Trammell Crow Center is an elegant tower of glossy charcoal granite that alludes to the classic forms of early skyscrapers through its three-part composition of base, shaft, and pointed top. The somewhat excessive Chase Bank Tower of 1987 is memorable for the five-story slit that penetrates the building near its top (actually a practical, as well as iconographic, gesture that reduces wind load). Keating's third skyline contribution – Renaissance Tower – is exactly what it looks like: a plain 1970s glass box (by Hellmuth, Obata & Kassabaum, with Harwood K. Smith & Partners) that was redecorated with a new curtain wall pattern and adorned with whimsical towers on top. These protrusions reflect the same impulse that resulted in the giant weather beacon atop the Republic National Bank Building of 1955. Another notable skyline shape is the now-endangered Mercantile Bank's four-sided clock with spire – a quirky composition that could pass for contemporary "retro." Some views of this once-dominant 1940s icon have been obscured by the bank's new building – Philip Johnson's Bank One Center of 1987, with its colossal barrel-vaulted copper roofs.

The Scene Downtown. The tall buildings that emerge so abruptly from the core of the city do so with varying degrees of finesse and amenity at ground level. Most make at least some ingratiating gestures to pedestrians – bronze sculptures at the base of Trammell Crow Center, for example. Two of the most ambitious tower-related public spaces – the sunken plazas at One Main Place and

NationsBank Plaza – lack the appeal of similar gestures in denser urban environments where open space offers such a welcome relief. Even in the densest zones of downtown Dallas, one scarcely ever escapes a sense, if not a glimpse, of the wide open spaces beyond.

After its inauspicious beginnings as a mundane grid with one token public block, the city has managed through the years to take a number of steps toward downtown urban grandeur. Actually, the first major departure from the regular grid was due less to fore-thought than a lack thereof. Still in its infancy, the city grew beyond John Neely Bryan's original plat via an adjoining plat whose orientation deviated from the original by 30°. The result is a sometimes confusing, but always potentially interesting, departure from rectilinearity such as that seen in the leftover triangle that became Thanks-Giving Square and that has informed the geometry of buildings such as One Dallas Center, Energy Plaza, and 1700 Pacific.

In 1910, community leaders expressed their aspirations for a more beautiful (and less flood-prone) city by hiring George Kessler, of Kansas City and St. Louis, to create a city plan. Though Kessler's grand vision was never fully implemented, his legacy is significant. Public spaces attributable to his influence include Ferris Plaza, across from Union Station; the infamous Dealey Plaza, whose role as the city's western gateway has been superceded by its place in history as the site of the Kennedy assassination; Central Expressway, originally designed as a grand boulevard linking downtown to points north; and that most conspicuous nod to the City Beautiful Movement, the scenic Turtle Creek Parkway leading northward to Dallas' most affluent neighborhoods. [Special Moment: A leisurely drive northward along Turtle Creek Boulevard.]

Ascending Aspirations. As in any American city, vast portions of the built environment in Dallas have been shaped by an absence of aesthetic ambition among those who build – a void often filled by pragmatic sensibilities and an emphasis on minimizing cost to maximize profit. In some cases architectural ambition is squelched by a conservative bent that keeps buildings safely removed from the cutting edge. In other cases, high ambition is reflected in desperate, misguided attempts at monumentality (as in that ubiquitous bloated and grotesquely proportioned tract house type known as the "North Dallas Special," a modern-day caricature of classic architectural styles.) But there are also instances in which entrepreneurial spirit, civic pride, and high architectural aspirations have coalesced in Dallas to produce exceptional public buildings and places.

During the 1930s – in a well-orchestrated promotional coup not unlike the civic collaboration that brought the railroads to Dallas – the city succeeded in being selected over older, more historically significant cities to host the 1936 Texas Centennial

Exposition, a world's fair celebrating the 100th anniversary of
Texas' independence from Mexico. In less than a year, a mammoth
design and construction effort coordinated by Dallas architect
George Dahl yielded a collection of exhibition buildings and museums on the grounds of the State Fair of Texas that collectively represent Dallas' grandest architectural vision and purest Beaux-Arts
sensibilities. Designated a National Historic Landmark, Fair Park is
built around the grand Hall of State as its centerpiece. The Hall is
notable for its Art Deco style and as a collaborative effort involving
architects, artists, and craftsmen. **[Special Moment: A stroll from Fair
Park's Parry Avenue gate along The Esplanade to the Hall of State.]**

It wasn't until 1978, with the opening of I.M. Pei's monumental
Dallas City Hall, that the city began to reassert itself architecturally
through its civic institutions. (Much of the energy behind this
process is credited to mayor Erik Jonsson, who hired Pei even before
the architect's reputation had been fully established.) The City Hall
– with its aggressive forms and tilted facade, set against a vast open
plaza – marked Dallas' debut as a player in the upper echelons of
contemporary American architecture. The City Hall was followed
by Fisher & Spillman's Central Research Library, located directly
across the plaza as an architecturally sympathetic complement to
Pei's design. Just west of City Hall, the Dallas Convention Center
(built in 1957 and unsympathetically extended three times since
then) does its job of delivering the air-conditioned space and loading docks required for large-scale national conventions.

As early as 1977, the city began defining a 20-block area in the
northwest zone of downtown (between Ross Avenue and Woodall
Rogers Freeway) as the Arts District. Its first architectural manifesta-
tion was the Dallas Museum of Art, which opened to rave reviews
in 1984 as an elegant continuation of the Modernist lineage of
Edward Larrabee Barnes. A 140,000-sq.-ft. addition designed by
Barnes, the Hamon Building of 1993, uses the same scored Indiana
limestone and pure geometric forms to create a seamless extension
of the original rather than an obvious appendage.

Linked to the museum at the other end of the district via Flora
Street (the landscaped central spine) is yet another civic-architecture
tour de force – the 1989 Morton H. Meyerson Symphony Center
by I.M. Pei. Also built in Indiana limestone, the Meyerson features
an austere, yet grand, multilevel lobby – with both flat and circular
expanses of glass curtain wall – that gives way to the intimate,
wood-clad Eugene McDermott Concert Hall within.

After years of no further progress, the Arts District seems
poised to move into its next phase of development, beginning with
the proposed Nasher Sculpture Garden, two acres of outdoor
sculpture donated by developer Raymond Nasher along Flora and
Harwood Streets. A proposed performing arts center would provide

space for the Dallas Opera, the Dallas Theater Center, the Dallas Children's Theater, and other groups. Also being planned is a mixed-use development between Pearl and Olive that would include residential and retail functions.

Just across Woodall Rogers from the Arts District, as if taking a cue from its neighbors, the Federal Reserve Bank of 1992 makes another stunning architectural statement. Designed by Kohn Pederson Fox of New York, and Sikes Jennings Kelly & Brewer of Houston, this landmark building combines the high-tech look of aluminum and glass with the stability of limestone, a curved blade of which slices through the tower as a signature element. Standing in contrast to the contemporary feel of the bank is Philip Johnson's nearby mixed-use postmodern stage-set, The Crescent.

Corporate Suburbia and Beyond. Architectural monumentality does not end in Dallas with the CBD; in a sense, the corporate havens of the suburbs is where it really begins. At Legacy, for example – a master-planned business community in Plano – one is struck, not so much by the architectural quality of the corporate complexes built there, but by their sheer magnificence. Big buildings on the land. Big manicured lawns. Big pools and fountains. And big, big skies. (Similar impressions of large scale occur at Ross Perot Jr.'s innovative industrial airport complex at Alliance, in north Fort Worth, where mammoth distribution and manufacturing facilities sit like big white boxes in acres of green). Design-wise, among the dozen corporate facilities at Legacy – such as EDS, JC Penney, Fina, Dr Pepper/Seven Up – the Frito-Lay National Headquarters of 1984, by Lohan Associates, sets a superb example in the way it gently nestles into its hilly site so as to span part of a small lake.

Another corporate enclave – actually a total community that also includes residential, commercial, industrial, and recreational uses – is notable for replicating the Dallas paradigm of growth through the force of will. Las Colinas, in Irving, represents the realization of a grand vision by landowner Ben Carpenter, who built an urban center around a 125-acre lake with a canal and Venetian-style water taxis. Among the office towers, housing hundreds of multinational companies, is Williams Square, a skillfully executed three-building ensemble by Charles Bassett of Skidmore, Owings & Merrill San Francisco that surrounds an expansive open plaza on three sides. The major attraction of the plaza is Robert Glen's monumental bronze sculpture of nine stampeding mustangs.

Perhaps the most satisfying corporate setting of all is Solana, a 900-acre development ten miles north of D/FW Airport, with IBM as its principal tenant. Here is a remarkable collaboration among Legorreta Arquitectos, Mitchell/Giurgola, and Peter Walker/Martha Schwartz that resulted in an idyllic setting of connected ponds, streams, meadows and groves into which technical and office buildings, shops and a hotel have been artfully planted. These are predominantly simple, square-windowed buildings of similar height. Moving from one complex to another, the rigorous order imposed by Mitchell/Giurgola is offset by the playfulness of Legoretta's colorful planes and pylons. [Special Moment: Delighting in the punctuating colors of Solana.]

Also beyond Dallas proper, though not within the corporate realm, are at least two "regional highlights" that belong on the area-architecture must-see list. One is the Kimbell Art Museum in Fort Worth, by Louis Kahn, wherein the play of light along marble-sheathed cycloid vaults makes for a masterful building of international stature. [Special Moment: One's first real-life glimpse of Kahn's Kimbell.] The other regional must-see is actually a category: the county courthouses set prominently in the nearby town squares of Waxahachie (a favorite), Decatur, Denton and Hillsboro. Here one experiences not only the artful design of architects J. Riely Gordon and W.C. Dodson, but also enduring imagery from young communities on the rise – buildings as expressions of pride and exuberance. [Special Moment: Taking in the town square, Waxahachie, Texas.]

Closer to Home. In contemplating architecture, we often focus on the large-scale hyper-achievements that assert themselves as isolated objects in space – particularly in Dallas (Big "D"), where thinking big happens almost by default. But to do so is to downplay the significance of the city fabric as a whole, and the smaller-scale elements within it. *Dallas Morning News* Architecture Critic David Dillon – an urgent voice for high standards in Dallas architecture and urban design since the early eighties – has often made a compelling case for more attention to these little things that serve as the interface between people and the city itself: things like street furniture, handrails, bus stops, little parks – even decorative paving and manhole covers. Dallas still makes many more environmental concessions for automobiles than for pedestrians, but it is making strides. We can delight not only in the fact that an auto-age city like Dallas even *has* a DART light-rail system, for example, but also in The Oglesby Group's lively transit stops, with their arcing steel canopies.

Evidence that smaller is sometimes better is found in the 1931 Highland Park Village shopping center – that wonderfully accessible retail assemblage, with its fine plateresque detailing, executed under Spanish folk and early Renaissance influences. [Special Moment: Browsing Highland Park Village while sipping a fresh caffe latte.] In contrast to the grand corporate palaces such as the JC Penney complex, for example, it is refreshing to admire the pristinely integrated geometric forms of the smaller and more readily comprehensible Triangle Pacific building by New York's Gwathmey-Siegel.

Other great lessons in the art of small buildings can be found
in the work of several Dallas architects. Gary Cunningham's serene
and provocative Cistercian Chapel ranks among the best Dallas-
area architecture of the recent past, and his Power House conversion to a residence remains a continuing source of fascination.
Landry and Landry's trapezoidal Mausoleum and Chapel for
Emanu-El Cemetery builds on a tradition of powerful design that
began in 1956 with Temple Emanu-El, by Howard Meyer and
Max Sandfield. Corgan Associates has enhanced the small-building
category with projects such as its work at Farmers Market and its
warehouse-to-residential conversion, the snappy 2220 Canton
Street lofts. Franchise architecture has received a big boost with the
new Crate & Barrel store (by Jacque Verlinden, with Good Fulton
& Farrell), an extension of the Knox Street renaissance begun by
Good Fulton & Farrell's Knox Street Village mixed-use development that sensitively combines existing commercial facades with
new construction. And The Oglesby Group's Key Cataract Surgery
Center and its Northern Trust Bank are exquisitely crafted small
buildings, worthy of emulation.

In uptown Dallas, we find lively streets and commercial strips
with engaging, ad hoc qualities (McKinney, Lemmon Avenue,
Lovers Lane, Oak Lawn). And this zone, as well as downtown
itself, is a setting for a number of admirable small-scale multifamily
residential projects, such as Gary Cunningham's Cole Avenue
Apartments, Ron Wommack's Parkwood Terrace, and Lionel
Morrison's work on Springbrook. But only after factoring in that
often-belittled and neglected building type – the single-family
house – can the full significance and appeal of Dallas architecture
be appreciated. We would expect, after all, that the personal wealth
of an affluent citizenry – and the sophistication implied therein–
would be manifested in that most personal form of architectural
expression. And, indeed, Dallas has perhaps more than its share
of truly significant houses, some by imported "name-brand"
architects, others the product of local design talent.

In the former category, we find post-1950 examples from
Frank Lloyd Wright, Harwell Hamilton Harris, Edward Durrell
Stone, E.L. Barnes, Charles Moore, and Philip Johnson. More
recent projects include Antoine Predock's site-specific, geometrically
complex fortress above Turtle Creek in Highland Park, and three
houses in Preston Hollow: Richard Meier's pristine house-as-gallery
for a single investor; Steven Holl's lyrical Stretto House; and a
22,000-sq.-ft. Neo-Georgian compound by Robert A.M. Stern.

Through the turn of the century, Dallas architects built in the
popular period styles, as evident in the neartown Swiss Avenue
Historic District, a veritable open-air residential museum. [Special
Moment: A slow drive up Swiss Avenue, and back.] But more imagi-

native explorations began in the late 1920s with David Williams, whose work (best illustrated by his Elbert Williams Residence) reflects cultural influences and domestic building traditions indigenous to the Texas region. The mantle of "regionalism" – whose fundamental tenet remains sensitivity to place – was also assumed in Dallas by architects such as O'Neil Ford, prior to his move to San Antonio, and A.B. Swank, who collaborated with Ford on memorable houses (see the Bromberg residence) and on the highly regarded "Little Chapel in the Woods." Two Ford contemporaries – the popular Charles Stevens Dilbeck and C.D. Hutsell – were active in Dallas' prestigious residential neighborhoods in the 1930s and beyond, working in their own picturesque, yet somewhat idiosyncratic, hybrid styles. [Special Moment: Observing Hutsell Houses as they step down the hill on Lakewood Boulevard.]

The history of Dallas' notable residential architecture in the ensuing decades is dominated by a relatively small number of architects, whose most significant works are included in this guide. Collectively, they produced houses that reflect a certain degree of originality, in addition to skillful siting, detailing, and use of materials, as well as sensitivity to climate, and – often – a Modernist bent. Some of the most familiar names in this group are Howard Meyer, Enslie Oglesby and James Wiley (The Oglesby Group), and Frank Welch. Dallas' newest generation of architects known for distinguished houses includes Max Levy (whose "House with a Sky View" has received critical acclaim), Gary Cunningham (see his painterly composition in stucco on a North Dallas suburban lot), and Lionel Morrison (whose pair of houses for clients on adjoining lots stands as testimony to the merits of Modernism).

In the highest levels of Dallas society, financial success is not its own reward; it is owning the right house. But it's also owning it in the right *neighborhood*. And while a number of these are "desirable" (Lakewood, Preston Hollow, and Bluffview, for example), there are none quite so lovely and idyllic as those in the park cities – Highland Park and University Park, both of which capitalize on the scenic beauty of the Turtle Creek corridor. [Special Moment: Strolling the length of Lakeside Drive in Highland Park.] Here one is enchanted not only by individual houses – grand, mostly traditional expressions of wealth – but by the whole gestalt: curving streets, changing vistas, trees and water, stone bridges, with thriving grass and greenery all around. Here we find the heavenly reward for worldly success. Perhaps even more than that bundle of skyscrapers erupting from downtown, this is quintessentially Dallas. And John Neely Bryan would be proud. – *Larry Paul Fuller*

1 Downtown Dallas

When architect James Flanders arrived in Dallas in 1874, the buildings, he wrote, "were of the flimsiest and most temporary kind. Nobody expected to remain here permanently...and their idea was to make all the money they could while the town lasted."

The town did last, of course, but even buildings that were no longer flimsy – elaborate theaters, hotels, stores, and office buildings – were quickly disposed of when money could be made from the deal. However, Dallas has always had the virtue of its defect, which is to say that destruction simply made way for construction, and the energy Flanders mistook in 1874 as fly-by-night stayed around to reinvent the modern city many more times.

Downtown Dallas, snugly encircled today by the freeway ring consisting of Woodall Rogers, Central Expressway, I-30 and I-35, welcomes the architecturally-minded visitor with the trademark shimmer of all modern, glass-clad cities. Dallas patrons have had an appetite for buildings with sculptural form, which is why the Hyatt Regency with its 50-story raised geodesic dome and the Dallas City Hall with its floors cantilevered at a 34° angle have become landmarks. The skyline abounds with the shapes of towers – and one Flying Red Horse – that scrape the sky in all manner of ingenious ways and, as a Dallas tradition, are boldly lighted at night. A closer, street-level approach (particularly within the original core of mercantile activity, defined by Elm, Main, and Commerce) reveals historic buildings that have survived Dallas' purges and have won a belated respect from citizens and from architects whose new buildings seem to frame and dignify them.

Five distinct districts make up the whole of downtown. Besides the commercial core and the Civic Center, an area known as West End has been designated historic for its fine industrial buildings (c.1900-1930), which emerged on the west side of the railroad tracks that once ran along Pacific. (The tracks were removed in 1921 at the urging of planner George Kessler and, ironically, the Dallas Area Rapid Transit has appropriated the same thoroughfare for its downtown light-rail system.) Built as warehouses in the ornamental style of Chicago commercial architecture, these structures have been restored for multiple uses. In combination with the Farmers Market district where new apartments have recently gone up (there are now 10,000 housing units in and near downtown), the West End has played a major role in turning the moribund urban life of the 1970s-era downtown into its current lively, mixed-use incarnation. With the Arts District, which is home to the Dallas Museum of Art and the jewel-like Meyerson Symphony Center, downtown has reached a maturity and grace that Dallas is certain to cherish, in spite of its (still restless) self.

1 Downtown Dallas

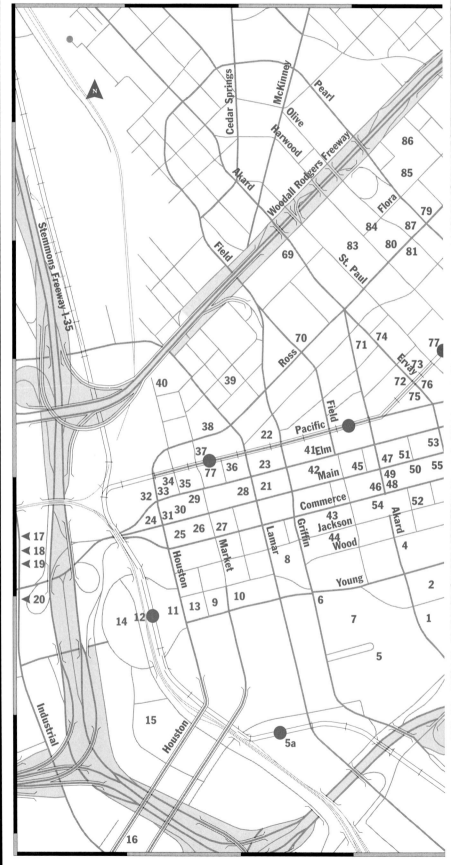

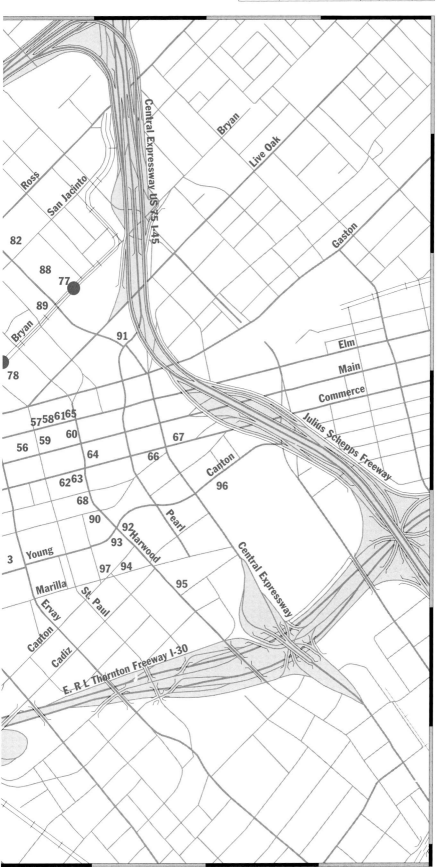

1 Downtown Dallas

Nathaniel Lieberman

1

Dallas City Hall, *1978*
1500 Marilla Street
I.M. Pei & Partners; Harper & Kemp
I.M. Pei's heroic City Hall anchors Dallas'
sprawling civic center complex on the southern edge of the central core. Its 12-acre site
was carved from a district of warehouse buildings, inaugurating downtown's first significant
attempt at urban renewal. The front facade
cantilevers outward at a 34° angle, creating
an abstract and monumental composition
rigorously delineated by the use of monolithic
cast-in-place concrete. The wind-swept ceremonial plaza reinforces the precise geometry
of the building, displaying as its focal point
Henry Moore's bronze sculpture **(2) The
Dallas Piece,** 1978.

3

J. Erik Jonsson Central Library, *1982*
1515 Young Street
Fisher & Spillman
Dallas' Central Library occupies its prominent
corner location with as much dignity as can
be mustered in the face of City Hall across
the street. The building attempts to match
Pei's monumentality while at the same time
being reverentially contextual and subordinate
– a premise that doesn't quite work. Inside,
there are several exceptional spaces, including
the **(3a) Declaration of Independence Room,**
1995, by Max Levy, a splendid shrine-like
exhibit hall.

4

Old Federal Reserve Bank Building, *1921*
400 S. Akard Street
Graham, Anderson, Probst & White (Chicago)
Grayson Gill, addition, 1960
It is hard to imagine that the Federal Reserve
Bank of Dallas ever fit into this building,
which served as its headquarters for 71 years.
The Chicago firm Graham, Anderson, Probst
& White, architects of the Wrigley Building
and other Loop landmarks, designed the
building in Neo-Classical style with a three-
story Doric-columned entrance loggia supporting an entablature and figural sculpture.
Decorative steer heads and garlands under
the cornice represent one of the earliest
attempts in Dallas at incorporating southwestern motifs into the design of a large
institutional building.

Original, 1957

Al Assid/Studio Etc.

6
Pioneer Plaza, *1994*
Griffin Street at Young Street
Slaney-Santana Group, landscape architect
When it was first proposed in 1990, this
sculpture park of fifty trailing longhorns initiated heated debate over the nature of public
art and its message about Dallas' place in the
Texas myth. Equally controversial was the
site, formerly designated as a location for a
future convention hotel and sharing a common boundary with the sacred ground of
(7) Pioneer Cemetery, 1848, the resting place
of Dallas' early prominent citizens. Despite
these criticisms, Pioneer Plaza has developed
into a hugely popular tourist attraction.

Expansion, 1993

5
Dallas Convention Center, *1957*
650 S. Griffin Street
George Dahl
Harrell & Hamilton, expansion, 1973
Omniplan, expansion, 1984
JPJ Architects; Loschky, Marquardt & Nesholm
  (Seattle), expansion, 1993
The Dallas Convention Center grew to
its present mammoth size in four phases,
creating in the process a hopeless jumble
of disparate additions and incoherent circulation. A new master plan, completed in 1990
and currently being implemented, will hope-
fully address some of these problems, even
though the 1993 expansion contributes to the
stylistic confusion. The best piece of this
2,000,000-sq.-ft. puzzle is the original 1957
civic center component facing Dallas City
Hall across Akard Street. Designed by George
Dahl, the 9,800-seat arena and adjacent theater wing demonstrate the architect's articulate use of form, structure and materials,
albeit within a '50s idiom. It's too bad subsequent architects took no clues from the
original. Somewhere under the 1993 expansion and accessible from Lamar Street is the
(5a) DART Convention Center Station, 1996,
by HOK, offering one of two alternative
modes of transportation to the Convention
Center (a Heliport is on a nearby roof).

8
Founders Square, *1914*
900 Jackson Street
Lang & Witchell
JPJ Architects, adaptive reuse, 1984
Starting in 1914, the Higginbotham-Bailey-
Logan Company built this large brick structure to house their wholesaling and apparel
manufacturing business. Two subsequent
expansions, plainly visible on the south facade
(west to east), were added over the next nine
years, continuing the horizontal banding
and Prairie-esque detailing evident in the
prominent corner towers. This building was
designed while Lang & Witchell were also
completing a similarly scaled and detailed
warehouse for Sears-Roebuck on Lamar
Street. In 1984, a full-height atrium was
inserted into the building as part of its successful conversion to office space – one of the
first such adaptive reuse projects downtown.

Doric columns. Located behind Union
Station, on the original passenger platforms,
is the **(12) DART Station,** 1996, HOK.

9
One Ferris Plaza, *1985*
400 S. Record Street
Omniplan
This 17-story granite-clad headquarters for
the media giant A.H. Belo Corporation sits
on a raised podium within a five-block zone
of parks and plazas stretching from Union
Station east towards Founders Square. A
quasi-octagon in plan, its thin facade faces
symmetrically onto Ferris Plaza, while the
opposite side looks down upon **(10) Lubben
Plaza,** 1992, Omniplan, one of the most
successful sculpture parks in the city.

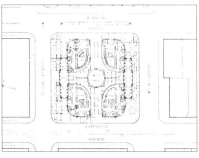

13
Ferris Plaza, *1920*
Houston Street at Young Street
George Kessler (St. Louis), landscape architect
George Kessler, in his 1911 City Plan for
Dallas, identified the need for a public park
as a critical element in the urban design for
Union Station. The symmetrical composition
of building and plaza represents Dallas'
modest contribution to the City Beautiful
Movement. This shady downtown oasis is
slightly recessed from street level and has as
its central focus the city's first public fountain.

11
Union Station, *1916*
400 S. Houston Street
Jarvis Hunt (Chicago)
Wyatt C. Hedrick (Fort Worth), renovation, 1950
JPJ Architects, adaptive reuse, 1977
The construction of a new passenger station
in 1916 consolidated five other terminals
used by the nine railroad lines serving Dallas.
Jarvis Hunt, the Chicago architect responsible
for Kansas City's majestic Union Terminal,
designed a gleaming enameled-brick monument in the Beaux-Arts style. The vaulted
waiting room on the second floor is expressed
on the front facade by a deep, double-story
loggia with openings framed by stalwart

14
Hyatt Regency Hotel and Reunion Tower, *1978*
300 Reunion Boulevard
Welton Becket Associates (Los Angeles)
When it was built by the Hunt brothers in
1978, the Hyatt Regency initiated a downtown development boom that continued well
into the 1980s. The standard Hyatt architectural formula, perfected by John Portman and
copied in numerous American cities, is given
a high-octane charge here, due, in part, to the

site's spectacularly visible location near the confluence of I-30 and I-35. The shimmering silver volumes of the hotel are balanced against the 50-story raised geodesic dome, creating a synergy that invigorated Dallas' moribund skyline. The nearby **(15) Reunion Arena,** 1980, HKS, Inc., is significant only in its recollection of the utopian La Reunion settlement established in west Dallas by French and Belgian colonists in 1855.

16
Houston Street Viaduct, *1912*
Houston Street, southwest of Downtown
Hedrick & Cochrane (Kansas City), engineers
The first permanent bridge to connect Dallas with the early suburb of Oak Cliff was, at the time of its construction, one of the longest reinforced concrete arch viaducts ever built. Following the disastrous Trinity River flood of 1908, county engineers advertised for competitive plans for the new bridge. Ira G. Hedrick's graceful winning design consisted of 51 concrete arches, in addition to a steel girder spanning the riverbed to allow for extra vertical clearance for anticipated barge traffic.

17
Frank Crowley Criminal Courts Building, *1989*
133 N. Industrial Boulevard
HDR
The heap of brown buildings on the east levee of the Trinity River is a disappointing collection of county and state justice facilities. The first component, the **(18) Sterrett Justice Center,** 1982, Justice Center Architects, was the county's first jail built outside of the downtown freeway loop. Subsequent additions, consisting of the Crowley Courts Building and the **(19) North Tower,** 1989, HDR, continued the dismal repudiation of Texas' rich legacy of county courthouse architecture. Across Commerce Street, the State of Texas added the **(20) Jesse R. Dawson State Jail,** 1995, Morris Architects (Houston), innovative as a design-build facility constructed for the State by private developers.

21
NationsBank Plaza, *1986*
901 Main Street
JPJ Architects
Dallas' tallest building rises in a dramatic shaft of silver reflective glass and aluminum spandrel panels to a height of 72 floors (921 feet) ranking it among the 35 tallest buildings in the world. The plan is a square pulled apart at its diagonal corners, which, when combined with its sculpted crown, creates a tower of constantly changing imagery. Its location on the edge of the central core, free from surrounding high-rise buildings, assures its long-term prominence on Dallas' skyline.

22
DART West End Bus Transfer Station, *1996*
Griffin Street at Pacific Street
Lockwood, Andrews & Newnam
Dallas Area Rapid Transit has been more successful with its rail station architecture than with facilities accommodating buses. This project, and one similar to it on the east side, were designed as transfer points between downtown bus routes and the nearby transit corridor.

23
Milliners Supply Company, *c.1880*
911 Elm Street
One of the oldest extant buildings downtown retains little of the character of its original Victorian Italianate facade. Downtown streets were lined with thousands of these small commercial buildings, which were built after the arrival of the railroads in 1872.

West End Historic District

24
Dealey Plaza, *1940*
Elm, Main, and Commerce Streets at
  Houston Street
Hare & Hare (Kansas City), landscape
  architects

Situated between Houston Street and the
triple underpass, Dealey Plaza marks the original townsite of Dallas, where John Neely
Bryan first set up his trading camp in 1841
on the banks of the Trinity River. The present-
day configuration dates to a series of public
works projects initiated during the 1930s to
address flood control and traffic congestion.
The meandering river was relocated to its
present channel, and the three main downtown
streets, Elm, Main and Commerce, were
realigned to converge into a triple underpass
beneath the railroad tracks leading into Union
Station. The project was completed by a pair
of Art Deco concrete peristyles, which mark
the site as the western vehicular gateway to
downtown. Dealey Plaza is largely unchanged
since the assassination of President John F.
Kennedy on November 22, 1963.

25
Dallas County Courthouse ("Old Red"), *1892*
500 block of Main Street
Orlopp & Kusener (Little Rock)
James Pratt, restoration, 1999

The sixth courthouse to occupy this site since
1846 is a massive Romanesque Revival structure that expressed the new-found economic
prowess of the state's then-largest city. The
polychromatic masonry and roof tiles suggest
lingering influences of the Victorian era,
while the heavily textured granite and sandstone walls, engaged turrets, arched openings
and contrasting horizontal string courses represent typical elements of H.H. Richardson's
mature Romanesque style. Richardson's
Allegheny County Courthouse in Pittsburgh,
completed four years earlier, was a strong
influence on M.A. Orlopp's design. Originally
surmounted by a central tower 205 feet in
height (removed in 1919 due to structural
concerns), "Old Red" served as the center of
county government until 1928.

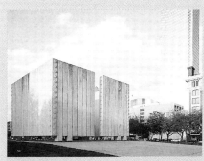

26
John F. Kennedy Memorial, *1970*
600 block of Main Street
Philip Johnson (New York)
Johnson's disquieting cenotaph, sitting isolated in the center of an otherwise featureless
plaza next to "Old Red," is a 50-ft. square
formed by 72 slender concrete elements
strapped together by post-tensioned cables.
The memorial attempts to express the empti-
ness and anguish of a city and nation in the
years following the 1963 assassination.

27
MKT Building, *1912*
701 Commerce Street
H.A. Overbeck
Thomas E. Woodward, renovation, 1978
This seven-story terra-cotta and masonry
office building served as the national headquarters for the Missouri-Kansas-Texas
Railway Co. (the "Katy"), which operated a
railroad empire extending from the Gulf
Coast to the lower Midwest. H.A. Overbeck's
design employed transitional window proportions with gilded ornamentation, accompanied by standard academic detailing at the
projecting cornice.

28
El Centro College, *1910*
801 Main Street
Lang & Witchell
Oglesby Group, adaptive reuse, 1977
Dallas' finest example of the Chicago School
of high-rise commercial architecture is this
eight-story former department store built by
the Sanger Brothers. With its large windows,
Sullivanesque terra-cotta ornament and slender vertical piers expressing the structural steel
frame, this building was sensationally modern
in a city comprised largely of heavy masonry
commercial structures. A projecting cornice
was removed in the 1960s.

29
John Neely Bryan Cabin, *c.1845*
600 block of Elm Street
Records suggest that this is the last of three
cabins, and the first permanent home,
erected by Dallas' entrepreneurial founder.
Reconstructed from many of the original
hewn cedar logs, this cabin was actually one
half of the original "dog-trot" structure (two
enclosed rooms separated by a covered open
porch). This remnant of Bryan's pioneer settlement served for years as the center of the
social, political, and economic life of Dallas.

West End Historic District

30
Dallas County Records Building, *1928*
509 Main Street
Lang & Witchell
Smith & Warder; Broad & Nelson; Jack M.
 Corgan, addition, 1955
Adjoining the Criminal Courts Building is this
block-long Neo-Gothic Revival structure that
reveals the broad stylistic repertoire of Dallas'
most prolific firm, Lang & Witchell. The
articulated limestone facade, with its planar
composition and vertical emphasis, anticipates
the imminent arrival of Classical Moderne.

31
Dallas County Criminal Courts Building, *1913*
501 Main Street
H.A. Overbeck
Overbeck's handsome Renaissance Revival jail
and courts building stood in sharp stylistic
contrast to the old county courthouse across
the street. Behind the richly-detailed facade
the architect inserted a programmatically and
technically innovative design for this early
justice facility, which once counted as its residents Clyde Barrow and "Pretty Boy" Floyd.

32
Texas School Book Depository, *1901*
411 Elm Street
Burson, Hendricks & Walls, adaptive reuse,
 1979
Hendricks-Calloway, Sixth Floor Museum, 1988
North of the courthouse district can be found
numerous mid-rise commercial and wholesale
warehouse buildings that confirm the economic prosperity experienced in Dallas during
the first two decades of the 20th century.
Many of these warehouses served as branch
distribution centers for farm implement manufacturers based in Chicago, among them
the Southern Rock Island Plow Company,
the original owner of the School Book
Depository. The Chicago business connection
brought with it architectural influence, as
evidenced here in the building's transition
between the traditional Romanesque and the
newer Chicago commercial style.

Paul Hester

33
501 Elm Place, *1902*
Hubbell & Greene
Corgan Associates, adaptive reuse, 1986
Herbert M. Greene confidently interpreted
the Chicago commercial style in this warehouse building for the John Deere Plow
Company. Heavy corner planes and thick
vertical piers acknowledge the aesthetic
constraints of load-bearing masonry walls.

34
Southern Supply Company, *1911*
211 N. Record Street
James Riely Gordon (San Antonio);
*   H.A. Overbeck*
Corgan Associates, adaptive reuse, 1985
This is the only remaining building in Dallas
designed by the great San Antonio architect
famous for his numerous county courthouses.
The taut masonry skin and facade composi-
tion of diminishing arches were strongly
influenced by Adler & Sullivan's Walker
Warehouse in Chicago, completed in 1889.

35
Purse & Company, *1905*
601 Elm Street
H.A. Overbeck
Originally built for the Parlin and Orendorff
Implement Company, this slender, block-long
building deftly introduced classical detailing
within a typical Chicago School facade.

36
Awalt Warehouses, *c.1905*
208 N. Market Street
This six-story corbelled brick warehouse
benefited from its frontage on the Texas &
Pacific Railroad lines that ran down the center
of Pacific Avenue. The removal of these tracks
in 1921 initiated a decline in the warehouse
district's dominant position as a wholesale
distribution center.

37
Texas Moline Plow Building, *1903*
302 N. Market Street
H.A. Overbeck
Corgan Associates, adaptive reuse, 1984
By 1891, Dallas had replaced Kansas City
as the nation's largest distribution center for
farm equipment. After 1900, large warehouses
such as this replaced the smaller Victorian
commercial buildings that proliferated in the
area following the arrival of the Texas &
Pacific Railroad in 1873.

38
Old City Jail, *1906*
705 Ross Avenue
Corgan Associates, adaptive reuse, 1983
Two-story pilasters with Prairie-style capitals
contrast with the classical entry pediment in
this diminutive building, which served as
Dallas' police headquarters until 1917.

39
Dallas World Aquarium, *1924*
1801 Griffin Street
Adaptive reuse, 1992, 1997
One of the most sophisticated adaptive
reuse projects in downtown is this privately
funded aquarium and rain forest exhibit
imaginatively inserted behind the brick
walls of two small warehouses.

40
West End Marketplace, *1911*
1701 N. Market Street
Barglebaugh & Co., addition, 1924
Demarest & Wells; Ceria & Coppell (Houston),
*   adaptive reuse, 1985*
Consisting of three contiguous warehouse
structures built for home furniture, this seven-
story brick building – the tallest of the West
End's warehouses – was renovated in 1985
into a popular festival market.

41
Renaissance Tower, *1973*
1201 Elm Street
Harwood K. Smith & Partners; Hellmuth,
* Obata & Kassabaum (St. Louis)*
Skidmore, Owings & Merrill (Houston),
* renovation, 1987*
By the mid-1980s, Dallas' first "glass box"
tower (and Texas' tallest building until 1981)
was aesthetically obsolete, prompting an
image makeover by SOM's Richard Keating:
his second, and least successful, major project
downtown. Keating utilized blue, silver, and
green glass to create a curtain wall pattern
that highlighted the building's vertical column
lines and structural "X"-bracing. On the roof,
underscaled spires appear as a gimmicky after-
thought. Only in the renovation of the plaza
can be seen the same level of architectural
craft and ingenuity that is evident on
Keating's other two downtown skyscrapers.

42
One Main Place, *1968*
1201 Main Street
Skidmore, Owings & Merrill (New York);
* Harwood K. Smith & Partners*
The most significant downtown building of
the 1960s is this elegant, 34-story concrete
tower designed by Gordon Bunshaft of SOM.
The only drawback is the sterile sunken plaza,
a failed attempt at mixed-use development.

43
Santa Fe Building, *1926*
1114 Commerce Street
Whitson & Dale
The Santa Fe Railroad built this quasi-
Spanish Renaissance office and terminal
warehouse complex above a vast underground
complex of railroad tracks. Part of the com-
plex has been renovated as the **(44) Santa Fe II**
Condominiums, Corgan Associates, 1999.

elaborate cornice and attic ornamentation, capped by a distinctive mansard roof and bronze crest. The hotel's lower floors are equally impressive, particularly the piano-nobile arcade on Commerce Street and the segmented arch trimmed with sculptural relief marking the original entrance on Akard Street.

45
Davis Building, *1926*
1309 Main Street
C.D. Hill
Coburn & Fowler, addition, 1931
Corgan Associates, renovation, 1988
Characteristic of many 1920s Dallas skyscrapers is this 20-story Classic Revival headquarters for Republic Bank. The gilded rooftop cupola conferred extra height over a nearby banking competitor.

47
Kirby Building, *1913*
1509 Main Street
Barnett, Haynes & Barnett (St. Louis);
  Lang & Witchell
Corgan Associates, adaptive reuse, 1999
This 17-story, U-shaped office building, also financed by Adolphus Busch, opened the year following completion of the Adolphus Hotel. The Busch Building (as it was originally named) is an exuberant Late Gothic Revival tower lavishly clad in terra-cotta panels and crowned by a battlement of tracery and finials. Together with Cass Gilbert's Woolworth Building in New York City, it was one of the first American skyscrapers to be built in the Commercial Gothic style, marking an architectural shift in Dallas away from the Chicago School and a return to historic eclecticism.

46
Adolphus Hotel, *1912*
1321 Commerce Street
Barnett, Haynes & Barnett (St. Louis);
  C.D. Hill
Jerde Partnership (Los Angeles); Beran &
  Shelmire, renovation, 1980
Dallas' grand hotel was constructed by St. Louis beer magnate Adolphus Busch. No expense was spared in creating this exuberant Edwardian Baroque masterpiece, with its

48
Magnolia Building, *1922*
108 S. Akard Street
Alfred C. Bossom (New York); Lang &
  Witchell
Guy Thornton (Denver); Gensler (Denver),
  adaptive reuse, 1999
Alfred C. Bossom, an English architect working in New York from 1903 until 1926, enjoyed healthy patronage in Texas, where he designed high-rises in Dallas, Houston, and Galveston. Bossom designed this limestone-clad Renaissance Revival skyscraper around a central light well that dramatically separates symmetrical office wings rising from a three-story base. These wings are joined by a flying segmental arch at the 17th floor, and are each capped by a recessed attic story with a hipped tile roof. As the headquarters of the Magnolia Oil Company (a predecessor of Mobil Oil), this 29-story landmark tower symbolized the growing influence of oil in the city's commercial activities. When completed in 1922, the Magnolia Building was the 16th tallest skyscraper in the U.S. and the tallest south of Philadelphia. It remained the tallest building in Dallas until World War II. In 1934, the **(48a) Flying Red Horse,** J.B. McMath, signmaker – a 30-foot high red neon revolving sign – was erected atop a 50-foot tower on the building's roof. "Pegasus" quickly became the city's unofficial trademark and has remained one of the most endearing features of the Dallas skyline. **(49) Pegasus Plaza,** 1994, Brad Goldberg, sculptor, is a small plaza with stone water sculptures located on the north side of the Magnolia Building.

50
1530 Main Street, *1927*
Coburn & Smith
Corgan Associates, renovation, 1985
This 16-story tower, built by the Dallas National Bank, is designed in the Gothic-Revival style as a perfect accompaniment to its slender, vertical proportions. Across the street, **(51) 1525 Main Street,** c.1895, is a remnant of the 19th century brick commercial structures that proliferated in the central business district.

52
Dallas Power & Light Co. Building, *1931*
1506 Commerce Street
Lang & Witchell
The former DP&L headquarters consists of a 20-story office building and a three-story public lobby linking it with Commerce Street. Due to the narrow mid-block frontage on Commerce, the office tower was pushed one-half block to the south, facing onto Jackson Street. While the brick and terra-cotta tower represents the Zigzag Moderne style, with its step-back massing, strong vertical emphasis and Art Deco accents, the lobby element suggests the Classical Moderne influences of Bertram Goodhue and Paul Cret, through its elegant use of materials and handsome architectonic forms.

53
Wilson Building, *1903*
1621 Main Street
Sanguinett & Staats
Sanguinett & Staats; J. Edward Overbeck,
  addition, 1911
Corgan Associates, adaptive reuse, 1999
Dallas' most incomparable early 20th century
office building is this splendid Second Empire
elaboration of two famous Chicago landmarks: Adler and Sullivan's Auditorium
Building (1889) and H.H. Richardson's
Marshall Field Store (1887). Built by the
rancher and banker J.B. Wilson, the building
originally housed the department store
Titche-Goettinger on its ground floor, with
seven office levels above. To provide natural
light to the offices, two deep light wells were
inserted above the contiguous ground floor
and mezzanine levels, breaking the long Ervay
Street facade into three distinct pavilions.
Like other Victorian-era office buildings, the
eight-story facade is divided into five horizontal bands, each with a different fenestration
pattern and exuberant ornamentation.

54
One Bell Plaza, *1987*
208 S. Akard Street
JPJ Architects
Bell Plaza is a collection of monotonous, volumetric, travertine-clad towers comprising the
regional headquarters of Southwestern Bell.
The building complex is organized around a
generously landscaped public plaza, with the
Adolphus Hotel providing a stunning backdrop along its northern edge.

55
Neiman Marcus, *1914*
1618 Main Street
Herbert M. Greene
The flagship of Dallas' world-famous fashion
retailer is the only original department store
still in use downtown. A monument to classical rationalism, its terra-cotta facade has
barely enough detail to relieve the building's
overwhelming proportions.

Richard Payne

56
Bank One Center, *1987*
1717 Main Street
Philip Johnson/John Burgee (New York); HKS
Johnson/Burgee's second Dallas office building is modeled after the same firm's 1983
RepublicBank Center in Houston, which
consists of a banking hall pavilion and separate office tower, both sharing similar distinctive roof shapes. In Dallas the barrel-vaulted
banking hall and tower take a few visual cues
from the Wilson Building across the street,
and graciously give it some breathing room
by not crowding the street.

57
Tower Petroleum Building, *1931*
1907 Elm Street
Mark Lemmon
Built to provide office space for Dallas' burgeoning oil and gas industry, Tower Petroleum marked a significant stylistic departure from the classically inspired skyscrapers of the 1920s. The strong, vertical emphasis with step-back massing and fine Moderne detailing suggest the lingering influence of Eliel Saarinen's widely published entry in the Chicago Tribune Tower competition of 1922. Next door, **(58) Pacific Place,** 1984, Sikes Jennings Kelly (Houston), is a sensitive infill high-rise sandwiched between two landmarks.

59
1900 Elm, *1929*
1900 Elm Street
Greene, LaRoche & Dahl
Thomas, Jameson & Merrill, addition, 1955
Meckfessel Associates; Graham Greene, adaptive
    reuse as Dallas Education Center, 1994
Oglesby-Greene, adaptive reuse, 1997
The year of the stock market crash also saw the completion of Dallas' largest department store, an eight-story Renaissance Revival palazzo designed by George Dahl. With its three-story rusticated base and balconied attic

level of Venetian windows, this building for Titche-Goettinger expressed cautious optimism in the face of the coming depression. Both the original store and its 1955 addition have been renovated into loft housing and a downtown university consortium, respectively. In the same block, the 14-story **(60) Aristocrat Hotel,** 1925, Lang & Witchell, Conrad Hilton's first high-rise, displays Sullivanesque composition and Beaux-Arts detailing.

61
Majestic Theater, *1921*
1925 Elm Street
John Eberson (New York); Lang & Witchell
Oglesby Group, restoration, 1983
Designed by John Eberson, one of America's great theater architects, the Majestic Theater was the grandest in Dallas – the only survivor from an era when Theater Row on Elm Street was the glittering home to more than a dozen vaudeville and movie palaces. Built by Karl Hoblitzelle as the flagship and headquarters of his Interstate Amusement Co., the Majestic was one of seven theaters Eberson designed in Texas, and marks a tentative transition between his palatial style (executed here in Renaissance Revival) and his trademark atmospheric style. The highly-ornate terra-cotta facade and lavish "Roman Garden" interior were restored in 1983 by the City of Dallas.

62
Dallas Grand Hotel, *1956*
1914 Commerce Street
William Tabler (New York)
When completed in 1956, the 1,000-room Statler Hilton Hotel was the city's most sensational modern building. Tabler employed an innovative cantilevered flat-slab structural system to give the inflected facade a luxuriously urbane appearance. With the **(63) Dallas Public Library,** 1953, George Dahl, this is the best block of 1950s architecture in the city.

64
Police and Municipal Courts Building, *1914*
106 S. Harwood Street
C.D. Hill; Mauran, Russell & Crowell
(St. Louis)
Mark Lemmon; Smith & Mills, addition, 1956
In 1914, Dallas' majestic new City Hall must have had an architectural impact similar to what I.M. Pei's replacement had 64 years later. The only missing element was a City Beautiful plaza to accompany it. As the state's finest Beaux-Arts monument, City Hall demonstrated the mature Neo-Classical prowess of architect C.D. Hill. Hill's symmetrical design features corner pavilions bracketing giant Corinthian pilasters on each facade, a continuous cornice and frieze, an attic story

with balustrade and cartouches, and a crested Mansard roof with delicate oriel dormers.

65
Hart Furniture, *1888*
1933 Elm Street
This three-story brick warehouse is the finest 19th century Italianate structure remaining in downtown. The tall narrow windows and shallow bracketed cornice exemplify High Victorian commercial architecture.

66
KLIF Building, *1920*
2120 Commerce Street
Lang & Witchell
In the 1920s, the east end of Commerce Street saw a concentration of many automotive-related businesses, including this flatiron-shaped service station for Magnolia Petroleum Co., and the Prairie-style **(67) Automobile Showroom and Garage,** c.1920, at 2210 Commerce Street. The service station was an innovative design featuring an elaborately decorated office floor atop arched vehicular bays clad in stone. The motif is commercial Gothic with Prairie-esque flourishes on the parapet.

68

Lone Star Gas Co. Building, *1931*

301 S. Harwood Street

Lang & Witchell

The second of Lang & Witchell's two Moderne office buildings completed in 1931 is this 12-story former headquarters for the Dallas Gas Co. Adjoining an earlier Sullivanesque office building, the architects carried the existing polished granite base across to the new tower and set upon it a sculpted, set-back mass of cream-colored masonry. This tower lacks the soaring verticality and spirited detailing of the Dallas Power and Light Building.

70

Fountain Place, *1986*

1445 Ross Avenue

I.M. Pei & Partners (New York); Harry Weese
& Associates (Chicago); WZMH; Dan Kiley
(Charlotte, Vermont), landscape architect

The most extraordinary of Pei's three Dallas towers built during the 1980s is a 60-story, minimalist sculpture sheathed in shimmering green glass. As an object standing in isolation, the tower recalls similar bravura forms of Philip Johnson's Pennzoil Place in Houston. Its six-acre plaza and sublime water garden carved from the building's base demonstrate a subtle interplay of hard-edged geometry and supple nature. Plaza and garden have emerged as one of the great urban spaces in America.

69

Cumberland Hill School, *1888*

1901 N. Akard Street

A.B. Bristol Company

Burson & Hendricks, adaptive reuse, 1972

Dallas' oldest extant public school building was constructed in five phases beginning in 1888, and served the north side of downtown until its closure 70 years later. A 1972 renovation by future governor William Clements was the first substantive act of historic preservation in the city's history.

71

Lincoln Plaza, *1984*

500 N. Akard Street

HKS, Inc.

This wedge-shaped speculative office building built by Lincoln Property Company during

the height of the '80s boom conspicuously
borrows its saw-tooth window bays and
dark granite skin from the Bank of America
Building in San Francisco, completed in 1969.

Richard Payne

72
Energy Plaza, *1983*
1601 Bryan Street
I.M. Pei & Partners (New York)
Henry Cobb obviously enjoyed designing
high-rise towers along the juncture of Dallas'
oblique street grids. This time the plan is an
equilateral triangle rising in a polished, prism-
like form to its ultimate height of 49 stories.
The generous corner plaza is an act of dignified deference to Thanks-Giving Square.

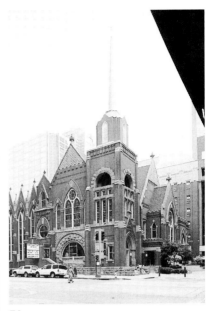

74
First Baptist Church, *1890*
1707 San Jacinto
Albert Ulrich
Clarence C. Bulger, renovation and addition,
 1928
The sanctuary of America's largest Baptist
congregation is downtown's finest remaining
Victorian-era structure, combining Gothic
Revival and Romanesque details in a confident
display of Mannerist design. Unfortunately,
Ulrich's original polychromed corner spire has
been replaced by the current pre-fab steeple.

73
U.S. Post Office and Courthouse, *1930*
400 N. Ervay Street
Office of the Supervising Architect
 (Washington D.C.)
Chief Architect Louis Simon was responsible
for this featureless and mundane federal
building with its minimal Renaissance Revival
detailing. To make up for its myriad architectural deficiencies, including the absence of a
suitable entrance, the building was awkwardly
dressed with an overly-detailed belt course
and comic strip-like terra-cotta panels.

Richard Payne

75
Thanks-Giving Square, *1977*
Pacific Street at Ervay Street
Philip Johnson/John Burgee (New York)
Philip Johnson, expansion and renovation, 1998
This intimate urban triangle, nestled deep in
the shadows of the financial core, borrows
elements from Philip Johnson's earlier design
for the Fort Worth Water Garden. The
recessed, sculpted park is defined by perimeter
walls and bisected by angular pathways. Its
spaces are abstract compositions of grass,
paving and cascading fountains, all balanced
against the helical form of the chapel.

76
Republic Towers, *1955*
Pacific Street at Ervay Street
Harrison & Abramovitz (New York);
Gill & Harrell
Harrell & Hamilton, addition, 1964
Omniplan, addition, 1978
Corgan Associates, renovation, 1999
Downtown's first major post-war project was
a 36-story office building and eight-story
banking pavilion for Republic National Bank,
designed by Wallace K. Harrison, architect of
the U.N. Headquarters. Harrison cloned his
earlier Alcoa Building in Pittsburgh, reutiliz-
ing its aluminum panel cladding in this
bankerly conservative and elegant complex.

Michael Lyon

77
DART Transitway Mall, *1996*
*Two stations on Pacific Avenue, two stations
    on Bryan Street*
Sasaki Associates, landscape architects;
    Oglesby Group; Haywood Jordan McCowan
Dallas' light-rail line emerges from the tunnel
under Central Expressway at the northeast
corner of downtown, before entering an
exquisitely designed transit mall along Bryan
Street and Pacific Avenue. A boulevard-like

ambience is maintained along the diverse
corridor through a tightly controlled palette
of hardscape materials and poles. The most
notable features of the corridor are the four
300-foot long stations (Pearl Street Station
pictured) spaced at three-block intervals.
Consisting of multiple shelters on each side of
paired tracks, the stations are similar in form,
structure and articulation, but vary in materials
and color to more closely associate with their
immediate context. Each shelter is covered by
an elegant, rolled steel plate suspended from
columns resting on a masonry base.

Wes Thompson

78
One Dallas Centre, *1979*
350 N. St. Paul Street
I.M. Pei & Partners (New York); Fisher &
    Spillman
At 30 stories, One Dallas Centre had little
impact on the Dallas skyline; its significance
was in its architectural distinction as a speculative office building. Henry Cobb designed
a rhomboid-shaped tower for developer
Vincent Carrozza as a response to the nearby
30° intersection of two downtown street
grids. The resulting sculptural volume is
enclosed in a taut, mullionless, glass and aluminum membrane, with two vertical notches
that accentuate the tower's angular mass.

79
Cathedral Guadalupe, *1902*
2215 Ross Avenue
Nicholas Clayton (Galveston); J.E. Overbeck
Characteristic of the work of Nicholas
Clayton, Galveston's great 19th century
architect, is this High Victorian Gothic
cathedral for the Roman Catholic Diocese
of Dallas. The well-proportioned facades and
prominent corner tower are enriched and
unified through the architect's deft use of
color and texture. The two front towers were
originally designed with soaring Victorian
spires; unfortunately they were never built.

80
Trammell Crow Center, *1984*
2001 Ross Avenue
Skidmore, Owings & Merrill (Houston)
Booziotis & Co., renovation for the Margaret
    and Trammell Crow Collection of Asian
    Art, 1998
The first of Richard Keating's three downtown office buildings is this 50-story campanile on the edge of the Arts District. The
tower's cruciform shape, classical composition,
distinctive silhouette and richly-animated
facade introduced a new high-rise vernacular
to the Dallas skyline. At its base, the tower is
surrounded by a public sculpture plaza and

low-rise art pavilion, both of which help to
integrate the huge development with the
surrounding Arts District.

81
First United Methodist Church, *1924*
1928 Ross Avenue
Herbert M. Greene; R.H. Hunt
Having abandoned an earlier downtown sanctuary in 1916 to disperse to suburban congregations, the church reversed its philosophy
several years later and attempted to reunite in
this new facility designed in a revival style of
Late English Perpendicular Gothic.

82
Chase Bank Tower, *1987*
2200 Ross Avenue
Skidmore, Owings & Merrill (Houston)
SJKB/Croft, Plaza renovation, 1998
By 1987, the Texas real estate boom, which
witnessed the construction of over a dozen
office towers in downtown Dallas, was in a
dizzying death spiral. This 55-story headquarters for Texas Commerce Bank was the
final boom-time skyscraper to be completed
in the state. Its predominant skyline feature is
a five-story carved slit extending between the
41st and 49th floors, serving the pragmatic
function of reducing the structural wind load
on the building. The slender rectangular shaft
is handsomely detailed and contains contextual references to neighboring office buildings. The tower is separated from Ross
Avenue by a 1.5-acre arduously landscaped
plaza, with fanciful fountains and other scale-
establishing elements, including a domed
pavilion in the northeast corner on axis with
the entry to the Meyerson Symphony Center.

Arts District

83

Dallas Museum of Art, *1984*

Edward Larrabee Barnes (New York); Pratt,
Box & Henderson

Edward Larrabee Barnes (New York), Reves
Wing addition, 1985

Edward Larrabee Barnes (New York); Thomas
& Booziotis, Hamon Wing addition, 1993

The pivotal component of the Arts District
is Edward Larrabee Barnes' sprawling Dallas
Museum of Art. In plan, the museum is a
collection of simple volumes and courtyards
organized around an internal circulation spine
longer than the Grand Galerie of the Louvre.
This gently sloping hallway connects pedestrian and vehicular entrances at opposite ends
with a ceremonial entrance in the middle.
The building's trademark barrel vault aligns
with Flora Street at this location. The permanent collection galleries are arranged on four
descending trays on the west side of the spine,
with other museum spaces ingeniously tucked
underneath. In Barnes' extensive museum
oeuvre, the DMA shares many similarities
with his earlier commissions in Pittsburgh
and Minneapolis: the same rational logic in
plan, mixed with a steady devotion to the
underlying precepts of orthodox modernism,
as filtered through the work of Luis Barragan.
At the DMA, Barnes has produced a work of
great simplicity, integrity, and elegance.

84

Arts District/Flora Street Streetscape, *1984*

Flora Street between Harwood Street and
Leonard Street

Sasaki Associates (Watertown, Massachusetts),
landscape architects

The Dallas Arts District comprises 18 blocks
of mostly empty real estate in downtown's
northeast corner. Its original vision as a
pedestrian-oriented district, mixing big
cultural facilities with shops and cafes along
Flora Street, was quickly subverted by spiral-
ing land prices, then was dealt a final blow
by economic recession. District identity is
currently maintained by Sasaki's intensive
streetscape design, which also provides a
visual connection between the DMA and
the Meyerson Symphony Center.

Richard Payne

85
Morton H. Meyerson Symphony Center, *1989*
2301 Flora Street
I.M. Pei & Partners (New York)
The elegiac 1980s ended on a high note in
Dallas with the opening of the Meyerson
Symphony Center, which provided the Arts
District with the critical mass and architectural distinction it needed to be recognized as
a viable entity. I.M. Pei rotated the shoebox
form of the concert hall 26° off the surrounding street grid and embraced it on three sides
by a circular glass lobby topped by skylight
lenses. This rotation opened the building
toward the downtown skyline, while simulta-
neously acknowledging the DMA at the
opposite end of Flora Street. The curvilinear
forms evident on the exterior have an even
more dramatic impact inside, where Pei softened his usual rigid geometry with sinuous
curves and complex, free-flowing spaces. By
exploiting the Late Baroque as a general stylistic source, Pei achieved a space of Piranesian
grandeur: mysterious, sensual and infinite.
By contrast, the Eugene McDermott Concert
Hall interior is a warm and richly-detailed
room notable for its gymnastic acoustical
devices, including the suspended movable
canopy over the stage and ceiling-level rever-
beration chambers. Next to the Meyerson
is **(86) Annette Strauss Artist's Square,**
1990, Sasaki Associates, a minimalist outdoor
festival venue.

Nathaniel Lieberman

87
Belo Mansion, *1888*
2101 Ross Avenue
Hubbell & Greene, renovation, 1900
Burson, Hendricks & Walls, adaptive reuse,
  1978
This Classical Revival residence built by A.H.
Belo, founder of the *Dallas Morning News*,
is the only downtown mansion surviving
from an era when Ross Avenue served as the
city's most affluent address. The neo-classical
portico was added in the 1900 renovation.

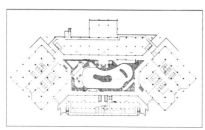

88
Plaza of the Americas, *1980*
703 N. Pearl Street
HKS, Inc.
HKS, Inc., renovation, 1992
Downtown's most substantial mixed-use project is this static composition of twin glass-
box office buildings separated by a 15-story
atrium and hotel. The meager vocabulary of
the towers is contrasted against the repetitive
textural grid of the hotel's facade, as well as
the spiral form of the attached parking ramps.
Across the street, **(89) Bloch Celebration of
Life Plaza,** 1998, Milosav Cekic (Austin), is
an exuberant adaptation of an existing aerial
skyway node into an urban park.

90
First Presbyterian Church, *1912*
401 S. Harwood Street
C.D. Hill
Oglesby Group, restoration, 1989
While other congregations were building new
downtown sanctuaries in the Gothic Revival
style, Dallas Presbyterians chose a classical
temple form as their prototype. C.D. Hill
developed a refined Beaux-Arts repertoire on
the pediment facades and shallow dome in
preparation for his Neo-Classical masterpiece
down the street.

91
John D. Carpenter Plaza, *1980*
Pearl Street at Central Expressway
Robert Irwin, sculptor
Similar to Dealey Plaza on downtown's west
side, Carpenter Plaza serves as the eastern
vehicular portal to the CBD. Robert Irwin's
thin wall of rusted steel dramatically slices
through grassy mounds and street intersections as it attempts to mitigate the overwhelming presence of Central Expressway.

92
Scottish Rite Cathedral, *1913*
500 S. Harwood Street
Hubbell & Greene
Continuing the Neo-Classical promenade
down Harwood Street is this Beaux-Arts
temple to freemasonry, designed by Herbert
M. Greene. The building's prominent and
ample site, symmetrical massing dominated
by a monumental colonnaded portico, and
elegant use of contrasting materials make
this a preeminent City Beautiful landmark.

93
Masonic Temple, *1941*
501 S. Harwood Street
Flint & Broad
Dallas' second Masonic edifice was one of
the last downtown buildings constructed
prior to World War II. It offers a rare stylistic
comparison with the Scottish Rite Cathedral
across the street: the same building type
separated by a span of 28 years. The Masonic
Temple suggests the lingering influence of
Classical Moderne, filtered through architect
Donald Nelson's work at Fair Park.

94
Desco Tile Company, *1923*
1908 Canton Street
The Venetian Gothic facade of this tile showroom demonstrates the imaginative use of tile
patterns and terra-cotta ornament to enrich
small-scale commercial buildings.

95
Farmers Market, *1941*
1010 S. Pearl Street
Corgan Associates, Shed No. 2, 1993
Corgan Associates, Resource Center, 1994
What began in the early 1900s as an open-air
public market has slowly developed into
Dallas' most authentic and pleasant pedestrian
experience. The first sheds were added prior
to World War II, followed by an enclosed
shed in 1993. This new addition, despite its
sensitive architectural congruity with the
original structures, has been a programmatic
failure due to its exclusion of vehicles.
Another planning blunder occurred with the
1993 re-routing of Central Expressway
through a corner of the original complex,
causing the loss of a shed, as well as incom-
prehensible traffic circulation for the entire
area. It is remarkable that the Farmers Market
has survived these efforts to undermine its
spontaneous vitality. The most recent addition is Corgan's 1995 Resource Center, a
properly scaled, contextual building that
employs pseudo-industrial forms and
materials to mimic a farm vernacular.

96
2220 Canton Lofts, *1925*
2220 Canton Street
Corgan Associates, adaptive reuse, 1996
The austere concrete frame and brick infill
facade of this 1925 warehouse provides a
suitable gridded backdrop to the lively pattern
of black metal balconies. Downtown's first
significant loft conversion initiated the
spate of similar adaptive reuse projects in
the late 1990s.

97
Warner Brothers Film Exchange, *1929*
508 Park Avenue
Weiss, Dreyfous & Seiferth (New Orleans)
During the 1920s, the residential neighborhood southeast of downtown developed into
a district of film distribution businesses in
support of Dallas' theater district on Elm
Street. This Zigzag Moderne gem, designed
by the New Orleans firm responsible for the
Louisiana State Capitol, is a spirited outpost
of Hollywood glamour.

2 Deep Ellum/Fair Park/ Near East and South

There is no better measure of Dallas' early growing pains than the changing nature of the neighborhoods that grew up around John Neely Bryan's original city. For it was here, particularly to the south and east, that folks attempted to settle down. The wealthy, who were years away from embracing the notion of commuting, built grand mansions within walking distance of their businesses, without realizing how soon those residences would be compromised by the encroaching city. The oldest of such elite neighborhoods, The Cedars, was in decline in 1890 only ten years after its first grand houses were built. From then on, the peregrinations of the wealthy charted a course east to Peak's Suburban Addition then south toward South Boulevard and Park Row, and on to lower Swiss Avenue and Munger Place before finally heading north in the early 20th century to Highland Park. Surviving mansions, well-protected now by the Dallas Historic Preservation League, still evoke an inner-city lifestyle that has only recently begun to be revived.

There is another neighborhood, however, whose evolution was a bit more organic. Deep Ellum – what the African American population called the area consisting of Elm Street, Main, and Commerce east of the Houston and Texas Central Railroad – sprang into existence following the Civil War as a haven for freed slaves. Deep Ellum was rough – fraught with violence and prostitution – but it was also a community. Businesses, including hotels, vaudeville houses, and pawn shops owned by African Americans, flourished. And, in the 1920s, musicians like Blind Lemon Jefferson and Huddie "Leadbelly" Ledbetter played the blues in the neighborhood's clubs. Deep Ellum was a freedman's world in the purest, most expressive meaning of the word.

The essential Bohemian atmosphere of the neighborhood has changed little over the years although it has accommodated art galleries, design firms, and loft dwellers in its renovated warehouses. Deep Ellum has gained such an appreciation of its own quirky vitality that it has taken steps to protect itself from the kind of city planning that would have cleaned it up and turned it into the ceremonial boulevard leading to Fair Park from downtown.

Plans for ways to connect the historic grounds of Fair Park to downtown Dallas have been discussed since the park was finished in 1936. It was here, on the site of the yearly Texas State Fair, that Dallas staged the 1936 Texas Centennial Exposition, and brought national recognition to the city. The Centennial occasioned a complex of exquisitely detailed, celebratory buildings and helped lift the city out of the Depression. A designated National Historic Landmark, Fair Park continues to attract more than 7 million visitors a year.

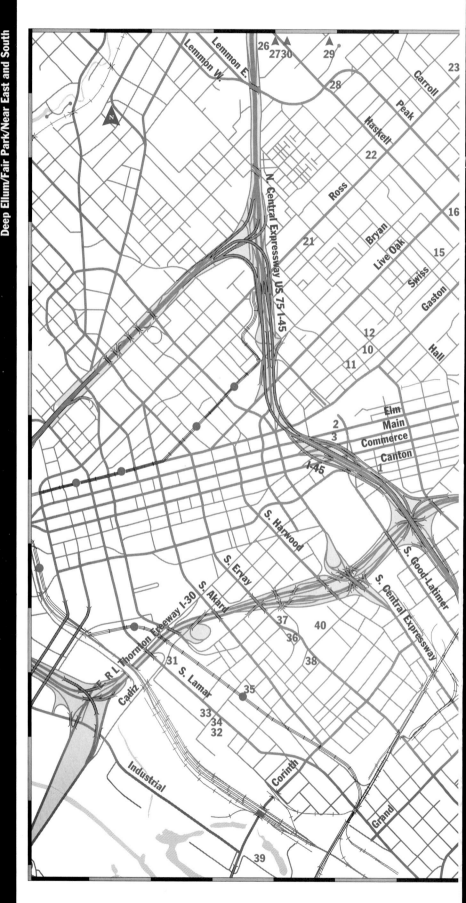

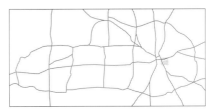

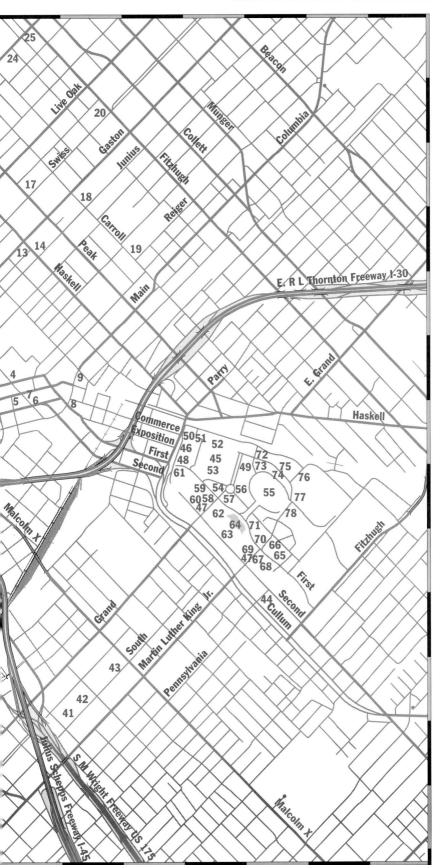

2 Deep Ellum/Fair Park/ Near East and South

1
Adam Hats Lofts, *1914*
2700 Canton Street
John Graham (Seattle)
Corgan Associates, adaptive reuse, 1997
Anchoring the southwest corner of Deep
Ellum, and adjacent to the former Houston
& Texas Central tracks, is this four-story,
brick and terra-cotta factory building built
by Henry Ford for the assembly of Model-T
automobiles. The architect was John Graham
of Seattle, who designed several of these
regional Ford plants between 1914 and 1918.

3
Deep Ellum Storefronts, *c.1900*
2500 block of Elm Street
This block of two-story commercial storefronts is largely intact from the early 1900s,
when it was the center of a thriving commercial district serving the city's growing black
and immigrant population. Many of the
stores' facades sported cast iron columns,
which allowed for increased window area
without heavy masonry piers. This is one
of the few remaining cast iron storefronts
in Dallas.

2
Union Bankers Building, *1916*
2551 Elm Street
William Sidney Pittman
The former Pythian Temple once presided
with authority over the core of Dallas' black
commercial district. Designed by William
Sidney Pittman, the state's first black architect
and the son-in-law of Booker T. Washington,
this Renaissance-inspired building is dominated by two-story arched openings on the top
floors, along with cornices and an ornamental
parapet. It was Pittman's largest built work.

Willis Winters

4
Continental Lofts
3309 Elm Street and 232 Trunk Avenue, 1888
212 Trunk Avenue, 1912
3301-33 Elm Street, 1914
Oglesby-Greene, adaptive reuse, 1997
This intact complex of early industrial buildings is a potent reminder of the role cotton
played in the Texas economy at the turn of
the century. The Continental Gin Company,
originally owned by R.S. Munger, was the
largest manufacturer of cotton-processing
equipment in the United States. Munger's
factory grew in several phases, beginning in
1888 with a series of narrow, brick vernacular
warehouses along the T&P tracks and culmi-
nating in 1914 with the more substantial
office and factory group facing Elm Street.
The surviving buildings form one of the
most significant landmarks of industrial
architecture in the state.

5
3200 Main Street Lofts, *1913*
3200 Main Street
Graham Greene, adaptive reuse, 1991
Dallas' emergence as a regional center for
trade and commerce can be attributed to two
key events: its designation in 1913 as a new
port of entry by the U.S. Customs Service,

and in the following year, its selection as
headquarters of the Federal Reserve Bank,
Eleventh District. This six-story structure of
cubic proportions was built by the Interstate
Forwarding Company as Dallas' first U.S.
Customs warehouse. It was one of the earliest
utilitarian industrial buildings in the city to
employ an expressed, reinforced concrete
structural frame infilled with brick and glass.

6
Murray Building, *1921*
3401 Commerce Street
Oglesby-Greene, adaptive reuse, 1996
Indicative of the smaller, second-generation
commercial structures in Deep Ellum is this
three-story brick building that originally
served as a fabrication plant for the Dallas
Tent & Awning Company. The five-bay wide
rational facade has minimal cast stone accents
and – in a solitary gesture toward classicism –
displays a dentilated cornice. Architect
Graham Greene was responsible for the
adaptive reuse of this building, and many
others in Deep Ellum, including the nearby
(7) Farm and Ranch Lofts, 1920, Oglesby-
Greene, adaptive reuse, 1997.

8
Exposition Plaza, *1986*
Commerce Street at Exposition Avenue
James Pratt
The 1911 Kessler Plan recommended linking Fair Park with downtown via a grand ceremonial boulevard. While this Haussmann planning gesture never materialized, Deep Ellum's version of Place de l'Etoile was implemented as the centerpiece of the proposed processional, as well as a gateway to Fair Park. Although it has never become the catalyst for surrounding re-development as anticipated, James Pratt's lively plaza is nevertheless a critical beautifying amenity anchoring the east end of Deep Ellum.

9
3800 Main Street/Silos, *1945*
3800 Main Street
Eugene Davis
Phillips/Ryburn Associates, adaptive reuse, 1989
Grain elevators provide vertical punctuation in the Deep Ellum industrial landscape. The smallest of these silo projects was built after World War II by Frito-Lay as the first of several "chip" plants that Dallas would become famous for (in 1958, Texas Instruments would begin production of a different kind of chip). The imaginative renovation of this facility in 1989 was Deep Ellum's first significant adaptive reuse project.

Wilson Block

10
Wilson House, *c.1898*
2922 Swiss Avenue
Keith Downing, restoration, 1981
The lone survivor of the grand Victorian mansions that once covered east Dallas in the late 19th century is this Queen Anne-style residence built by cattleman Frederick Wilson. This house, together with the remaining houses in the 2800 and 2900 blocks of Swiss Avenue (the Wilson District) were restored by the Meadows Foundation in 1981.

11
Beilharz House, *c.1885*
2800 Swiss Avenue
Keith Downing, restoration, 1981
With its prominent octagonal tower and gambrel roof, this Shingle-style residence built by Theodore Beilharz is a suitable bookend to the two-block length of the Wilson District. Beilharz was a master stonecutter responsible for the masonry on "Old Red" and the Ellis County Courthouse in Waxahachie.

12
Meadows Foundation Headquarters, *1992*
3003 Swiss Avenue
Keith Downing, 1992
The architect responsible for the restoration of the Wilson District houses also designed this office building headquarters for the Meadows Foundation. The insertion of a

large building into the surrounding historical neighborhood is successfully mitigated by the Victorian-esque appendages and detailing.

13
Criswell College, *1902*
4000 Gaston Avenue
Charles W. Bulger (Galveston)
Mark Lemmon, addition, 1940
Phillips Swager Associates, adaptive reuse, 1990
Heavy-handed Neo-Classicism marks this imposing edifice designed for the Gaston Avenue Baptist Church. Architect C.W. Bulger practiced in Galveston for 12 years before moving to Dallas in 1904, when he was joined by his son, a recent graduate of the University of Chicago. Together, Bulger & Son were responsible for over 100 churches (primarily Baptist) throughout the southwest, as well as Dallas' first skyscraper, the Praetorian Building, completed in 1909. Bulger later adopted his Gaston Avenue design for a near duplicate church in Texarkana. The current fiberglass dome is a mere ghost of the ornately clad original.

15
Stearns Hall, *1929*
3909 Swiss Avenue
C.H. Griesenbeck
Fisher & Spillman, renovation, 1974
The earliest component of the Dallas Theological Seminary campus is this former YMCA facility designed by Clyde Griesenbeck in a vague Mediterranean style. Flanking the pleasant quadrangle dominated by Stearns Hall and the adjacent Davidson Hall is perhaps the finest building on the campus: the two-story **(15a) Mosher Library,** designed by Fisher & Jarvis, 1959. In the early 1970s, Fisher & Spillman updated the school's architectural vocabulary in the newest quadrangle facing Live Oak Street.

14
Grace United Methodist Church, *1903*
4105 Junius Street
W.A. Caan (St. Louis)
The Gothic Revival style provided Dallas' earliest suburban Methodist congregation with a suitable neighborhood landmark as a counterpoint to the Neo-Classical Baptist church across the street. Grace United Methodist, along with First Baptist downtown, are the two finest examples of this ecclesiastical style in the city. The most notable feature of this church is its soaring corner tower, confidently detailed with buttresses, lancet windows, corner turrets and a finialed steeple. The two primary elevations facing Junius and Haskell are equally resourceful and picturesque.

16
Lincoln Hall, *1921*
1206 N. Haskell Boulevard
Herbert M. Greene & Co.
Herbert Greene's Georgian sensibilities are beyond reproach in this former boarding house for the YWCA. The three-story brick and stone building rests on a raised basement and features a symmetrical facade framed by subtly projecting pavilions with two-story stone pilasters. Greene was one of Dallas' most successful architects throughout his prolific career, which included prominent partnerships with J.W. Hubbell and George Dahl.

Peak's Suburban

In 1879, Peak's Suburban Addition was carved from the family plantation of real estate pioneer Jefferson Peak, following the arrival of the railroads in the eastern part of the city in 1872. Today, the area is a microcosm of primarily builder-designed residences, reflecting myriad architectural styles during the primary period of development between 1890 and 1930.

17
Mirajah Brooks House, *c.1905*
4303 Swiss Avenue
The symmetrically balanced facade of this impressive house has a full-height porch with paired Corinthian columns supporting a classical pediment. The one-story wraparound porch behind the main portico is a rare feature of the residential Neo-Classical style.

19
Private Residence, *1912*
4503 Reiger Avenue
Lang & Witchell
This diminutively scaled Mission-style house is enriched by the use of stone detailing in the porch railing and piers (each topped by a Prairie-style orb), gable coping and the slightly overscaled quatrefoil attic windows.

18
Private Residence, *c.1900*
4503 Junius Street
This fine Queen Anne-style house is the only brick Victorian remaining in east Dallas. The hipped roof, turret and front-facing gable, in combination with an asymmetrical porch supported by classical columns, are common features of this style.

20
Viola Courts, *1923*
4845 Swiss Avenue
Antonio Guidera, designer
Located across from the entry gates to prestigious Swiss Avenue, Viola Courts represented Dallas' development into an increasingly sophisticated and high-density urban city. The mixed bag of stylistic references can be attributed to the well-intentioned naivete of Antonio Guidera, the builder-designer.

21
Fishburn Buildings, *1907*
3200 Ross Avenue
By 1910, commercial structures had begun
to invade the opulent promenade of Ross
Avenue mansions extending northeast out of
downtown for almost two miles. One of the
largest encroachers was this two-story brick
and cast stone building for Fishburn's
Laundry, an overwhelming presence set in
the midst of an elite residential neighborhood, prompting its rapid demise. The excru-
ciatingly repetitive facade of this building
is bifurcated by continuous vertical piers.

22
Oriental Rug Cleaning Co., *1926*
3907 Ross Avenue
Sadler & Russell
Architect Luther Sadler was responsible for
this Moorish facade, with its odd bay rhythm
of ground-level arched openings and compara-
bly sized second-floor windows. By 1920, the
decline of Ross Avenue as the city's elegant
residential street was complete, its desirability
as an elite neighborhood was superceded by
newer, deed-restricted developments such as
Highland Park and the nearby Munger Place.
During the 1930s, Sadler was one of the city's
most progressive designers, responsible for
several important Moderne buildings.

23
Dallas Women's Forum, *1906*
4607 Ross Avenue
Sanguinett & Staats
One of only three remaining residences
from among hundreds of mansions built
during Ross Avenue's Gilded Age is this
Neo-Classical palace constructed by banker
Charles Alexander. Its cubic massing and
rational application of Neo-Classical ornament suggest the hand of architect C.D. Hill,
who managed the Dallas office of Sanguinett
& Staats.

24
Claremont Apartments, *1924*
4636 Ross Avenue
The four-unit Claremont was typical of
two- and three-story apartment buildings that
proliferated in east Dallas during the 1920s
along streetcar lines. Its Mission Revival
styling was fashionable, albeit uncommon,
for this building type.

25
James W. Fannin Elementary School, *1915*
4800 Ross Avenue
Lang & Witchell
Fannin Elementary was built to serve the
burgeoning population of east Dallas, which
tripled in size between 1900 and 1920. The
exquisitely detailed central pavilion marks
Lang and Witchell's tentative foray into
Gothic Revival, a style the firm would return
to 13 years later in their Dallas County
Records Building.

27
ACS Headquarters, *1971*
2828 N. Haskell Boulevard
Fisher & Spillman
This dignified pre-cast concrete office building served as the headquarters of the Southland Corporation for 18 years, before its move to more imposing quarters across the street. Understated and sparingly detailed, it is one of the best tall buildings in the Central Expressway corridor.

28
Mallallieu Methodist Church, *1909*
2200 N. Haskell Boulevard
James Flanders
The assured Prairie-style composition of this humble neighborhood church marks the late style of James Flanders, Dallas' first professional architect.

26
Cityplace Tower, *1989*
2711 N. Haskell Boulevard
Cossutta & Associates (New York)
When it was first announced in 1983, the master plan for the Cityplace development included 18 million square feet of office, hotel and residential space on 130 acres of inner-city real estate straddling Central Expressway. Within four years, as the first of two proposed 43-story office towers was nearing completion, the price of oil had dropped from $32 to $18 a barrel, Dallas possessed an office vacancy rate of biblical proportions and the Southland Corporation – the developer of Cityplace – had assumed massive debt to avoid a hostile takeover. All that was left of Aldo Cossutta's mammoth urban vision was a single, forlorn tower adjacent to a newly constructed boulevard. The tower consists of two vertical slabs of office space rising on each side of stacked, three-story sky lobbies. The lobbies form a continuous vertical slit on the building's east and west faces, matching the similar vertical thrust of the primary office facades. Cityplace Tower is a highly articulated skyscraper – the tallest outside of downtown – that suffers from both unvariegated coloration and slightly stunted proportions. It is nevertheless a striking architectural landmark anchoring the southern extremity of Central Expressway.

29
Alex Spence Middle School, *1939*
4001 Capitol Avenue
Mark Lemmon
Mark Lemmon designed numerous public schools in Dallas before assuming the all-powerful position of consulting architect for the Dallas Independent School District in 1946. Among Lemmon's many fine campuses is this Classical Moderne junior high, executed with crisp stone and aluminum detailing.

30
Private Residence, *1936*
5103 Pershing Street
Charles Dilbeck
Cochran Heights is a pocket neighborhood
wedged between Henderson Avenue and
Central Expressway. Its two primary streets –
Pershing and Milam – contain dozens of
small cottages designed by Dallas' most idiosyncratic architect, Charles Dilbeck. This
white-washed, cubic assemblage is one of
the neighborhood's three Moderne-style residences designed by Dilbeck; the remaining
houses are predominantly in his Ranch and
French Eclectic idioms. The Moderne houses
are the treasures of Cochran Heights, serving
to substantially modify Dilbeck's eclectic
legacy. Examples of Dilbeck's three cottage
styles are located at 5203 Pershing (Moderne);
5028 Milam (Ranch); and 5029 Milam
(French Eclectic).

31
Good Luck Service Station, *1939*
904 Cadiz Street
Wilemon Bros., designers
Renovation, 1993
This delightful Streamline Moderne service
station is a survivor of the 50-station Good
Luck Oil Company (Gloco) empire that
spread throughout Dallas in the 1930s. The
30-foot scalloped stucco tower, now denuded
of its neon signage, bears striking propor-
tional similarity to Philip Johnson's 62-story
Bank One Center.

32
Sears-Roebuck Warehouse, *1914*
1409 Lamar Street
Lang & Witchell
Lang & Witchell, additions, 1915, 1916
Concurrent with their warehouse commission
for the Higginbotham-Bailey-Logan
Company, Lang & Witchell also designed
this behemoth distribution center and
wholesale store for Sears-Roebuck. The first
phase, completed in 1914, encompassed
850,000 square feet on nine floors. Like the
Higginbotham warehouse, projecting towers
added up to two additional floors in height.
Windows are organized between continuous,
wide horizontal headers and narrower, discon-
tinuous sills. Prairie-style decorative patterns
mark the upper floors of each tower and –
in a salute to Sullivan – luscious, foliated
pier capitals grace the main entrance. Lang &
Witchell continued this progressive expression
on two subsequent additions, as well as
painting the horizontal bands on an extant
commercial warehouse across the street at
(33) 1325 Lamar Street. Adjacent to the
distribution center, Lang & Witchell also
designed the **(34) Sears Roebuck Club,**
1914, in a more stringent Prairie style.

35
DART Cedars Station, *1996*
1112 Bellevue Street
Hellmuth, Obata & Kassabaum
Of the twelve DART stations that utilize
the prototype model originally developed by
HOK, the Cedars Station is the most elemental in execution. It is an elegant and spare
design, refreshingly uncluttered by applied
public art.

36
Ace Baking Company, *1903*
1401 S. Ervay Street
Between 1880 and 1890, "The Cedars" developed as Dallas' first affluent residential neighborhood. One of the area's earliest residents was Dr. John Hughes, who also built a series of factory buildings across from City Park for the manufacture of soda water, vinegar, jelly and candy. This five-story brick building, with handsome segmental and flat window arches and corbelling underneath three horizontal cornices, is the only remaining component of the original Hughes Bros. Manufacturing Company complex.

37
Ambassador Hotel, *1905*
1312 S. Ervay Street
Despite the influx of industry, and the resulting decline of The Cedars, City Park continued to serve as a strong attraction for surrounding development, including the city's first suburban luxury hotel – the Park – and the nearby **(38)** **Eagle Apartments,** 1615 S. Ervay Street, 1920, a sophisticated, classically detailed apartment house resting atop an enclosed parking garage.

40
Old City Park, *1876*
1717 Gano Street
The property for Dallas' first public park was acquired in three phases beginning in 1876. Within nine years, a 19-acre site had been assembled, including the land comprising Browder Springs, the city's privately owned water supply. Improvements were made throughout the 1880s and 1890s, including gazebos, greenhouses, a bandstand and a miniature zoo: attractions successful in elevating the park's popularity and influencing the city's southward expansion over the next decade. Since 1969, Old City Park has been administered by the Dallas County Heritage Society as an architectural and cultural heritage museum. Thirty-three historic structures, representing the period from 1840 to 1910, have been relocated to the park from sites around north Texas. The most significant of these is **(40a)** **Millermore** (photo above), a marginal Greek Revival plantation house built between 1855 and 1862. The house was located nearby on Bonnie View Road and was the first historical structure brought into the park. Adjacent to Millermore is the original Miller log cabin (1847), the oldest structure at Old City Park. Recent land acquisition has greatly expanded the park's boundaries, which are defined by a characteristic iron and stone fence.

39
Longhorn Ballroom, *1950*
216 Corinth Street
High camp is the trademark of these kitschy Wild West facades that conceal Dallas' beloved Country-Western performance venue.

South Boulevard/Park Row

43
Private Residence, *1913*
2707 South Boulevard
J. Edward Overbeck
A classic example of the Mission Revival style
is this imposing two-story residence designed
by J. Edward Overbeck for Levi Marcus.
The centrality of this house is initiated by
the prominent "Alamo" dormer perched on
the hipped roof, and confirmed by the
Mission-style parapet over the impressive
entry portico, which displays a corbelled arch
and diagonal buttresses. Overbeck succeeded
C.D. Hill as the manager of Sanguinett &
Staats' Dallas office, before leaving to establish
his own practice. This residence was one of
his first independent commissions.

41
Private Residence, *1914*
2419 South Boulevard
Lang & Witchell
By 1915, residents of the Cedars had fled to
newer, more stable neighborhoods. Dallas'
prominent Jewish families favored residential
subdivisions farther south that were developed
along two stylish streets – South Boulevard
and Forest Avenue – and served by a nearby
relocated synagogue. This house by Lang &
Witchell features strong Prairie-style detailing
applied to a more traditionally proportioned
cross-gable house type. Notable features
include the dramatic porch arches with elegant cast stone trim, a tile roof with deep
eaves, and a secondary shed roof supported
by brick piers similar to those employed by
the same architects on their Mission Revival
house at 4503 Reiger Avenue.

44
Joe Lewis Field House, *1982*
1702 Cullum Boulevard
Parkey & Partners
Clarity and restraint characterize this public
school field house located on the southern-
most corner of Fair Park. The lobby end of
the gymnasium is a series of taut, heavily-
gridded planes of aluminum and glass which
align with the projecting edges of the building's shed roof. The farthest extension of the
roof plane forms the lowest cornice line,
cleverly marking the public entrance.

42
Private Residence, *1913*
2527 South Boulevard
Another South Boulevard mansion of mixed
architectural provenance is this intriguing
blend of Tudor and Craftsman design motifs.
While the upper floors are generally Tudor
in character, the lower floor is undeniably
Craftsman. In addition, Craftsman details,
consisting of triangular knee braces and
elaborated rafter ends invade the attic level.

Fair Park

In 1936, Texas commemorated the 100th anniversary of its independence from Mexico with a series of state-wide celebrations. A central exposition was proposed, with four cities waging a sometimes bitter campaign to secure the rights to stage this event. At stake for the host city was unparalleled national exposure and a strong economic boost in the midst of the Depression. Using the existing grounds and buildings at Fair Park as the basis of its bid, Dallas out-hustled its competitors and was selected to host the Texas Centennial Exposition. The fair was planned by chief architect George Dahl, with legions of designers and artists, who collaborated to produce one of the great American world's fairs of the 1930s.

45
The Esplanade (Reflecting Basin), *1936*
George Dahl
The principal axis of the Exposition developed along the existing layout of the fairgrounds, which dated to George Kessler's City Beautiful-inspired master plan of 1904. Dahl strengthened Kessler's formal axis by adapting existing, unrelated exhibition halls with new, monumental facades and projecting porticos on each side of a 700-foot long reflecting pool. These porticos establish the visual framework of the Esplanade and accentuate the grand perspective leading up to the Hall of State. Monumental artwork was deftly combined with additional site features to complete the visually complex and awe-inspiring spectacle. Of these secondary elements, only a pair of pylons executed by artist Pierre Bourdelle remain. At night, the Esplanade was transformed into an ethereal vision by a bank of 24 powerful searchlights radiating from behind the Hall of State.

46
Parry Avenue Entrance, *1936*
Lang & Witchell
This symbolic entrance to Fair Park (made obsolete by parking expansion during the 1980s) is the largest of four entry gates designed by Lang & Witchell. A singularly striking 85-foot high pylon greeted the pedestrian hordes upon disembarkation at the streetcar terminus on Parry Avenue. The base of the pylon displays a sculptural frieze by Texas artist Buck Winn. The plaza surrounding the pylon has been altered, although the secondary **(47) Grand Avenue and M.L. King, Jr. Boulevard Entrance Gates,** are still intact. Nearby is the **(48) Texas Vietnam Veteran's Memorial,** Martratt/Garmon, 1990.

Willis Winters

49
Hall of State (State of Texas Building), *1936*
Texas Centennial Architects; Adams & Adams
(San Antonio)
Thomas & Booziotis, renovation, 1987
The terminus of the Esplanade and the archi-
tectural centerpiece of the Exposition was the
State of Texas Building, now known as the
Hall of State. When the consortium of ten
Dallas firms hired to design the building
failed to produce a plan acceptable to the
State Board of Control, Dahl called in
Houston architect Donald Barthelme, who
quickly produced a synthesis of the previous
schemes and had it approved. Barthelme's
design for the Hall of State illustrates the
discernible influence of Paul Philippe Cret,
whose Folger Shakespeare Library and, more
particularly, his Aisne-Marne Memorial –
both dating to 1932 – provide authoritative
previews of this monumental edifice.
Barthelme worked in Cret's office in the early
1930s, prior to returning to his hometown of
Galveston. He undoubtedly brought with him
Cret's Classical Modern aesthetic, which was
abundantly applied in stone to the building's
central exedra and flanking lateral wings. The
building's towering achievement, however,
was in its incorporation of art as a propa-
ganda vehicle to express the history, culture,
and geography of Texas. A team of international, national, and regional artists was
assembled to augment the Art Deco architecture, a collaborative effort that produced
some of the most splendid and inspiring interior spaces in the United States.

Willis Winters

50
Hall of Administration Building, *1910*
C.D. Hill, Coliseum
George Dahl, renovation, 1935
Dallas' first coliseum was constructed by
the State Fair primarily for horse shows, but
was also utilized for musical entertainment
throughout the year. Its location along the
front boundary of the fairgrounds, immediately inside the front gate, allowed access
from inside the park during fair time,
as well as direct access from Parry Avenue. In
1935, Dahl renovated the Coliseum into the
Centennial Exposition's administration building by removing the original porticos and
applying a new Art Deco facade on its south
face. The central arched opening of this elevation contains a mural by Carlo Ciampaglia
as backdrop to Raoul Josset's sculpture, the
Spirit of the Centennial. The building is
currently being renovated as the Women's
Museum: An Institute for the Future, by
F&S Partners and Wendy Evans Joseph of
New York. Adjacent to the Hall of
Administration is the **(51) D.A.R. Building,**
originally designed by M.C. Kleuser – in yet
another Dallas attempt at Mount Vernon – as
the Conoco Travel Bureau Hospitality House.

Fair Park

Willis Winters

52
**Centennial Building (Transportation
  Building, Chrysler Building),** *1905*
James Flanders (State Fair Exposition Building)
George Dahl, renovation and addition, 1936
ArchiTexas, restoration, 1999
The Centennial Building was originally constructed in 1905 as the first steel and masonry
exhibition building on the fairgrounds. In
1904, after a series of events that caused stag-
gering financial losses, the State Fair agreed to
deed the fairgrounds to the City in exchange
for cash to pay off its debt. Funding for a
major new exhibit hall was included in the
deal, and James Flanders, fresh from his work
at the St. Louis World's Fair of 1904, was
hired as the architect. Flanders' design consisted of three large bays, each with a gabled
roof and projecting entrance portico. Dahl's
renovation in 1936 continued this tripartite
layout, only on a much grander scale. He
built three new porticos as part of a frontal
expansion of the building, extending it consi-
derably to almost twice its original length.
Similar gymnastics were performed on the
opposite side of the Esplanade, where Dahl
also incorporated an existing building into
the new axial ground plan. The current **(53)
Automobile Building,** Walter Ahlschlager,
1948, replaced the original structure that
burned. Matching porticos were added in
1986. Dahl's design for the two buildings
incorporated a pair of murals by Carlo
Ciampaglia under each portico, monumental
sculptures by Pierre Bourdelle and Raoul Joset
in front of each portico and cameo reliefs
by Bourdelle.

54
**Old Mill Inn (Flour Milling Industry
  Building),** *1936*
W.C. Conkranty
Clad in fieldstone and incorporating heavy
timber details, this building was one of the
few outside of the Midway that did not
utilize Art Deco styling in its design. It pre-
sents a startling contrast to the neighboring
Magnolia Lounge.

55
Cotton Bowl (Fair Park Stadium), *1930*
Mark Lemmon
George Dahl, renovation, 1936
*Chappell, Stokes & Brenneke, engineers,
  additions, 1948, 1949*
Hellmuth, Obata & Kassabaum, addition, 1993
Constructed on the old racetrack infield,
the original Fair Park Stadium was a concrete
bowl, partially below grade, giving it a distinctly different presence in the middle of
Fair Park than it possesses today. With a
seating capacity of 46,200, it was the largest
stadium in the south. The capacity was
increased by the addition of upper decks
in 1948 and 1949.

Willis Winters

56
Tower Building (U.S. Government Building),
  1936
George Dahl
ArchiTexas, restoration, 1999
The 179-foot high triangular tower of the
U.S. Government Building marked the geographic center of the Centennial Exposition.
Its design is attributed to Donald Nelson,
who previously worked on the 1933 Chicago
Century of Progress Exposition, and was
coaxed, along with others, to join Dahl's staff
at the fair's conclusion. These strong ties
account for the similarity of the federal buildings at both expositions. Nearby, **(57) Grand
Place,** Gill & Harrell, 1954, is an impover-
ished reminder of Albert Kahn's extravagant
Ford Motor Co. Exhibit Building, which was
located on this site during the Centennial.

Willis Winters

58

Magnolia Lounge (Magnolia Petroleum Building), *1936*

William Lescaze (New York)

Thomas & Booziotis, restoration, 1987

This little-known project by New York architect William Lescaze introduced European Modernism to Texas in 1936. Lescaze's rapid climb to fame occurred four years earlier when his work was included by Philip Johnson in the Museum of Modern Art exhibition on modern architecture. Although his design for the Magnolia Petroleum Building includes elements commonly found in Art Deco, its overall image was radically different from that of any other structure at the Exposition. Solid volumetric massing was supplanted by floating planes and cantilevered decks. Slender metal piers replaced monumental colonnades. The effect was avant-garde and exhilarating. The Magnolia Petroleum Building would serve as Modernist inspiration to a generation of Dallas architects. Adjacent to the Magnolia Lounge are the former **(59) Hall of Religion,** George Dahl, 1936; and the **(60) African American Museum,** Arthur J. Rogers, 1993.

Willis Winters

61

Fair Park Music Hall (General Motors Building), *1925*

Lang & Witchell

Peterman & Peterman, renovation, 1936

Jarvis Putty Jarvis, renovation and addition, 1972

In 1925, the City of Dallas finished construction of this cavernous 3,500-seat music hall located to the south of the Parry Avenue entrance. The building designed by Lang & Witchell was the winning entry in a limited design competition sponsored the previous

year. Their design incorporated Spanish Colonial Revival detailing, primarily in the dominant square towers on the building's north side and in the paired octagonal towers on the east and west facades. For the Centennial, the Music Hall was the only existing building not extensively altered; its conversion to display General Motors automobiles required interior modifications only. In 1972, the building was sensitively expanded by Jarvis Putty Jarvis, who utilized the octagonal shapes of the original building as a plan-generating device for the new additions.

Willis Winters

62

Dallas Museum of Natural History, *1936*

Mark Lemmon; C.H. Griesenbeck; John Danna Needham-McCaffrey, renovation, 1988

South of the Midway, Dahl arranged the city's future cultural institutions informally around a peaceful lagoon. The first of these was the Museum of Natural History, designed by Mark Lemmon and Clyde Griesenbeck as a monolithic, rectangular box, with little architectural detail. The entrance is marked by three vertical window bays with decorative aluminum mullions, and is flanked by paired pilasters with shell-motif capitals. The remainder of the building is conservatively clad in cream limestone. In 1988, Needham-McCaffrey livened things up in their reclamation of the museum's basement for administrative and support space. The northeast corner of the building was excavated and gingerly exposed via a delightful series of curvilinear, landscaped terraces designed by the Mesa Design Group.

Fair Park

63

Science Place I and Imax Theater (Museum of Fine Arts), *1936*
DeWitt & Washburn; Herbert M. Greene, LaRoche & Dahl; Ralph Bryan; Henry Coke Knight; Paul Philippe Cret
Roscoe DeWitt, addition, 1963
Corgan Associates, renovation as Science Place, 1985
Corgan Associates, IMAX Theater addition, 1996

The museums comprising the cultural district were envisioned as the legacy of the Centennial Exposition to the citizens of Dallas. In a single gesture, the city received the endowment of a substantial new civic center. The most important of the new facilities was the Museum of Fine Arts, which – like the Hall of State – was designed by a consortium of Dallas architects. This spartan building, clad in cream limestone and shellstone, was the centerpiece of the picturesque **(64) Lagoon** area, and was located on axis with the plaza and entry to the stadium. Corgan's 1996 IMAX Theater addition gave the Science Place a new monumental entry that is shifted off the Centennial axis. Despite its mass, the theater is surprisingly contextual within this architecturally sensitive district.

65

Science Place II (Domestic Arts Museum), *1936*
Anton Korn; J.A. Pitzinger
Emil Fretz, addition, 1973

The transition to large-scale public architecture proved to be a difficult one for Anton Korn, whose primary experience was in residential design. Nearby, the **(66) Texas Star Ferris Wheel,** the second tallest in the world, is easily Fair Park's most visible structure.

67

Dallas Horticulture Center (Horticulture Museum), *1936*
Arthur E. Thomas; M.C. Kleuser
Pratt, Box and Henderson, addition, 1971
Good, Fulton & Farrell, renovation, 1990
AAE, Inc., renovation, 1999

Of all the museum facilities in the original cultural district, this building bears the least resemblance to its original appearance. The most notable feature is the extraordinary minimalist glass Blachly Conservatory, added in 1971. In the gardens behind the main building can be found the **(68) Dallas Horticulture Education Building,** designed by Bubi Jessen of Austin as the Portland Cement Model Home for the Centennial, and restored by Dallas AIA in 1984. Three other nearby model homes were moved off-site after the close of the fair.

Willis Winters

69

Fair Park Band Shell (Band Shell), *1936*
W. Scott Dunne; Christensen & Christensen
Christensen & Christensen, addition, 1941
AAE, Inc., restoration, 1999

The concentric plaster arches of the Band Shell comprise an essentially Art Deco composition, while the reinforced concrete back-stage building is infused with elements of Streamline Moderne. The gently-sloping, 5,000-seat amphitheater is surrounded by lighting pylons. Scott Dunne was a noted theater architect in Dallas.

Willis Winters

70
Dallas Aquarium at Fair Park (Aquarium),
1936
Fooshee and Cheek; Hal Thomson; Flint
& Broad
Booziotis & Co., addition, 1993
The Aquarium represents a highly complex
building type that was only beginning to be
developed in the 1930s. The intuitive techno-
logical solution developed by the architects is
not apparent on the building's exterior, which
consists of the traditional raised entrance
pavilion and loggia with flanking wings. This
entrance, interesting for its vestigial display
of elements from both Streamline and Zigzag
Moderne, is formally aligned with the center
axis of the Bandshell. The expanses of blank
wall surfaces successfully incorporate a series
of alternating brick planes and recessed sculptural panels that impart a lively rhythm to
the facade. Adjacent to the Aquarium is the
(71) Education Annex, Luther Sadler, 1936;
AAE, Inc., restoration, 1998, originally the
Christian Science Monitor Pavilion.

72
Food and Fiber Pavilion (Agriculture
  Building), *1936*
George Dahl
Good, Fulton & Farrell, restoration, 1999
Dahl consolidated the livestock and agricul-
tural facilities on the north side of the
Cotton Bowl. The main axial approach into
the district utilizes the matching porticos
of the Food and Fiber Pavilion and the **(73)**
Embarcadero Building (Foods Building),
George Dahl, 1936, as foreground objects
to frame the perspective view and to focus
attention on a distant pylon. Nearby, is the

(74) Creative Arts Building (Foods Building),
George Dahl, 1936.

75
Pan American Arena (Livestock Coliseum),
  c.1929
Architect unknown
George Dahl, renovation, 1936
As he did on the Esplanade, Dahl incorporated
existing buildings into a much larger facility,
and faced them with a new Art Deco facade.
The new entrance was symmetrically aligned
with the north entrance of the stadium, ter-
minating a much longer planning axis that
extended south to the Museum of Fine Arts.
Within this contiguous building are various
livestock barns, one of which has been renovated into the **(75a) Dallas Police Mounted**
Unit Headquarters, Gary Garmon, 1998.

Willis Winters

76
Swine Building (Livestock Building No. 2),
  1936
George Dahl
Dahl's most accomplished single building
for the Centennial is this livestock facility
on the northeast corner of Fair Park.
Dahl proved that he was capable of great
Exposition architecture without the
encumbrance of Beaux-Arts baggage.

77
Fair Park Coliseum, *1959*
Harper & Kemp
While its architectural virtues can be
applauded – particularly the folded plate roof
and cantilevered facade – this massive metal
barn could use lessons in neighborly decorum.

78
State Fair of Texas Building (Police, Fire,
  Hospital and WRR Building), *1936*
Bertram Hill
George Mills, renovation, 1994
This small brick building provided standard
City services to the 6.5 million Centennial
visitors. In 1994, it was converted to adminis-
trative offices serving the State Fair of Texas.

The State Fair Grounds in East Dallas have for so long reflected the city's sense of itself – a big city in a big state – that it is surprising to learn of an 1886 feud over the location of the event. A contingent of farm implement dealers who had strong connections with the agrarian settlers to the north of Dallas wanted it to be held on John H. Cole's homestead in the community then known as Cedar Springs. Their efforts resulted in two fairs that year, although the eastern site has prevailed ever since.

When the dust of both events had settled, it became clear that the fair on Cole's farm would have a more far-reaching effect on Dallas than anyone could have guessed. It would effectively launch the city's move northward that has continued unabated even until today. Ross Avenue already occupied the northern edge of downtown and was soon (in 1887) to spawn the nearby State-Thomas neighborhood of grand Victorian homes. But the fair had given developers a sense of the potential for residential neighborhoods in the tracts of land further north. To that end, they ran a streetcar from downtown out to Cole's farm and beyond, traversing a landscape that a Methodist minister had already dubbed Oak Lawn.

The streetcar did encourage a flurry of construction on Cedar Springs, McKinney Avenue, Maple Avenue, and Oak Lawn, which produced some of the most extraordinary, though ill-fated, mansions Dallas had yet produced. Their powerful owners may have shifted the center of gravity away from southern and eastern neighborhoods, but Dallas had only taken a baby's step further north. It would take an act of God to realize the dreams of Dallas' most insightful developers, and, in 1908, that's exactly what they got.

When the devastating flood of 1908 assaulted downtown, it provoked overwhelming interest in the Highland Park enclave on the far northern edge of Oak Lawn (which had begun to be platted in 1907) and it prompted city leaders to hire urban planner George Kessler of Kansas City to develop a new master plan for Dallas.

Kessler seized upon the idea of tying together a system of parks along Turtle Creek. The resulting parkways and boulevards through the area turned Oak Lawn into a welcome transition from the grind of downtown to the lush gardens and lovely homes along Turtle Creek and its various subdivisions, like Northern Hills and Perry Heights. Oak Lawn also became a serene passageway for those headed further north to Highland Park.

But Oak Lawn's greatest contribution now is its spirit of urban life. A diverse, youthful population, densely housed in apartments and condominiums, animates the streets and keeps the city's finest (and funkiest) restaurants and shops healthy. And, because office buildings intermingle with apartment towers here, many walk to work – after stopping off at Starbuck's for morning coffee.

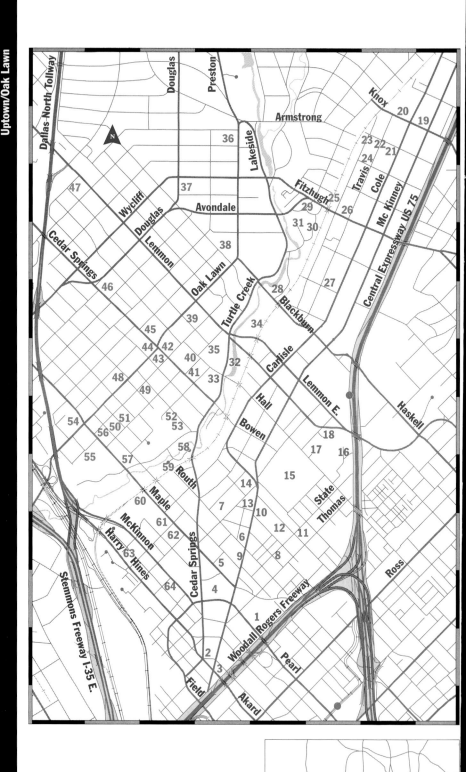

1

Federal Reserve Bank of Dallas, *1992*
2200 N. Pearl Street
Kohn Pedersen Fox (New York); SJKB (Houston)
While the Federal Reserve Bank's new Dallas
facility is not technically a "public" building –
only a few non-employees are likely to set
foot in its stone and glass lobby – its design
still makes a meaningful public statement.
Impressive massing and classic materials effectively convey the institution's hoped-for image
of "stability, dignity, and security." Equally
important is the respect with which the building treats the neighborhood surrounding this
important site just north of downtown. Even
though it can present a fortress-like appearance to pedestrians, from a distance – which
is how it is most often viewed – it nicely fills
the gap between the Crescent complex and
the Morton H. Meyerson Symphony Center.

2

Offices of HKS (Adleta Building), *1998*
1919 McKinney Avenue
HKS, Inc.
For its new headquarters office on McKinney
Avenue, Dallas-based HKS added contemporary touches to a nondescript warehouse –
wrapping portions of the building in corru-

gated metal panels, and creating a new entry
court accented by a minimalist plaza. The
interior offers a variety of comfortable, refined
spaces, while preserving many rustic features
of the original warehouse.

3

Woodall Rogers Tower, *1984*
1845 Woodall Rogers Freeway
Omniplan
This rational office tower is worth noting for
its first seven floors of parking, which are
beautifully disguised by the same skin used
for the offices. An assortment of cut-out corners yields a massing that works equally well
from the freeway or up close, while balconies
and simple stainless steel banding on the window wall help to reduce the building's scale.

Richard Payne

4
The Crescent, *1985*
Cedar Springs Road at Pearl Street
Johnson-Burgee (New York); Shepherd &
 Partners
Not Philip Johnson's best work, to be sure, but
still worthy of its landmark status. Ironically,
the Crescent represented the height of opu-
lence and conspicuous consumption in Dallas
when it was built in 1985 – the same time
that the city and state were tumbling into a
near depression that would last for the rest
of the 1980s. Despite this bad timing, however, the project has been viewed largely as
a success, with the hotel and office portions
becoming quite popular, and the retail space
managing to maintain a prestigious image, if
not full occupancy.

5
Hotel St. Germain, *1906*
2516 Maple Avenue
In 1888, Maple Avenue was still an unpaved
trail through the underbrush between Dallas
and Cedar Springs. Edwin P. Cowan opened
the street for development and attracted the
wealthy with construction of his own magnificent Queen Anne-style residence (since
demolished). This elegant Victorian mansion – now serving as a popular four-star
European-style hotel and gourmet restaurant
– is the best remaining example of Maple
Avenue's turn-of-the-century role as the city's
silk-stocking district.

6
Hard Rock Cafe (Formerly McKinney Avenue
 Baptist Church), *1910*
2601 McKinney Avenue
C.W. Bulger & Son
This touristy chain of eateries likes to make
a big impact with heavy, imposing structures.
In Dallas they found a willing convert in the
old McKinney Avenue Baptist Church, which
has now devoted itself to the worship of gui-
tars, t-shirts, and overpriced hamburgers.

7
The Quadrangle, *1966*
2828 Routh Street
Pratt Box & Henderson
RTKL Associates, renovation and office tower,
 1986
The Quadrangle was revolutionary when
it was constructed – its intimate scale and
unpredictable layout an appealing alternative
to the generic shopping centers that were
taking hold of the suburbs. Additions and
renovations have erased some of the charm,
but it remains a pleasing and popular place.

State-Thomas Neighborhood

Once a thriving center of African-American life, State-Thomas suffered the dual ravages of freeway construction and land speculation, and entered the 1980s as a small cluster of restored homes and acres of vacant lots. Today the 100-acre area is enjoying significantly improved fortunes, thanks to a visionary master plan by RTKL Associates, and an urban-living revival that has created strong demand for new apartments and townhomes.

8
Private Residence, *1892*
2615 State Street
This turn-of-the-century Victorian bungalow is typical of the homes that make up the 15-acre State-Thomas Historic District, although a variety of other styles (particularly Prairie) are also well-represented.

10
The Worthington on McKinney, *1992*
2800 McKinney Avenue
KSNG Architects, Inc.

11
The Heights of State-Thomas, *1998*
2400 Allen Street
RTKL Associates, Inc.

9
McKinney Avenue Trolley, *1989*
Huitt-Zollars
Before 1900, it was the extension of street railway lines into this area that made residential development feasible this far from town. One hundred years later, the restoration of the McKinney Avenue trolley plays an important role in the success of McKinney's retail shops and restaurants. It helped to create a distinct identity for the strip, and also tied it to the nearby Arts District and thousands of potential customers in the Central Business District.

12
5-7-9 Townhouses, *1998*
2902-2914 Woodside Street
RTKL Associates, Inc.

13
Office Building, *1985*
2811 McKinney Avenue
Morrison-Seifert
A restrained materials palette and well-planned courtyard give this low-key three-story office complex a lot of class for its relatively small size. One notable occupant is the
(13a) AIA Dallas Chapter Offices, 1990,
Stacy Architects; Willis Winters. To stay within the organization's limited budget, the architects finagled free or at-cost materials from area suppliers, and much of the labor was donated by Dallas AIA members.

14
Columbus Square, *1996*
Allen Street at Howell Street
KSNG Architects, Inc.; Good Fulton & Farrell
Ground-level retail and restaurant spaces help to establish a pedestrian scale at this 220-unit apartment complex. Structured parking is thoughtfully concealed, and the buildings surround a secluded courtyard.

15
Greenwood Cemetery, *1896*
3020 Oak Grove Avenue
On the northeast edge of State-Thomas, Greenwood Cemetery is the final resting place for many of the city's political and business luminaries, and home to a large variety of impressive tombstones. The area also includes the historic **(16) Freedmen's Cemetery,** with a memorial currently under construction.

17
Temple Emanu-El Mausoleum, *1998*
3430 Howell Street
Landry & Landry
Three concrete trapezoids are arranged to create a crypt-lined triangular courtyard. The hand-crafted semicircular tiles that are inlaid between the poured-in-place panels are an interesting and thoughtful detail.

18
Key Cataract Surgery Center, *1985*
2801 Lemmon Avenue West
The Oglesby Group
Proof that a small, multiuse building on a stingy site can be engaging and memorable, without sacrificing efficiency or economy. The architects used a small but varied palette of materials to animate an otherwise sleek facade.

19
Crate & Barrel, *1997*
3104 Knox Street
Good Fulton & Farrell; Jacque Verlinden
(Chicago)
A clean, contemporary home for this outpost
of the Chicago-based housewares and furniture retailer. Two masonry boxes intersected
by a glass vestibule create an interesting composition, and the resulting full-height atrium
facilitates smooth traffic flow and enhances
retailing opportunities on the store interior.

Charles Davis Smith

20
Knox Street Village, *1994*
3300 block of Knox Street
Good Fulton & Farrell
This conversion of a stretch of 1920s storefront buildings into modern retail space
helped to spur a Knox Street revitalization.
The plan called for the demolition of all
but the facades of the two-story structures –
creating a series of open, light-filled spaces.

James F. Wilson

21
Private Residences, *1997*
4431-4437 Cole Avenue
Cunningham Architects
Here is another small-scale residential project
designed by the neighborhood's most prolific
and perhaps most talented practitioner of the

genre. This one includes six simple, rectangular units and a small courtyard situated
behind a wall-like brick facade. Just across
the street is yet another notable example of
Cunningham's work, **(21a) 4438 Cole
Avenue,** 1998.

22
Armstrong Townhouses, *1982*
Travis Street at Armstrong Avenue
The Oglesby Group
Designed to maximize density, this development of 15 townhouses utilizes two plans:
one oriented to the street, and one to an interior walkway. Repetitive articulation in the
facade establishes the complex as a whole,
rather than as a group of individual units.

23
Private Residence (Power House), *1923*
3321 Armstrong Avenue
Dallas Power and Light Company
Cunningham Architects, adaptive reuse, 1988
An outstanding reuse of an abandoned
electrical switching station on the edge of
the upscale Highland Park neighborhood.
The interior celebrates the home's working-
class roots by utilizing an industrial materials
palette and relying on existing finishes in
many areas. The home is still decidedly luxurious however, with a new parlor, study, wine
cellar, and library; a grand ballroom on the
third floor; and a sculpture court behind the
enormous steel gate.

James F. Wilson

24
Concrete Townhouses, *1996*
4401 Travis Street
Cunningham Architects
This small townhouse development, consisting of four 1,700-sq.-ft. units, utilizes tilt-wall construction on three sides, with equally inexpensive fiber concrete siding on the rear wall. A deep (10 feet) cantilever over the garage entries helps to maximize the project's square footage.

27
Travis Street Condominiums, *1984*
3920 Travis Street
Morrison-Seifert
More security-conscious than many of the Oak Lawn projects that have been completed in recent, more-gentrified times, this 25-unit condominium project still displays some enduring Modernist sensibilities. Detailing on both the exterior and interiors is simple and restrained, and the designers made creative use of the sloping site to help conceal a ground-floor parking structure.

25
Parkwood Terraces, *1993*
4241 Buena Vista Street
Ron Wommack
A successful transformation of a decaying 1960s garden apartment complex into stylish rental units. In addition to major changes to the complex's appearance and the layout of individual units, one fundamental alteration to the site plan – shifting the focus of the units away from a courtyard and toward the street – is credited with spurring a neighborhood renaissance. The architect has since completed several other new or renovated projects in the area, including: **(25a) 4242 Buena Vista,** 1992; **(25b) 4214 Buena Vista,** 1995; **(26) 4141 Travis,** 1997; and **(26a) 4231-33 Travis,** 1994.

28
Private Residence, *c.1926*
3828 Turtle Creek Drive
J. Allen Boile
This Spanish Colonial home is one of the best examples of the Turtle Creek Park neighborhood's distinguished residential architecture. While most of Turtle Creek Boulevard has evolved over the past century into a zone for high-rise condominium projects, this "hidden" neighborhood near the northern end of the boulevard has maintained its single-family character since it was originally platted in the 1920s. Other notable residences in the neighborhood include: **(29) 3500 Rock Creek Place,** 1937, Goodwin & Tatum; **(29a) 3514 Rock Creek Place,** 1936, Ford & Swank; **(29b) 3520 Rock Creek Place,** 1950, Ralph Merrill; **(30) 4007 Stonebridge,** 1974, The Oglesby Group; and **(31) 3520 Arrowhead,** 1934, Hal Thomson.

32
Turtle Creek Boulevard, *1911*
George Kessler (Kansas City)
In 1910, a group of civic leaders invited
Kansas City landscape architect George
Kessler to develop a plan for the growing
city. Kessler's ambitious recommendations
for grand parks and boulevards were largely
unimplemented, with Turtle Creek Boulevard
being one of the few components visible
today. Development along the boulevard has
strained – but not destroyed – its popularity
and charm.

33
Apartment Building, *1957*
3525 Turtle Creek Boulevard
Howard Meyer
Meyer's often-used combination of Mexican
brick and textured concrete, along with a
distinctive series of concrete sun screens, has
stood the test of time at this high-rise apartment building. 3525 Turtle Creek was one
of Dallas' first apartment towers, and its
thoughtful siting and sensitivity to its surrounding neighborhood set a standard that
few successors have followed.

34
Kalita Humphreys Theater, *1959*
3636 Turtle Creek Boulevard
Frank Lloyd Wright
While Wright's only public theater presents a
graceful, elegant exterior, the original design
offered less-than-optimal conditions to theater
performers and audiences. As a result, there
have been a number of expansion and renovation projects over the years – such as adding
storage space and improving lighting. One
unwelcome "improvement" was the paving of
a large portion of the sloping site to create
additional parking spaces.

35
Arlington Hall, Lee Park, *c.1939*
3300 block of Turtle Creek Boulevard
Works Progress Administration
This two-third scale replica of Robert E. Lee's
home in Virginia sits – along with a bronze
statue of General Lee himself – in the former
Oak Lawn Park (renamed Robert E. Lee Park
in 1936). The park also includes the notable
(35a) **Toilet Building,** c.1915, William Martes.

36
Third Church of Christ Scientist, *1932*
4419 Oak Lawn Avenue
Mark Lemmon
This assortment of Romanesque elements
may have been unusual for a Christ Scientist
church in the 1930s – when classical styles
were dominant – but the design has helped
the church to remain a distinguished landmark through the years.

38
Holy Trinity Catholic Church, *1941*
3811 Gilbert Avenue
J.M. McCammon
A good deal more understated than the
nearby Third Church of Christ Scientist,
Holy Trinity still manages a big impact with
its impressively scaled facade and subtle
details such as ornate cast-stone archways
and window frames.

37
Townhouses, *1986*
4102-4110 Douglas
Arquitectonica (Miami)
Designed during Arquitectonica's "playful"
period, every other roof on this small townhouse complex was rotated 90 degrees, and
then they were all shifted five feet off center
to cover the walkways between the units.
Accentuating this whimsical design was the
architect's original paint scheme, which utilized five shades of purple.

39
Mirasol Courts Apartments, *1926*
3720 Rawlins Street
This Moorish three-story apartment house
is probably the city's most decorative
masonry building.

40
Lee Park Center, *1967*
3141 Hood Street
Ralph Kelman & Associates
Known for its work on a number of appealing
low-rise apartment and office projects around
the city, Ralph Kelman and Associates was
nearly as successful with this eight-story office
tower. Along a beautifully landscaped garden,
the building is notable for its unique structural
system, which treats the top level as a truss
from which the other floors are suspended.

41
Offices of WRW (John H. Miller House), *1904*
3510 Cedar Springs Road
The Miller House is the only known Shingle-style house left standing in Dallas, and one of the few remaining in Texas. Its construction began just a few years after Oak Lawn was opened for development.

44
Melrose Hotel, *1924*
3105 Oak Lawn Avenue
C.D. Hill
Originally designed as a residence hotel, the Melrose's simple "U"-shaped plan and straightforward brickwork are made more stately by a richly detailed limestone base and refined porte cochere.

42
The Centrum, *1987*
3102 Oak Lawn Avenue
Rossetti Associates
This was one of the city's first true mixed-use developments – with space for offices, retail, restaurants, and residences. The retail space, however, has proven to be more appropriate for ad agencies and architecture firms than retailers, with the exception of the popular **(42a) Star Canyon Restaurant,** 1994, Wilson & Associates.

45
Fire Station No. 11, *1909*
3828 Cedar Springs Road
Hubbell & Greene
Originally Fire Station No. 2 when it was built, this is now the oldest operating fire station in the city. The highlight of the Mission-style building is the series of elaborate cast-stone panels adorning the facade.

43
Oak Lawn United Methodist Church, *1913*
3014 Oak Lawn Avenue
C.D. Hill & Company
A combination of dark brick and buff cast stone create a dramatic facade for this strikingly ornate Gothic Revival church.

Charles Davis Smith

46
Oak Lawn Branch, Dallas Public Library, *1997*
4100 Cedar Springs Road
Good Fulton & Farrell
Kroger Food Stores offered this branch library as a turnkey project in exchange for development rights to the remainder of the site. The resulting facility is better funded – and better designed – than most other new branches.

47
Private Residence, *1940*
4524 Rawlins Street
Ralph Bryan
This house by architect Ralph Bryan, who
also participated in the design of Fair Park's
Hall of State, is a good example of the ante-
bellum style that found popularity – along
with other period styles – during the city's
period of tremendous growth in the 1940s
and '50s.

48
Office Building, *1958; 1960*
2727 Oak Lawn Avenue
Howard Meyer
Howard Meyer takes on the notoriously
unattractive "garden office building" and
comes up with a winner. Again he used his
trademark soft Mexican brick – this time
framed by an exposed steel structure – and
contrasted it with clean, elegantly proportioned window modules. His firm officed
here for many years.

49
Welborn Street Townhouses, *1980*
2800 block of Welborn Street
The Oglesby Group
Among The Oglesby Group's many contributions to Dallas architecture – in addition to
productive young firm graduates like Max
Levy, Ron Wommack, and Frank Ryburn –
are a number of well-designed townhouse
and apartment projects on and around Turtle
Creek. The Welborn Street Townhouses
include nine inwardly oriented units, each
defined by a barreled skylight, which also provides natural light in interior spaces. Notable
for their simple lines and exciting volumes
are the firm's nearby **(50) Fairmount/Hood
Townhouses,** 1981, at 3606 Fairmount.

51
Apartment Building, *1960*
2711 Hood Street
The Oglesby Group
This small apartment complex illustrates the
level of design creativity that was open to
architects creating apartment buildings in the
early 1960s – before the multifamily emphasis
shifted to larger, cookie-cutter projects in the
northern suburbs. Each of the three buildings
in this complex have their own unique identi-
ties, and individual units are differentiated by
rooflines, porches, and window units.

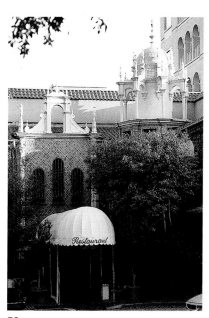

52
**The Mansion on Turtle Creek (originally
    Sheppard King Mansion),** *1925*
3417 Gillespie Avenue
J. Allen Boile
*Phillip Shepherd & Partners, renovations and
    additions, 1981*
The original Renaissance Italian villa was built
as a home for cotton magnate Sheppard King
and his family. Today the mansion – along
with its elegantly integrated 11-story addition
– is one of the nation's most luxurious hotels.

53
The Mansion Residences, *1994*
2801 Turtle Creek Boulevard
Haldeman Powell + Partners
Developed in the front yard of the Mansion
on Turtle Creek hotel, this new condominium
component is sensitive to its environment,
while still including the dramatic facade and

high-profile details needed to help justify
the eye-popping prices demanded for its
half-floor units.

54
Old Parkland Hospital, *1913*
3800 block of Maple Avenue
Hubbell & Greene
The existing brick structures (the first brick
hospital in Texas) replaced a wooden facility
that opened on the site in 1894. With the
help of the Dallas Chapter of the American
Institute of Architects, the buildings – which
had fallen into disrepair and eventual aban-
donment following Parkland's move to bigger
quarters in 1954 – are currently being restored
for use as a patient education center and home
to several non-profit healthcare agencies.

55
Texas Scottish Rite Hospital for Children,
    1977
2222 Welborn Street
HKS, Inc.; Rodney S. Davis Associates, Ltd.
This brutalist collection of heavy brick and
bronze-glass structures is intimidating on the
outside, but playful on the interior to reflect
the needs of the children and parents who use
the facility.

56
Loyd-Paxton Gallery, *1985*
3636 Maple Avenue
Burson, Hendricks & Walls; Loyd Taylor and
* Charles Paxton Gremillion, Jr.*
This Italianesque villa was reconstructed
in the mid-1980s for high-profile art and
antiques dealers Loyd Taylor and Paxton
Gremillion. In addition to the pair's gallery,
the building includes a luxurious penthouse
residence in a structure complete with towers,
arches, a tile roof, and cut-stone medallions.

57
Offices of Benson Hlavaty Architects, *1960*
2505 Turtle Creek Boulevard
Howard Meyer
A pair of floating canopies distinguishes this
small one-story office building on Turtle
Creek Boulevard. A combination of orange
and buff brick under a heavy exposed-steel
cap, along with simple aluminum-framed
windows, give the building a Miesian quality
often favored by Meyer. Excellent landscaping
accentuates the outdoor spaces created by the
linked canopies.

58
Private Residence, *1984*
2833 Park Bridge Court
Frank Welch
While Welch may be best known in architecture circles for "The Birthday," a stripped-
down regionalist retreat outside of Midland,
he is also widely respected for his work on
tasteful, restrained homes – like this one on
the banks of Turtle Creek. Also notable in
the area is the **(59) Private Residence,** 1998,
2706 Park Bridge Court, Jonathan Bailey.

60
Terrace House, *c.1965*
3131 Maple Avenue
Tom Sawyer
Concrete panels for spandrels and angular
balcony facings have a vaguely Wrightian
spirit on this high-rise apartment tower set
on the edge of Reverchon Park. This is quite
a contrast to the paper-thin look of recent
apartment facades.

61
Maple Terrace Apartments, *1924*
3001 Maple Avenue
Sir Alfred Bossom
Conceived by the same British architect that designed downtown's Magnolia Building, Maple Terrace was a luxurious and exclusive building when it was built in the 1920s. Today it shows some wear, but is still popular with residents, and is a likely candidate for renovation in the near future.

62
The Stoneleigh Hotel, *1923*
2927 Maple Avenue
Thanks to its low-key, classic design – and equally low-key, personalized service – the Stoneleigh has long been a favorite of people who are so famous they're trying to avoid the limelight. The destination for the truly well-connected is often the building's 7,000-sq.-ft., five-bedroom penthouse apartment.

63
KERA Studios, *1998*
3000 Harry Hines Boulevard
Rees Associates
Wrapping around the rear of KERA's existing studio and administration building, this thoughtfully designed two-story addition provided much-needed new studio and office space for Dallas' public television and radio stations. The open interior was designed to give visitors an inside look at the television and radio production processes.

Hedrich Blessing

64
Dallas International Center II, *1996*
2728 N. Harwood Street
DMJM-Keating & Associates (Los Angeles);
*   Gromatsky-Dupree*
The Centex Building at Dallas International Center is architect Rick Keating's response to the wave of modesty and cost-consciousness that spread over corporate America – and the real estate that houses it – in the 1990s. And Keating rises to the occasion by delivering a memorable, restrained box that conveys sophistication and class without the use of opulent materials or soaring spaces – proving that the need for good design didn't disappear with the market for 50-story office towers. Also in the development are a fine garden by The SWA Group and Keating's Dallas International Center III, 1999.

4 Market Center/Medical Center/Love Field

I n some ways, Stemmons Freeway is the quintessential Dallas roadway. Just as the Champs-Elysées gets at the heart of Paris and Fifth Avenue at the soul of New York, Stemmons takes you to an understanding of Dallas by virtue of its overwhelming presence and speed. It, too, partakes of the world of fashion – witness developer Trammel Crow's Trade Mart and International Apparel Mart – but its appeal is not the elegant stuff of runways and showrooms. (Those spaces are entombed inside of Crow's buildings.) Stemmons is more like a sixteen-lane back road, a service drive par excellence, the locus of loading docks, forklifts and containers on a grand scale. If it has never been easy for architects to design for this 8-mile strip, it is because Stemmons is about business that is fast, and if not dirty, exactly, then workmanlike and efficient. That said, it is, in a sense, the heartbeat of the city.

While Stemmons is the lifeblood of the Dallas Market Center, the InfoMart and the myriad assortment of smaller businesses off the freeway, it is also the sacred way for Dallas' sick and wounded. Home to Parkland Hospital, Children's Medical Center, the University of Texas Southwest Medical School, the Collier Learning Center, and the Zale Lipshy Hospital, the Southwest Medical Center, as it is called, tends to the universal business of protecting life. Its location, just off Stemmons on Harry Hines Boulevard, gives it the accessibility such an institution requires. A mixture of private, county and state funds means that the medical research that has made it famous, the excellence of its doctors and the cutting-edge nature of its facilities are available to all.

John Stemmons once reflected that the highway bearing his name was the best business deal he ever made. "I knew that construction of the freeway would benefit me and the city," he said, "because it got people from here to there." That function of getting people from one place to another was also performed beautifully by Love Field, the City's first international airport. Still in service now as the hub of Southwest Airlines, the airport's glamour belies the bus-terminal informality that helps market the company's inexpensive flights. Love Field dates from that moment when air travel was romantic, when just to walk through the terminal was to tread across the world as it was shaped out in the different colors of terrazzo beneath your feet. People dressed up to visit Love Field. Whole families came to Dallas from the surrounding towns to watch the planes take off and land. Those who value the iconographic power of architecture might find time to visit the airport. Back when Texas (and the world) were still provincial, it paid honor to travel, and there is something fundamentally humanizing about such a message.

4 Market Center/Medical Center/Love Field

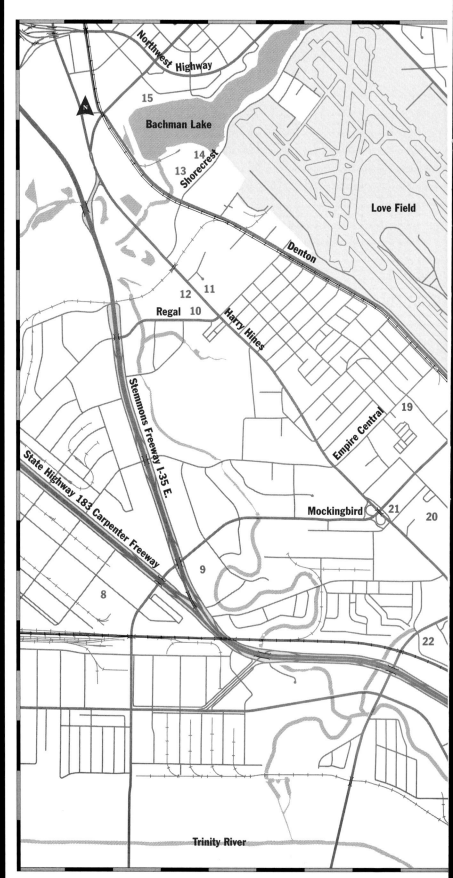

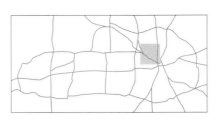

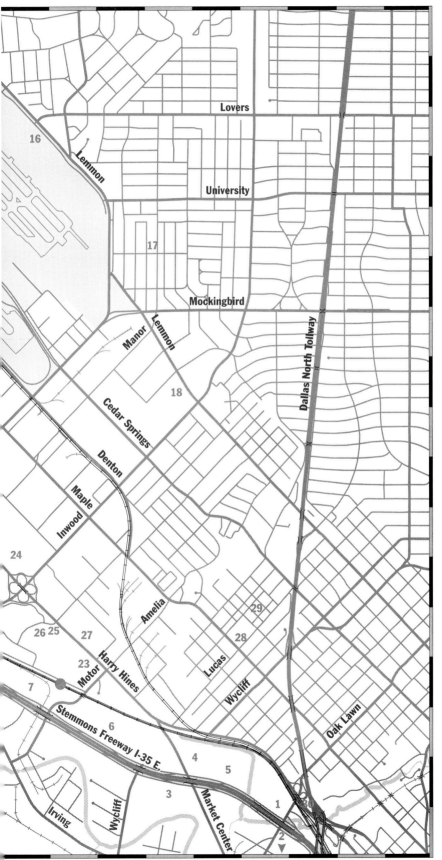

Lovers

16

Lemmon

University

17

Mockingbird

Manor

Lemmon

Dallas North Tollway

18

Cedar Springs

Denton

Maple

Inwood

24

Amelia

29

26 25

27

28

Lucas

23

Harry Hines

Motor

Wycliff

7

Stemmons Freeway I-35 E.

6

Oak Lawn

4

5

Irving

Wycliff

3

Market Center

1

2

4 Market Center/Medical Center/Love Field

Dallas Market Center

The rechanneling of the Trinity River in 1931 opened up thousands of new acres for commercial use, but it wasn't until after World War II that the area began to see wide-spread development. Then, in the mid 1950s, developers Trammell Crow and John Stemmons changed the face of the area when they began what would become a collection of wholesale bazaars known as Dallas Market Center – now the world's largest wholesale trade complex.

2
Decorative Center, *1954*
1500 Oak Lawn Avenue
Jacob Anderson
Beyond the unattractive new graphic inter-ventions, this collection of red-brick show-rooms represents a nice example of rationalist design. The buildings – sited around a central court – feature simple, refined details that give the project a timeless quality.

1
InfoMart, *1985*
1950 Stemmons Freeway
Growald Architects
Legend has it that Martin Growald once described his eight-story InfoMart as the Information-age equivalent of Joseph Paxton's industrial revolution landmark, the Crystal Palace. And, in fact, Great Britain's Parliament has recognized the building as the Crystal Palace's official successor. The project, which features a dramatic full-height atrium under its central barrel vault, continues to be a key component of the Dallas high-tech commu-nity – housing more than 100 technology- and telecommunications-focused businesses in 1 million square feet of office space, and hosting industry events and conferences in its exhibit hall.

3
Anatole Hotel, *1979; 1984*
2201 Stemmons Freeway
Beran & Shelmire
With more than 1600 keys, the Anatole is one of Dallas' largest hotels. Unfortunately, the project's exterior distinguishes itself with little more than sheer volume. The generally unarticulated facade does offer an artistic concession in the form of sculptured brick work at the building's base.

4
Dallas Trade Mart, *1959*
2100 Stemmons Freeway
Harwell Hamilton Harris; Harold Berry
Probably the best of the Trammell Crow
market buildings, the Trade Mart's exterior
reflects a level of detail and sensitivity missing
in many of its neighbors. Inside, Harris created a large "natural" atrium that he hoped
would have a restorative effect on harried
wholesale merchants and buyers. Saw-toothed
skylights allow extensive natural light while
limiting the effects of the harsh southern sun.

6
International Apparel Mart, *1964*
2300 Stemmons Freeway
Pratt Box & Henderson
This enormous fashion wholesale market
covers four square blocks and provides showroom space for more than 1,500 exhibitors.
The Great Hall, which won a 1965 TSA
Award, can seat more than 4,000 for fashion
shows, and features a mixture of textures and
abstract forms – as well as fountains and live
plants – that give it a very organic feel. The
open spaces in the firm's 1973 West Atrium
addition are more conservative and geometric,
but equally tasteful. Like other projects in
the Market Center, the Apparel Mart makes
liberal use of contemporary artwork to help
shake its utilitarian roots.

5
World Trade Center, *1974; 1976*
2100 Stemmons Freeway
Beran & Shelmire
Representing 1970s architecture at its most
brutal, the exterior of the massive World
Trade Center looks like the typical down-
and-dirty Trammell Crow warehouse concept
subjected to a very heavy steroid regimen.
Like many of his projects aimed at upscale
markets, however, the elder Crow couldn't
keep from slipping in a human touch – in
this case an assortment of bronze sculptures
in and around the building.

7

Stemmons Towers, *1962-1967*
2710 Stemmons Freeway
Harwell Hamilton Harris; Harold Berry
On a strip of freeway not known for well-designed office towers, these four buildings are a definite standout. The five-foot window setbacks create a very small floor-plate by modern standards, but they do result in a richer, more dynamic facade than most Dallas office buildings. The plaza Harris designed to connect the buildings – like his Trade Mart court – creates a pleasant, relaxing space out of what is often very inhospitable terrain.

8

Meyer & Johnson (Foremost Dairy), *c.1954*
999 Ambassador Row
Thomas, Jameson & Merrill (attributed)
Good Fulton & Farrell, adaptive reuse, 1996
Post-industrial materials and open interior spaces turned this abandoned dairy bottling plant into an "idea factory" for a progressive Dallas advertising agency. On the exterior, contemporary metal and glass detailing works with the existing Art Deco architecture to hint at the sophisticated audio and video production going on inside.

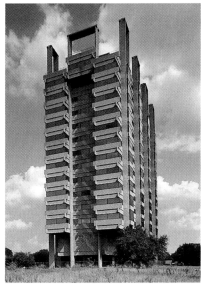

9

Brookhollow One, *1970*
Stemmons Freeway at Mockingbird Lane
Paul Rudolph (New York); Harwood K. Smith
& Partners
On the verge of the great thin-skinned, ultra-reflective glass-box era, Paul Rudolph offered an alternative – an all-precast building with a striking geometry and some very engaging expressions of structure in its facade and roof-line. But unfortunately for scores of blinded commuters, Dallas developers failed to see the beauty, and moved forward instead with millions of square feet of poorly differentiated mirrored-glass towers.

10
John D. Murchison Scouting Center, *1996*
8605 Harry Hines Boulevard
Good Fulton & Farrell
This regional headquarters for the Boy Scouts of America acknowledges an existing creek at the rear of the site by angling two limestone and brick volumes around the creek's bend. The volumes are joined by a light-filled two-story lobby space, and the subtle shift in their alignment is accentuated by a glass box that carries the facade of the front building past the entryway. The facility is part of the unique Pinecreek Commons development, a small business park serving well-funded non-profit organizations. Pinecreek Commons also includes the **(11) United Cerebral Palsy Headquarters,** 1997, by ROFDW; and the **(12) Child and Family Guidance Clinic,** 1992, by F&S Partners.

13
Dallas Water Utilities Northwest Operations Center, *1926*
2605 Shorecrest Drive
This multi-building complex, which has been added to over the years, includes a pump station, purification plant, and storage facilities. Most interesting is the large two-and-one-half-story main building. Its dark brick exterior – accentuated by cast-stone parapet trim and column caps – and arched windows make it a classic example of early Dallas industrial architecture.

14
Bachman Lake Boat House, *1988*
2827 Shorecrest Drive
Mullen Architects
Bachman Lake, just off the end of Love Field's main runway, is a remarkably popular urban recreation area – crowded on weekends with picnickers, joggers, and fishermen. This boathouse, which is home to the Dallas Rowing Club, is a durable, functional structure that reflects both its high-traffic location and its utilitarian purpose – without being defined by them. Viewed from the water, the building's roofline and siding pattern subtly suggest the form of an inverted rowing shell carried overhead.

15
Bachman Recreation Center, *1980*
2750 Bachman Drive
Parkey & Partners
This rambling one-story brick building offers 42,000 square feet of facilities – including a 25-meter pool, theater, and full-size gymnasium – designed to meet the recreational needs of people with disabilities. With simple geometry and clean details, the relatively large building avoids spoiling its park-like location between Bachman Lake and an adjacent tree grove.

16
Dalfort Aerospace (Braniff International),
1958
7701 Lemmon Avenue
Charles Luckman
Space-age style and rigorous symmetry –
both fundamental precepts of the aviation
industry – distinguish this former home of
Braniff Airlines at Love Field. The building's
low profile allows it to mix comfortably with
surrounding aircraft hangars, while its glass
window wall, shallow "V" roofline, and deep
roof overhangs suggest a range of uses that
includes more than just aircraft storage
and maintenance.

17
Polk Park Recreation Center, *1980*
6800 Roper Street
Hobbs Wiginton Fawcett
Leo A. Daly, addition, 1998
When a two-story gymnasium was added
in 1998 to accommodate growing use of the
Polk Park facility, the architects approached
the project with sensitivity to both the existing stucco structure and the surrounding
neighborhood. Most notable is the addition's
simple facade, where two-tone brick acknowledges the scale of the original building, and
pilasters split with downspouts suggest the
original's twin-column scheme.

18
Coca Cola Bottling Plant, *1963*
6011 Lemmon Avenue
Pitts Phelps & White (Beaumont, Texas)
A remnant of an era when big industrial
buildings were designed with an eye on some-
thing other than *just* functionality and cost.
The front of the building features a two-story

glass facade under a simple arched fascia, with
the second story shielded by a metal brise-
soleil. The facade makes a simple, discreet
transition to brick at the rear of the building.

19
Knights Branch Office Building, *1986*
2400 Empire Central Drive
Thomas Booziotis & Associates
This low key office building, which currently
includes the headquarters of Booziotis &
Company Architects, is nestled onto a densely
wooded site in a residential-scale neighborhood. Its simple, barn-like form, standing-
seam roof, and low-key materials palette give
it a "Texas" feel more often found in Austin
or San Antonio than in Dallas.

20
Exchange Park, *1955-1965*
6300 Forest Park Boulevard
Lane Gamble Huddleston
The three Modernist office buildings that
exist today were intended as just the first
phase of a much grander overall plan for this
early "suburban" development. Changes in
ownership, however, and the completion of
Stemmons Freeway – which facilitated prof-
itable development even further from the
CBD – meant that garden apartments, a
medical center, and additional office towers
were never realized. A notable feature of the
project is the landscape by Arthur and Marie
Berger, which remains in very good condition.

21
Salvation Army Offices, *1963*
6500 Harry Hines Boulevard
Grayson Gill
Originally home to the Great National Life
Insurance Company, this project is one of the
best of what was a largely undistinguished
crop of garden office buildings that sprang up
around Dallas in the early 1960s. Today the
building houses administration offices of
the Salvation Army, and is still thought of
by many as one of the city's most beautiful
buildings. The chapel addition in the back is
also interesting, if not entirely in character.

22
Callier Center for Communication Disorders,
 1968
1966 Inwood Road
Fisher & Spillman
This University of Texas at Dallas institution
houses a preschool, clinic, laboratories, and
library – all serving or benefiting individuals
with speech, language, or hearing problems.
The design and siting of the buildings reflect
the reawakening awareness in the 1960s of
the energy-saving benefits that could be
achieved by moderating the rays of the
intense southern sun.

23
Parkland Memorial Zale Lipshy Hospital,
 1990
5151 Harry Hines Boulevard
The Oglesby Group; Page Southerland Page
Zale Lipshy hospital was created to appeal
to the high-end of the healthcare market –
patients from around the world with complex, expensive-to-treat diseases and plenty
of money (or very good insurance) – and
the project's architecture reflects this market
position. Its beige concrete exterior, white-
framed windows, and tastefully animated
facade give it a more sophisticated look than
its often hulking competitors. The interior
is equally upscale, with country-club style
furnishings and decor in public areas, and
the hotel-like patient rooms that are now
common throughout the healthcare industry.

Southwestern Medical Center

What began in 1943 as a small wartime medical college has grown into The University of Texas Southwestern Medical Center at Dallas, a world-renowned research and teaching institution. The 60-acre main campus includes more than 3 million square feet of space, with the 152-bed Zale Lipshy teaching and referral hospital located nearby. Biomedical research facilities are located on an additional 30-acre parcel given to the University in 1987.

24
Simmons Biomedical Research Building,
1993
5700 Harry Hines Boulevard
Edward Larrabee Barnes & John Lee
  (New York); F&S Partners
The master plan for this rapidly growing research facility provides for the eventual construction of seven connected office towers, arranged diagonally along three large courtyards, and all served by the existing entryway.

25
Tom and Lula Gooch Auditorium, *1973*
5323 Harry Hines Boulevard
HKS, Inc.
As the medical center's closest brush with high-traffic Harry Hines Boulevard, this

1,200-seat auditorium plays an important role in establishing its architectural identity. While it is far from the institution's best foot, its heavy masonry "lid" resting on a dark, recessed base implies stability and confidence. Recessed panels help to bring the heavy column and roof elements down to a more human scale.

26
Administration Tower, *1974*
5323 Harry Hines Boulevard
The Oglesby Group
When the Medical Center entered the period of rapid growth that began in the early 1970s, it quickly recognized the constraints of its relatively small campus. To limit the amount of land area dedicated to administrative functions, The Oglesby Group minimized this building's footprint, spreading little more than 60,000 square feet out over 12 floors. The resulting verticality is played up with creative fenestration and exposed structure.

27

Carr P. Collins Social Services Center for the Salvation Army, *1986*
5302 Harry Hines Boulevard
F&S Partners
This facility consolidated a number of scattered Salvation Army housing programs in one location. It includes both overnight "shelter" accommodations, and longer-term, transitional housing for families and single adults. The design and construction are appropriately rugged, but avoid correctional-facility associations by focusing on a landscaped plaza accentuated by a chapel. Salvation Army officials chose the site primarily for its position in the social-services corridor that has developed along Harry Hines Boulevard near the public Parkland Hospital.

29

Cedar Springs Place, *1937*
2531 Lucas Drive
Walter Sharp; Lester Flint; Grayson Gill;
* Ralph Bryan; Anton Korn; Roscoe DeWitt;*
* Everett Welch; Herbert Tatum;*
* Arthur E. Thomas*
This outstanding example of the International Style was Texas' first New Deal public housing project. While it is often cited as an example of the International Style's failure as a low-income housing solution – and some of the buildings show significant deterioration – it still retains most of its architectural and planning integrity. Both the site plan and the design of individual buildings reflect the significant influence of German housing projects of the '20s and '30s – particularly Ernst May's Bruchfeldstrasse Estate (1925) in Frankfurt.

30

Sammons Center for the Arts (Dallas Water Utilities Turtle Creek Pump Station), *1981*
3630 Harry Hines Boulevard
ArchiTexas, adaptive reuse
C.A. Gill, original construction, 1909
This imposing structure began its life as the city water department's primary pump station – handling more than 15 million gallons of water per day. In 1981, it was renovated for use as a multipurpose arts facility. It houses performance, rehearsal, and meeting space, and it also is home to several Dallas nonprofit arts organizations. The building was declared a historic landmark in 1983.

28

Maria Luna Park Tower, *1987*
Maple Avenue at Lucas Drive
ArchiTexas
Located in a largely hispanic neighborhood, *La Torre de la Amistad* (The Tower of Friendship) combines Spanish and regional Mexican architectural influences like stucco, clay tile, painted ironwork, and exposed timbers to form a popular local landmark.

5 East Dallas/Lakewood

With the development of his Munger Place in 1905, Robert Munger, a cotton machine magnate, sought to solve the residential worries of Dallas' elite. Publicity for his 300-acre addition said "its occupants need never fear the encroachment of factories, shops, or any other undesirable class of neighbors within its boundaries." Deeds required owners to spend no less than $10,000 on a two-story house with a 60-foot setback.

Over the next 25 years, Munger Place attracted such a rich compendium of architectural styles, including Classic Revival, Prairie Style, Georgian Revival, English Tudor, Shingle Style and Italian Renaissance, that it has been called the finest intact area of early 20th-century architecture in the Southwest. But for all its grandeur and Munger's promised protection from encroachment, Munger Place – specifically Swiss Avenue, (the finest, most representative street) – began to be threatened in the early 1970s. It was then that the Dallas Historic Preservation League combined efforts with the National Trust for Historic Preservation and the Dallas Department of Urban Planning to put more mettle in Munger's promise. The neighborhood achieved historic zoning and Swiss Avenue is now listed on the National Register of Historic Places.

Like Munger Place, the Lakewood neighborhood was blessed with an owner and developers who were also committed to creating and maintaining the beauty of a place. In the 1920s, W. F. Pearson hired Albert Dines and Lee R. Kraft to develop his land "in the right way." Their interpretation of his directive – they saved trees, cut winding roads through the hilly land, and required generous setbacks from the streets – set the tone for the type of homes the neighborhood quickly attracted.

Some of Dallas' most important architects designed residences for Lakewood. Charles Dilbeck was particularly adept in the design of houses that used rough textures of stone and wood and whimsical architectural forms to conjure up picturesque cottages. C.D. Hutsell filtered a Spanish Eclecticism through his imagination and gave Lakewood its own version of the fashionable idiom. O'Neil Ford and Arch Swank, Dallas favorite son David Williams, Houston Modernist Donald Barthelme, and the traditionalist John Staub are some of the architects who enriched these winding streets.

Lakewood's mood is sleepy and peaceful, undisturbed by the kinds of incursions into its fabric that have so torn up Highland Park. Its proximity to the recreational opportunities and beauty of White Rock Lake further enhances its desirability.

To best experience the sites in this chapter, follow the spine of East Dallas on Gaston Avenue and Garland Road through Munger Place, Lakewood Shopping Center, past Lakewood Country Club, White Rock Lake, and the Dallas Arboretum.

5 East Dallas/Lakewood

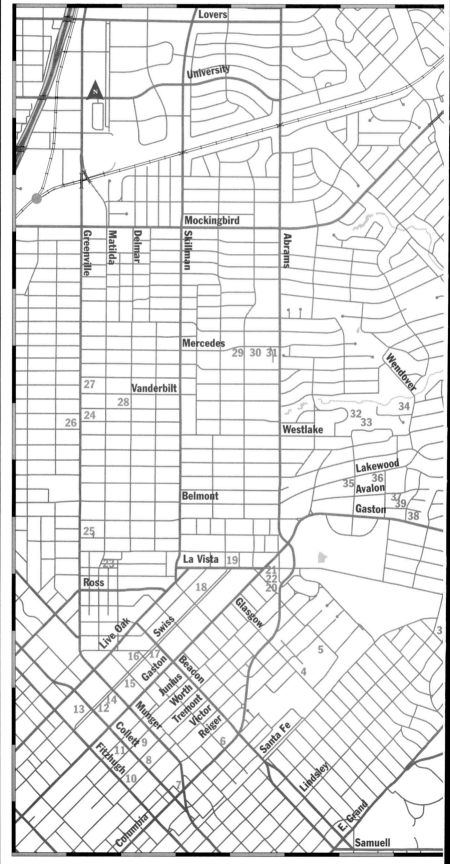

Lovers

University

N

Mockingbird

Greenville
Matilda
Delmar
Skillman
Abrams

Mercedes

29 30 31

Wendover

27
Vanderbilt
28

26 24

32 33
34

Westlake

Lakewood
35 36
Avalon
37 39
Gaston 38

Belmont

25

La Vista 19
18

21
22
20

Ross

Glasgow

Live Oak
Swiss

16 17
Gaston
15

Beacon

5
4

13 14
12

Junius
Worth
Tremont
Victor
Reiger

Munger

Collett 9

6

Santa Fe

11
Fitzhugh 8

10

7

Lindsley

Columbia

E. Grand

Samuell

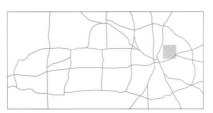

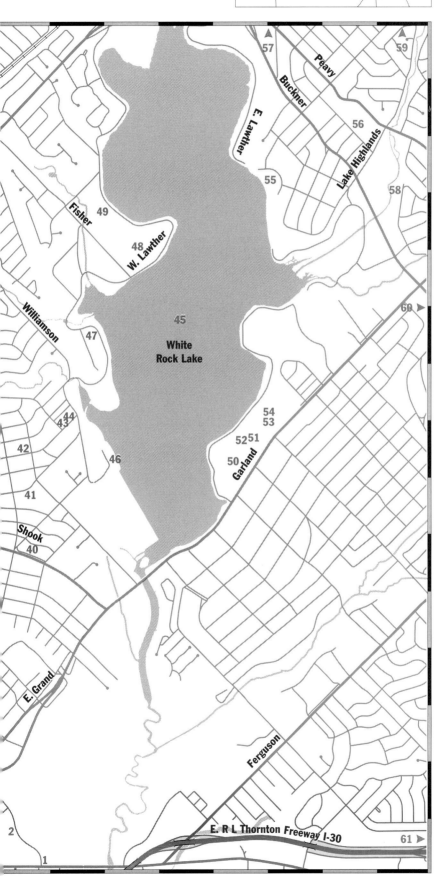

57

59

Peavy

Buckner

56

E. Lawther

Lake Highlands

55

58

Fisher 49

48
W. Lawther

60 ▶

Williamson

45

47

White
Rock Lake

54
53

44
43

5251

42

50

Garland

46

41

Shook
40

E. Grand

Ferguson

2

1

E. R L Thornton Freeway I-30

61 ▶

5 East Dallas/Lakewood

1
Tenison Memorial Park Entry Gates, *1928*
Samuell Boulevard at Tenison Parkway
Lang & Witchell
Marking the south entry to Tenison Park is
this pair of graceful, freestanding peristyles
executed by Lang & Witchell with quintessential, Neo-Georgian imagery. Behind
this noble portal is Dallas' oldest public golf
course, originally designed by the great Texas
golf architect John Bredemus. The nearby
(2) Tenison Park Driving Range, 1999,
McCarthy Hammers, continues the contextual use of stone in this historic park.

3
Lindsley Park Pavilion, *1998*
700 Tenison Memorial Boulevard
Brown Reynolds Watford
This striking masonry and timber picnic
shelter, topped by a pair of pyramidal roofs,
draws its architectural cues from the abundant
Tudor cottage residences found in Hollywood
Heights. During the post-war 1920s, residen-
tial builders in Dallas universally adopted the
Tudor cottage as the city's standard masonry
housing type.

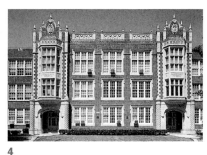

4
Woodrow Wilson High School, *1928*
100 S. Glasgow Drive
DeWitt & Lemmon
This Jacobean confection balances an
elaborately detailed central pavilion with
dual towers against calmer classroom wings
on each side. Together with **(5) J.L. Long
Middle School,** 1928, DeWitt & Lemmon,
the two campuses constitute a formidable
East Dallas landmark.

James F. Wilson

6
Columbia Avenue Arts Center, *1918*
5501 Columbia Avenue
H.A. Overbeck
Dan Shipley, adaptive reuse, 1992
One of the most successfully-restored former
fire houses in the city is this two-story brick
building notable for its combination of
Italianate and Prairie-style detailing.

7
Columbia Inn, *c.1925*
5101 Columbia Avenue
An outstanding example of the two-story
apartment buildings that proliferated in East
Dallas neighborhoods during the 1920s is this
well-balanced Craftsman composition.

Munger Place

Munger Place was the first residential development in the city to utilize deed restrictions and other modern planning innovations to achieve architectural uniformity and long-term stability. Opened as an elite residential district in 1905 by cotton gin magnate R.S. Munger, this neighborhood attracted Dallas' leading citizens and was an instant financial success. Pervasive Prairie-style influences are still evident among the historic district's restored houses.

8
Private Residence, *1914*
5007 Victor Street
Many of the houses in Munger Place were constructed from plans obtained through mail-order house catalogs. The provenance of this Craftsman residence, and a similar one on Reiger Street, is *Associated Architects' Fifty House Plans*, published in 1910.

10
Private Residence, *1913*
4915 Victor Street
Solid, two-story massing, simple roof forms, frame construction and substantial porches were common attributes of most Munger Place residences. A distinguishing feature of this house is its prominent Mission-style parapet, sheathed in shingles to simulate brick.

9
Private Residence, *1909*
5116 Worth Street
Grandiose frontality is achieved in this residence by its projecting Neo-Classical porch and balcony, an element also mirrored on the east side of the house. Each portico is topped by a rounded, hipped roof, which ties back into the taller pyramid roof form over the main house.

11
Private Residence, *1909*
4936 Junius Street
C.D. Hill
The prominent Dallas architect C.D. Hill built this transitional Prairie four-square residence for himself. Its flat roof and spare detailing – save for the Italianate brackets and continuous projecting cornice – suggest a Modernistic influence not found in other Munger Place houses.

Swiss Avenue

Swiss Avenue is one of the finest intact neighborhoods of early 20th-century residential architecture in the United States. Developed as the upscale focal point of Munger Place, and now a separate historic district, Swiss Avenue was envisioned by its planners as the home of Dallas' business and social elite. Along its eight-block length are numerous residences designed by the city's most important architects, representing 16 different historical styles.

12
Higginbotham Residence, *1913*
5002 Swiss Avenue
Lang & Witchell
Lang & Witchell's encompassment of the Prairie School style dates to the 1907 employment of C.E. Barglebaugh, a recent transfer from Chicago, where he worked for both Frank Lloyd Wright and Walter Burley Griffin after the turn of the century. During his nine-year tenure with Lang & Witchell, Barglebaugh was responsible for much of the firm's Prairie-style work, including this residence for Rufus Higginbotham, a prior client of the firm for a warehouse downtown. Barglebaugh had the "Wright stuff" in this mature, Prairie-style design; the finest of its type in Dallas, and possibly the state.

13
Private Residence, *1917*
4937 Swiss Avenue
C.P. Sites
One of three known Swiss Avenue residences designed by C.P. Sites is this two-story Prairie four-square with a flanking rear wing and porte cochere. Its simple, horizontal massing and low-hipped roof with broad overhangs recalls Frank Lloyd Wright's Winslow House in River Forest, Illinois, completed in 1893. Sites added an entry porch supported by slotted brick piers and accented with minimal cast stone ornament.

14
Private Residence, *1928*
5020 Swiss Avenue
Lang & Witchell
Next door to their house for Rufus Higginbotham, Lang & Witchell also designed this informal English country house for his son-in-law. Side-by-side, the two houses demonstrate the stylistic breadth of the firm's residential work, including their attention here to historical detail.

15
Private Residence, *1916*
5314 Swiss Avenue
Hal Thomson
Hal Thomson demonstrated considerable virtuosity in this asymmetrical, yet balanced, composition that blends Mediterranean and Adamesque elements within a Georgian milieu. By white-washing the facade, Thomson was able to unify these disparate details into a work of stark beauty.

16
Private Residence, *1916*
5439 Swiss Avenue
Hal Thomson
This expansive adaptation of English
Palladianism is one of the most bombastic
mansions on Swiss Avenue. Built by C.C.
Greer, the president of Magnolia Petroleum
Company, this house demonstrates Hal
Thomson at his symmetrical best, with a
large central pavilion flanked by tall loggias
and recessed wings. Profuse Georgian detailing
contributes to the eclectic energy of the
main elevation.

18
Private Residence, *1929*
5907 Swiss Avenue
Bertram Hill
Bertram Hill designed five houses on Swiss
Avenue between 1918 and 1929, ranking
him as the neighborhood's third most active
architect, behind Hal Thomson and Lang &
Witchell. This Georgian Revival residence
pays respect to Thomson's centralized compositions of the previous decade, most notably that of the Greer residence. Narrower lot
widths at this end of Swiss Avenue impacted
the houses with more vertical proportions
that, in this case, precluded the possibility
of matching loggias and side wings

17
Aldredge House, *1917*
5500 Swiss Avenue
Hal Thomson
The most accomplished of Thomson's symmetrical designs on Swiss Avenue is this
French Eclectic manor with elegant Renaissance detailing executed in stone. Thomson
exercised surprising restraint in the design of
this residence, which features slightly projecting pavilions with hipped roofs bracketing a
central, recessed entry elaborately defined in
stonework. Paired loggias are pushed behind
the plane of the main facade. A full-width
raised terrace and balustrade echo similar
designs on Thomson's other nearby houses.

19
Private Residence, *1925*
6243 La Vista Drive
A commanding terminus to Swiss Avenue
is this two-story, Jacobean-style manor clad
in brown brick, with stucco and brick half-
timbering on the front gables, and stone trim
on the projecting bay window and Tudor
entry arch. The green-tiled, gabled roof and
soaring chimneys, with triple brick and stone
flues, increase the visual prominence of this
impressive residence.

20
Rayworth Williams House, *1926*
700 Paulus Avenue
David R. Williams
David Williams' remarkable architectural tenure in Dallas spanned ten years, from 1923 to 1933. During this brief period he designed a number of seminal residences in Dallas and Corsicana that incorporated vernacular forms, native materials and local climactic responses in his development of a "regional" style of architecture. This compact house, Williams' third in Dallas, represented his final transition from overt Mediterranean/Spanish Eclectic imagery to the more indigenous style that marked subsequent commissions.

21
Old Lakewood Library, *1937*
6342 La Vista Drive
Lucius O'Bannon
Across from the Lakewood Theater is one of the earliest branch libraries in the city – a coup for Albert Dines and Lee Kraft, as they sought to bring distinction to their nearby commercial and residential development. This gracious public building, clad in Texas shellstone and trimmed with smooth limestone, stands in elegant contrast to the predominantly Modernistic shopping center.

22
Lakewood Theater, *1938*
1825 Abrams Parkway
Pettigrew and Worley
With its resplendent neon tower, the Lakewood Theater brought instant recognition to the surrounding shopping district and residential subdivisions being developed by Dines and Kraft. Interstate Circuit, Inc., Texas' largest theater chain, built the Lakewood as part of the company's ambitious suburban expansion scheme during the 1930s. The theater interiors were supervised by Texas Centennial Exposition artist Eugene Gilboe.

23
Duplex Residences, *c.1935*
5800 block of La Vista Court
Like its Tudor cottage kin, the two-story Tudor duplex was among the most widely used multifamily building types in East Dallas and Oak Lawn during the late 1920s and throughout the 1930s. This two-block length of La Vista Court boasts the highest concentration of these duplexes in the city. While no individual unit stands out, collectively, they form a remarkably cohesive neighborhood notable for its distinctive spatial character, as well as the congruity of its architecture.

Willis Winters

24
Retail/Private Residence, *1986*
2802 Greenville Avenue
John Mullen
This two-story mixed-use building is a wonderfully urbane adaptation of an early Texas
commercial structure to the high-density retail
corridor along lower Greenville Avenue. As
the adjacent subdivisions of Belmont, Vickery
Place and Greenland Hills were developed
during the 1920s and 1930s, Greenville
Avenue became the primary north-south
thoroughfare of East Dallas. Scattered along
its length are delightful retail enclaves that
served the adjacent neighborhoods. The best
of these were voluptuously clad in ceramic tile,
including **(25) 2100-18 Greenville Avenue.**
(26) 2815-31 Greenville Avenue and **(27)**
3024 Greenville Avenue represent the more
typical construction of patterned masonry
with cast stone ornamentation.

29
Private Residence, *1927*
6292 Mercedes Avenue
David R. Williams
During the 1920s, David Williams and his
young protégé, O'Neil Ford, travelled extensively throughout Texas documenting the
state's indigenous building traditions. This
house was one of the first to incorporate vernacular themes gleaned from these excursions.
Representative of his "Texas Colonial" style,
this residence features a two-story, white-
washed mass of irregular but balanced composition, with generous openings for cross
circulation. Traditional ornamentation and
detailing is conspicuously absent. Nearby is
the **(30) Private Residence, 6342 Mercedes,**
1932, one of O'Neil Ford's earliest houses,
demonstrating the influence of his mentor.

28
Robert E. Lee Elementary School, *1931*
2911 Delmar Avenue
DeWitt & Washburn
Boyle & Burke, addition, 1956
During the 1930s, DeWitt & Washburn
produced three of the most significant modernistic structures in Dallas. The first of these
was this remarkable experiment in cast-in-
place concrete. The consistently fine form-
work gives a subtle texture to the school's
facade, while the cast details and ornamentation are surprisingly intricate.

31
Private Residence, *1937*
3216 Jacotte Circle
Howard Meyer
This small residence for Eugene Sanger was
the first built work of Dallas' most accomplished Modern architect, Howard Meyer,
who began his Dallas practice in 1935, following a degree from Columbia, a year in Europe
studying the work of the masters, and brief
stints working for Bertram Goodhue and
Thompson & Churchill. His arrival in Dallas
coincided with William Lescaze's Magnolia
Lounge at Fair Park, a Modernist project of
immense local influence. (Meyer worked on
Lescaze's U.N. Headquarters competition
entry while a student at Columbia). With this
house, Meyer demonstrated confident, first-
hand knowledge of the International Style.

32
Marcus Residence, *1937*
1 Nonesuch Road
DeWitt & Washburn
After firing Frank Lloyd Wright for designing
a house that was unresponsive to the Dallas
climate, fashion retailer Stanley Marcus commissioned this restrained (by comparison to
Wright's design) exercise in the International
Style. It shares many similarities with Howard
Meyer's residence on Jacotte Circle of the
same year, including horizontal massing, a
flat roof with broad overhangs and a painted
masonry wall rising to the second floor window sill. Marcus was an extremely sophisticated architectural client; in addition to
Wright, he was responsible for bringing to
Dallas, over a period of 45 years, William
Lescaze, Eero Saarinen and I.M. Pei.

33
Private Residence, *1927*
6835 Westlake Avenue
Sir Alfred Bossom
The English architect responsible for the
Magnolia Building – Dallas' first skyscraper –
designed this baronial country estate for
Arthur Kramer, president of the downtown
department store A. Harris & Co. The structure of this house is more intriguing than its
architecture. Bossom insisted on installing an
earthquake-proof foundation with stainless
steel ball bearings that would allow the house
to move as the soil shifted. Steel structural
framing lent unnecessary additional solidity.

34
Bromberg Residence, *1939*
3201 Wendover Road
Ford & Swank
For three eventful years prior to World War II,
O'Neil Ford & Arch Swank were partners
in a small Dallas office that produced two of
the most critically acclaimed modern buildings in the United States during the late
1930s: a vacation house for Sid Richardson
on San Jose Island, and the Little Chapel in
the Woods at the Texas State College for
Women in Denton. Ford and Swank also
designed this house for Alfred and Juanita
Bromberg on a secluded East Dallas site.
With a rectangular, gabled volume framed
by chimneys and surrounded by screened
porches, the house was devoid of any architectural pretense. It represented the continuing exploration and refinement of a Texas
regional style initiated earlier in the decade
by Ford's mentor, David Williams.

35
Private Residence, *1934*
6676 Lakewood Boulevard
Anton Korn
This Italian Renaissance villa was designed
by Anton Korn, architect of numerous
Tudor mansions in Highland Park. Dines
& Kraft, the developer of Country Club
Estates, Westlake Park, and Monticello
additions (now collectively known as
Lakewood), engaged the services of Dallas'
most noted residential architects to design
speculative houses.

36
Private Residence, *1935*
6748 Lakewood Boulevard
George Marble
Richard Drummond Davis, renovation
    and addition, 1999
This French Eclectic residence shows the
indelible influence of Charles Dilbeck, who
moved from Tulsa to Dallas in 1932, and
partnered briefly with Dines & Kraft's
favorite architect, George Marble. The irregular roof silhouette, through-cornice dormers,
fieldstone walls with brick trim and massive
round chimney flue, would become signature
elements of Dilbeck's mature style.

38
Private Residence, *1936*
6851 Gaston Avenue
DeWitt & Washburn
Built as the Contemporary Model Home for
the Texas Centennial Exposition and moved
to this site following the fair, this was one of
the most widely visited Modern homes in the
state in 1936. Houston architect Donald
Barthelme assisted DeWitt & Washburn
in the design of this landmark house. Luther
Sadler designed a similar Modernistic residence at **(39) 6843 Lorna Lane,** 1936.
Nearby, at 2300 Auburn is the Masonite
House, also from the Centennial Exposition,
unfortunately altered beyond recognition.

37
Private Residence, *1940*
6820 Avalon Avenue
Charles Dilbeck
Charles Dilbeck was Dallas' most idiosyncratic residential designer, responsible for hundreds of French Eclectic and Ranch-style
homes distributed throughout the city. His
largest residence in Lakewood is this French
farmhouse clad in fieldstone, accented with
half-timbering and brick nogging. The "L" –
shaped plan parti, with a square tower
marking the juncture of the two wings,
was repeated by Dilbeck four years later at
6252 Mercedes. This farmhouse amply
illustrates Dilbeck's romantic philosophical
approach to his residences: quaint, picturesque composition, mixed with rugged
natural materials and finely crafted details.

40
Private Residence, *1953*
7122 Shook Avenue
A.B. Swank
Arch Swank continued to practice in Dallas
following O'Neil Ford's permanent relocation
to San Antonio after World War II. Following
a five-year partnership with Roscoe DeWitt,
Swank established his own office, with this
confident Modern residence representing
one of his first solo commissions. The two
adjacent houses, 7126 and 7132, are also
by Swank.

41
Private Residence, *1929*
7030 Tokalon Drive
Herbert M. Greene, LaRoche & Dahl
During the 1920s and 1930s, George Dahl
designed many prestigious residences for the
city's business elite, including this limestone-
clad French manor for R.G. Storey, an officer
with Republic National Bank.

C.D. Hutsell

42
Private Residence, *1930*
7035 Lakewood Boulevard
C.D. Hutsell

C.D. Hutsell designed and built 50 houses in Lakewood between 1926 and 1941. As an architect/builder, he played a critical role in fulfilling Dallas' manifest destiny of the 1920s: eastward expansion to the shores of White Rock Lake. His Spanish Eclectic homes on Lakewood Boulevard established the signature identity of the neighborhood through a unified architectural vocabulary consisting of cream-colored masonry, Spanish tile roofs, rough-hewn wood balconies and porches, distinctive chimneys, and elaborate decorative metal work. These elements are all present on this residence built for his own family in 1930, which also illustrates his favored plan type: an "L"-shaped scheme organized around an enclosed courtyard. Following a trip to California in 1929, where he was influenced by the home of cowboy movie star Tom Mix, Hutsell further enriched his vocabulary of design features by employing round turrets and parabolic arched stained-glass windows, accented by exterior canvas draperies.

43
Duplex Residence, *1938*
7301-03 Lakewood Boulevard
C.D. Hutsell

This Lakewood Boulevard duplex – often mis-attributed to Charles Dilbeck – is a departure from Hutsell's standard Spanish Eclectic recipe. Hutsell rendered this ingeniously planned Ranch-style compound in heavily textured shell-stone walls.

44
Private Residences, *1936-37*
7311-7315 Lakewood Boulevard
C.D. Hutsell

Beginning in 1936, Hutsell built eight split-level Spanish Eclectic homes along the eastern-most stretch of Lakewood Boulevard. These houses are miniature, highly elaborated variations of his own residence. When assimilated as a group, they form the most picturesque residential streetscape in Dallas.

45
White Rock Lake, *1911*
Opened in 1911 as the city's first water reservoir, White Rock Lake did not assume its current status as Dallas' most important urban park until a series of improvements were initiated by the Park Board in 1929. A swimming beach and bath house, boathouse and fish hatchery were constructed immediately, followed by a series of rock structures built by the Civilian Conservation Corps, giving the lake the rustic, national park-like character it is noted for today.

46
Water Operations Control Center, *1911*
2900 White Rock Road
City of Dallas Engineering Department
Parkey & Partners, adaptive reuse, 1983
The most prominent landmark on the lake's west shore is the original pump station and filtration plant constructed at the north end of the dam and spillway. Its handsome red brick facade with vertically proportioned windows, multiple string-courses and a decorative cornice suggest the unabated influence of the Victorian era on the city's second-tier municipal architecture.

47
Private Residence, *1998*
3535 W. Lawther Drive
Frank Welch
One of the newest houses on the lake's west side is this engaging Texas villa that follows in the regional building traditions established by David Williams and O'Neil Ford. The

unpretentious aspect of this house seems completely at odds with its more pompous west-side neighbors.

48
H. L. Hunt Mansion, *1929*
4009 W. Lawther Drive
This is the best of three replicas of Mount Vernon extant in Dallas, built by the oilman H.L. Hunt, who was reputedly the richest man in the world at the time of its construction. By virtue of its perpetually green lawn and stately promontory, the Hunt Mansion achieves a timeless grandeur unmatched by any other residence in the city.

49
Private Residence, *1939*
4321 W. Lawther Drive
Howard Meyer
Dallas' most accomplished Modern architect also designed the city's finest and most impressively sited Georgian mansion for Sydney Hohenberg. Meyer used great decorum in the proportions and composition of this graceful house.

Dallas Arboretum

50
DeGolyer House, *1940*
8525 Garland Road
Schutt & Scott (Beverly Hills)
The 66-acre Dallas Arboretum and Botanical
Garden is located on the southeast corner of
White Rock Lake, its boundaries encompass-
ing two former historic estates purchased in
the late 1970s for the development of a pub-
lic arboretum. Beautifully sited on the larger
of the two original tracts is this Spanish
Colonial Revival estate built by Everett and
Nell DeGolyer. The hacienda-like DeGolyer
House now serves as a splendid architectural
centerpiece of the restored 1940 gardens
designed by Arthur and Marie Berger.

51
Women's Council International Garden, *1997*
*Morgan Wheelock (Summerville, Massachusetts),
    landscape architect*
The coup de grace of this formal garden is
a stunning water-on-water perspective view
from the DeGolyer House terrace. Nearby
is the more informal **(52) Jonsson Color
Garden,** 1990, Naud Burnett.

53
Camp House, *1938*
8617 Garland Road
John Staub (Houston)
The Camp House is one of two extant houses
in Dallas by the great Houston architect John
Staub. In addition to his spirited eclectic
residences, Staub was also capable of a more
abstract austerity, as evidenced here by the
interplay of massing and texture as the

primary compositional parti. The primal simplicity of this residence, combined with its
sensitive response to the local climate, recalls
the regional motivation behind the work of
David Williams. Next to the Camp House
is the **(54) Lay Ornamental Garden,** 1989,
Boyd & Heiderich, an informal, English-style
garden.

55
Bath House Cultural Center, *1929*
521 E. Lawther Drive
Carson & Linskie
Spencer Design Group, renovation, 1997
In the late 1920s, the Park Board assumed
responsibility for developing recreational facilities around White Rock Lake. One of the
initial improvements was a mammoth bathing
beach and adjacent bath house, located on
the lake's east shore. The bath house was constructed of reinforced concrete, with fluted
piers interjecting a contrapuntal measure in
a decidedly horizontal composition. Its completion in 1929 makes it one of the earliest
Art Deco buildings in Texas.

56
St. John's Episcopal Church, *1963*
848 Harter Road
O'Neil Ford & Arch Swank
Utilizing an oval plan and saddle-shaped
roof, Ford & Swank succeeded in redefining
traditional liturgical forms in this highly
original Modern church. The two architects
collaborated frequently in the late 1950s and
early 1960s; this sanctuary is their best small-
scale work during that period.

57
Private Residence, *1960*
9729 Van Dyke Road
Donald Speck
This self-assured house utilizes a Wrightian
planning grid and formal vocabulary to
achieve its striking neighborhood presence.
The angular glass facade employs a variety
of effective devices for sun control, including
suspended vertical fins, which serve to
balance the horizontal emphasis of the
elevation, while also establishing a deceptive
monumental scale.

58
Private Residence, *1954*
1019 Waterford Drive
Glenn Allen Galoway
This exceptional Modern house was designed
by Glenn Allen Galoway, a little-known
architect who came to Dallas in the early
1950s after working for Philip Johnson in
New York. The influence of Johnson's earliest
residences is apparent in the taut planes of
brick and glass in combination with a flat
roof. As in Johnson's de Menil House in
Houston (1950), the plan is organized around
an interior court, with a linear facade facing
the street. In his abbreviated career, Galoway
built five residences in Dallas, of which three
remain, including a nearby house at 611
Buckner Boulevard.

59
Private Residence, *1959*
8931 Capri Court
John Barthel
In a neighborhood of fine 50s houses, this
residence by John Barthel stands out. Two
rotated square volumes under a pair of angular folded plate roofs create an elemental
abstraction with soaring geometric monumentality that belies the home's diminutive size.

60
Granger Community Center, *1961*
1310 W. Avenue F, Garland, Texas
Fisher & Jarvis
During their seven-year partnership, Herschel
Fisher and Duane Jarvis consistently designed
innovative Modern buildings, including an
inspired and structurally daring solution for
this municipal recreation center in Garland.

61
Mesquite Municipal Building, *1960*
711 N. Galloway Avenue, Mesquite
Caudill Rowlett & Scott
Caudill Rowlett & Scott were primarily
known for their innovative school designs
during the 1960s. This rationally planned
suburban city hall is one of their few projects
in the area.

I n 1845, soon after John Neely Bryan established his trading post on the north bank of the Trinity River, a William Hord and his family settled down on a high ridge along the south bank. Thus, the seeds of Dallas and its suburb Oak Cliff were sown, and the dynamic between the two areas was set in place. It began as a purely geographical distinction: Dallas was flat and prairie-like and Oak Cliff happened to have really steep cliffs and enormous oaks. And of course there was the river flowing between them.

In 1850, the population of Hord's Ridge (as it was first called) took it hard when it lost the election to become the county seat to Dallas. Like Dallas' annexation of Oak Cliff in 1903, there was dissension and bitterness on the south bank, and the suburb's reputation as a city within a city was born.

Oak Cliff's continued pride of place dates to 1887 when successful grocers Thomas Marsalis and his partner John Armstrong purchased 2,000 acres of prime property on the south bank and began to develop it. When Armstrong soon left the partnership, Marsalis pushed forward with an ambitious plan for a health spa and vacation resort. He built a hotel (patterned after San Diego's Hotel del Coronado), a three-story dance pavilion, an opera house, and a zoo, and he installed a steam-powered railway that ran across the river to the Dallas County Courthouse square. But Marsalis was caught overextended in 1893 when the economy crashed, moved to New York to begin again, and died a poor man two years later.

By 1900 the exclusive Oak Cliff had become home to more middle- and working-class people. Land was subdivided and a number of modest houses began to be built. But Oak Cliff never lost its allure; developers continued to open up new neighborhoods – Lake Cliff, Winnetka Heights (now a historic district), and the lovely Kessler Park, for example.

And yet, over time this southern suburb – which had once fancied itself the Cambridge to Dallas' Boston or (because of its views of the city) the Brooklyn Heights to its Manhattan – became run down and depressed. Banks redlined much of it in the 1970s, which stymied home-buyers and small businesses needing mortgages.

When Oak Cliff came out on the other side of those depressed years, newcomers discovered what loyal, older residents had known all along, that the neighborhood possessed some of the most varied and interesting architecture in the city, a mixture of ingenious vernacular structures and high-style, architect-designed buildings. Its population is diverse – the Hispanic community has turned old Oak Cliff's city center on Jefferson Street into its own, colorful Main Street – and the winding hilly streets still yield dramatic views of Dallas. Oak Cliff residents take in those views with pleasure and, one feels, without a trace of envy.

51
52
53

Sylvan

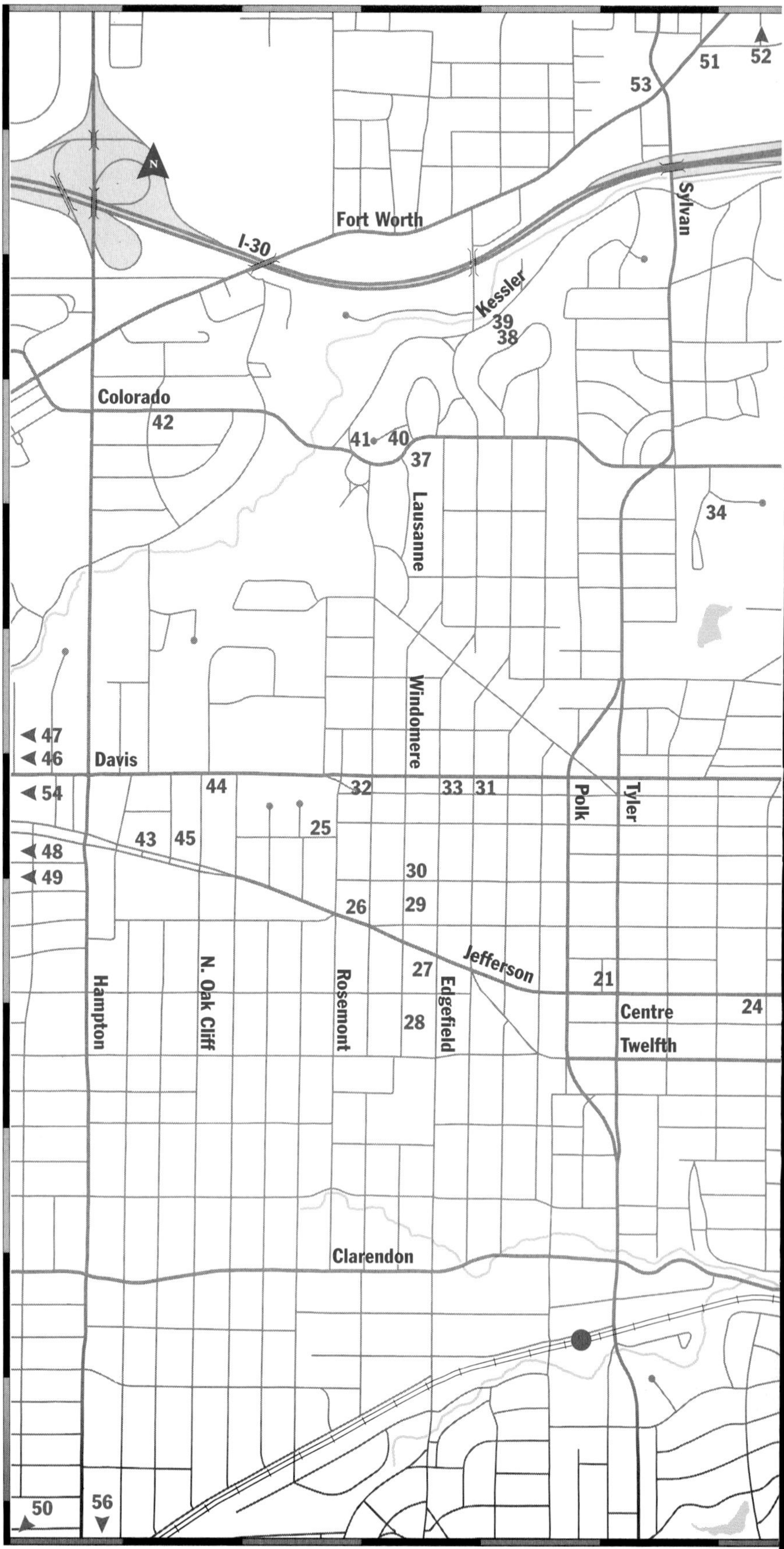

Fort Worth

I-30

Kessler
39
38

Colorado
42

41 40
37

34

Lausanne

Windomere

47
46
Davis
54

44
32
33 31

Polk
Tyler

45
43

25

48
49

30

26
29

Hampton

N. Oak Cliff

Rosemont

27
28

Edgefield

Jefferson

21

Centre
24

Twelfth

Clarendon

50
56

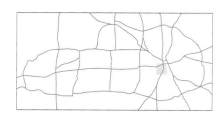

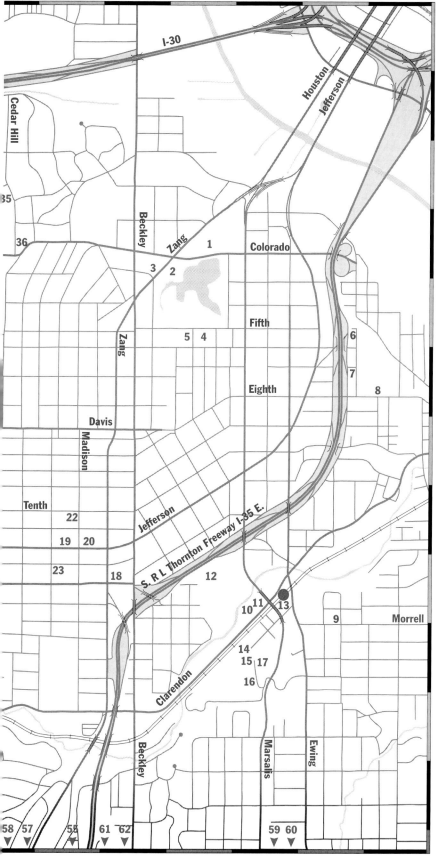

I-30

Cedar Hill

35

36

Beckley

Zang

Houston

Jefferson

1

Colorado

3 2

Zang

Fifth

5 4

6

7

Eighth

8

Davis

Madison

Tenth

22

Jefferson

19 20

S. R L Thornton Freeway I-35 E.

23

18

12

10 11 13

9

Morrell

14

15 17

16

Clarendon

Beckley

Marsalis

Ewing

58 57 58 61 62

59 60

6 Oak Cliff

1

Lake Park Retirement and Nursing Center, *1929*
329 E. Colorado Boulevard
Thomson & Swaine
Hal Thomson's sophisticated Cliff Towers was built by Charles Mangold as the most luxurious residential hotel in the state. It remains a resolute Oak Cliff landmark.

2

Lake Cliff Park, *1906*
300 block of E. Colorado Boulevard
Hare & Hare (Kansas City), landscape
*   architects*
Lake Cliff was a popular private amusement park developed by Charles Mangold and John Zang in 1906 to attract Oak Cliff development. Its financial demise led to acquisition by the City in 1913. The present-day character of the park dates to 1944 improvements carried out by Hare & Hare.

3

Casita Lupe Cafe, *c.1932*
1207 N. Zang Boulevard
Across from the park is the former Polar Bear Ice Cream stand: a compelling demonstration of vernacular architecture as billboard.

4

Private Residence, *1916*
406 E. 5th Street
Lake Cliff Park and its adjacent neighborhood to the south and east are part of the original Oak Cliff townsite laid out by Thomas Marsalis and John Armstrong in 1887. Despite annexation by Dallas in 1903, and the subsequent development of the park as an amusement attraction featuring carnival rides, dancing pavilions and a 2,500-seat casino, the park's immediate residential environs were slow to develop. Beginning in the mid-1910s, bungalows began to appear along the park's southern boundary, including this well-restored home exhibiting a four-square plan and Craftsman detailing. The projecting second-floor windows and through-cornice gabled dormers add a mischievous note of complexity to an otherwise simple Craftsman elevation. Down the street, the residence at **(5) 320 E. 5th Street,** 1925, is a more substantial Craftsman composition, with double front-facing gables and a raised, side-gable second story.

6

Kovandovitch House, *1914*
523 Eads Avenue
Joseph Kovandovitch, designer
One of the most maligned residential landmarks in Dallas is this isolated villa overlooking R.L. Thornton Freeway south of downtown. Its remarkable survival into the 21st century can be attributed to the enduring properties of reinforced concrete and the high-minded vision of its owner-builder, an immigrant restaurateur named Joe Kovandovitch.

7
Dallas County Government Center, *1961*
414 S. R.L. Thornton Freeway
Prinz & Brooks
By virtue of its conspicuous site and implacable early-60s aesthetic, this small office building achieves a provocative freeway presence. A folded plate roof is confidently lifted above adjacent office blocks that display varying elevations responding to site and programmatic influences. Nearby is the **(8) Yvonne Ewell Magnet High School,** 1995, at 1201 E. 8th Street, HKCP Jennings Hackler and John S. Chase FAIA.

9
Zion Hill Missionary Baptist Church, *c.1940*
907 Morrell Avenue
Many of Dallas' architectural anomalies can be found in the quixotic vernacular buildings of Oak Cliff, including this grandiose metaphorical exposition of ecclesiastical architecture.

Dallas Zoo

10
Administration Building, *1963*
621 E. Clarendon Drive
Tatum & Quade
Once serving as the main entry to the original Dallas Zoo, the Administration Building now offers passage to Zoo North. Substantial renovations to old Zoo facilities have recently occurred, including the **(11) Entry Plaza and Lemur Exhibit,** HKS, Inc., 1996, and the **(12) Exxon Endangered Tiger Exhibit,** F&S Partners and URSA International (Atlanta), 1999. Nearby, is the **(13) DART Zoo Station,** HOK and Vidaud+Associates, 1996.

14
Wilds of Africa, *1990*
Herb Reimer (New York); Design Consortium (New Orleans), landscape architects
The Dallas Zoo dramatically expanded its boundaries in 1990 to encompass an African theme park and monorail ride. Within the Wilds of Africa are several impressive exhibits, including the **(15) Hamon Gorilla Conservation Research Center,** Jones & Jones (Seattle) and F&S Partners, 1990, and the **(16) Kimberly Clark Chimpanzee Forest,** HKS, Inc. and the Portico Group (Seattle), 1996.

17
Meadows Animal Healthcare Facility, *1999*
Oglesby-Greene
Nestled against the slope of a verdant hillock is the Zoo's site-sensitive animal hospital: a highly refined and graceful building that recalls the WPA-era structures of Zoo North.

18
NationsBank Oak Cliff, *1965*
400 S. Beckley Avenue
Harwood K. Smith & Partners
Oak Cliff's tallest building is a pristine vertical slab which – together with the lower banking hall – rests upon a raised, landscaped plinth. The strictly regimented ground plane successfully modulates the scale of this urbane ensemble.

Willis Winters

19
Jefferson Tower, *1929*
351 W. Jefferson Boulevard
Jefferson Boulevard forms the nucleus of Oak Cliff's main commercial district along an eight-block stretch bounded by Zang Boulevard and Polk Street. East of Zang, Jefferson continues its alignment along the old curvilinear route of Thomas Marsalis' steam-powered railway, constructed to bring visitors from Dallas in the 1890s. By the 1930s, Jefferson Boulevard had developed into the most substantial commercial district in the entire city outside of downtown. Jefferson Tower was the boulevard's single largest project, consisting of an eight-story brick and terra-cotta office building and adjacent retail storefronts. Other significant early commercial buildings include Howard Hughes' polychromed **(20) Texas Theater,** 229 W. Jefferson Blvd., W. Scott Dunne, 1931, the largest suburban movie house in the southwest at the time of its construction, and the handsome Italianate building at **(21) 901 W. Jefferson Boulevard,** 1916.

22
North Oak Cliff Branch Library, *1986*
302 W. 10th Street
Good Haas & Fulton
This striking branch library features a raised triangular skylight as the building's central organizing element. Its dramatic extension into the parking lot is a boldly iconic – and functional – gesture.

23
Independence House, *1953*
334 Centre Street
Prinz & Brooks
The first building in Dallas to receive a national design award from the American Institute of Architects is this suave former home of Oak Cliff Savings. It has been profoundly altered by the addition of an elevator tower and white-washing of the exterior brick walls.

24
Ranchito Cafe, *1949*
612 W. Jefferson Boulevard
Charles Dilbeck
Charles Dilbeck's eccentric architectural vocabulary is a good fit for the former Red Bryan's Smokehouse restaurant. Dilbeck delighted in creating a mythical Ranch-style imagery that he applied to both his residential and commercial projects.

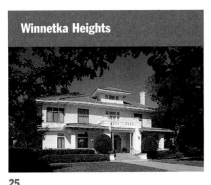

Winnetka Heights

25
Oak Cliff Society of Fine Arts, *1912*
401 N. Rosemont
The last major subdivision of the original
Oak Cliff townsite was Winnetka Heights,
platted in 1908 by a consortium of developers
including oilman J.P. Blake, who built this
modified Prairie four-square for himself in
1912. The neighborhood's predominantly
Prairie-style residences, including the masonry
four-square house at **(26) 101 N. Montclair
Avenue,** 1912, were designs adapted from
architectural pattern books of the period.

27
Private Residence, *c.1915*
215 S. Edgefield Avenue
The lower porch of this Neo-Classical residence passes uninterrupted behind the flat-
roofed, monumental portico. Another fine
example of the cross-gabled Craftsman style
is at **(28) 318 S. Windomere,** 1912.

29
Private Residence, *c.1915*
122 N. Windomere Avenue
The absence in this four-square residence of
any historical detailing and ornamentation
marks the Prairie style in its purest form.

Nearby is **(30) 200 N. Windomere Avenue,**
1925, a side-gabled Craftsman house with
paired porch columns and a large dormer.

31
Theater/Retail Building, *1941*
1214 W. Davis Street
This small theater and retail complex falls
into a stylistic domain somewhere between
the ebullience of Art Deco and the more
rational objectivity of Modernism. The
grandiose-looking theater entrance belies
the building's minute scale.

32
Sherman and Yaquinto Law Office, *1922*
509 N. Montclair
ArchiTexas, addition and renovation, 1986
This gambrel-roofed Colonial Revival house
is an oddity among Winnetka Heights' more
progressive architectural styles from the same
period. The mannerist expansion in 1986
cleverly mirrors the distinctive gambrel form
of the original.

33
Cannon's English Village, *1922*
1310-14 W. Davis Street
The affluence of Winnetka Heights attracted
stylish suburban retail development, including
this Jacobean complex located on the neighborhood's northern boundary. This building
represents the final step toward the planned
community shopping centers that would
appear in Dallas throughout the 1930s.

34
Private Residence, *1956*
718 Kessler Lake Drive
Prinz & Brooks
The topography and natural beauty of Kessler Park inspired some of the finest contemporary residences in Dallas, including this dynamic home for car dealer Earl Hayes. Architect Harold Prinz arranged a series of cantilevered pavilions that effortlessly float above the verdant banks of a small lake. The sedate front facade stands in contrast to this uninhibited structural exhibition.

35
Private Residence, *1951*
1435 Cedar Hill Road
David Braden
In the early 1950s, several young Dallas architects built small contemporary homes on dramatic Oak Cliff sites. Among this group were David Braden, his partner Harold Jones (418 West Clarendon Avenue, 1951) and J. Herschel Fisher (1630 Nob Hill Road, 1950). Braden's modest house occupies a forested slope amid luxuriant vegetation. The cantilevered wood deck is reputedly the first of its kind in Dallas. Down the street is Kessler Park's Streamline Moderne landmark, prominently sited on a bend in Colorado Boulevard: **(36) 1302 Cedar Hill Road,** 1939.

37
Private Residence, *1936*
1134 Lausanne Avenue
Charles Dilbeck
The most notable feature of this informal French farmhouse designed by Charles Dilbeck is the octagonal stair tower marking the juncture between two angled wings. The entry is squeezed between this turret and an adjacent massive chimney. Dilbeck's subtle, white-washed brickwork is somewhat overpowered by the heavy-handed application of contemporary roof shingles. Another picturesque Dilbeck compound can be found at **(38) 1125 Canterbury Court,** 1937.

39
Private Residence, *1948*
1934 Kessler Parkway
A.B. Swank
This austere residence by Arch Swank nestles securely into its densely wooded, sloping site. With its flat roof and regularly coursed block walls, this house must have been a disturbing post-war intrusion into Kessler Park's previously staid architectural environment.

40
Skillern Residence, *1925*
1177 Lausanne Avenue
Hal Thomson (attributed)
The lazy meander of Colorado Boulevard
through Kessler Park produced spectacularly
visible home sites, which few architects failed
to take advantage of. One of the most prominent houses in the area was this residence
built by drugstore heir R.A. Skillern, shortly
after the neighborhood was opened for development in 1924. The symmetrical composition, projecting loggias and the deft combination of both Mediterranean and classical
detailing suggest the hand of architect Hal
Thomson, whose Swiss Avenue mansions
bear striking similarities to this house.

41
Private Residence, *1958*
1553 W. Colorado
L.C. Cavitt
The cantilevered structural extensions at each
gable end provide a peculiar, albeit demon-
strative, lesson in roof framing. Like many
contemporary residences in Kessler Park, this
house seems to float above its undulating site.

42
Private Residence, *1936*
1950 W. Colorado Boulevard
This impressive Norman farmhouse substantially – and successfully – employs the French
idiom of Charles Dilbeck to create a wonderfully complex and richly textured composition. Only the non-elaborated chimney denies
Dilbeck's possible involvement in the design.

Willis Winters

43
Private Residence, *1940*
2237 W. Jefferson Boulevard
Charles Dilbeck
Following his arrival from Tulsa in 1932,
Dilbeck established a small practice that would
eventually dominate Dallas residential construction in the years leading up to World War II.
Not only did he design custom houses for private clients, he also supplied plans to developers who were acquainted with the widespread
appeal of Dilbeck's work and could depend on
its easy marketability. New subdivisions containing Dilbeck-designed cottages were preva-
lent in the late 1930s and early 1940s, including a small enclave between Davis Street and
Jefferson Boulevard, north of Sunset High
School. This diminutive Ranch house, facing
south onto Jefferson, suitably displays Dilbeck's
skillful artistry and the resulting thematic
effect. Other neighborhood cottages that
achieve similar ends include the split-level
Ranch duplex at **(44) 522 N. Oak Cliff
Boulevard,** 1941, and the French Eclectic residence at **(45) 410 N. Montreal Avenue,** 1941.

46
Santa Clara Catholic Church, *1995*
321 Calumet Avenue
Vidaud+Associates
This extensive parish complex achieves a
captivating, mission-like ambience through
its literal interpretation of Spanish Colonial
themes. The vividly hued stucco buildings
create a strong figural presence in the west
Oak Cliff landscape.

47
Louise Kahn Elementary School, *1997*
810 Franklin Street
Garza BRW Architects
With its well-proportioned plaza and surrounding cloister, this handsomely-designed
elementary school achieves a civic presence
rarely encountered in a primary educational
campus. Distinctive roof forms articulate a
performance hall and gymnasium on the
building's north side, where the sloping topography allows for additional building height.
An "L"-shaped pylon is carefully positioned
in the plaza to complete the campus' vertical
hierarchy and overall compositional effect.

48
Jefferson Drive-In Theater, *1948*
4506 W. Jefferson Boulevard
Jack M. Corgan
Jack Corgan designed hundreds of movie and
drive-in theaters throughout the southwest
after World War II. His kitschy, uninhibited
masterpiece, the Jefferson Drive-In, stands as
a mute sentinel in west Oak Cliff, fortunately
unaffected by development pressures. It is one
of the most important cultural icons in Dallas.

49
Moises Molina High School, *1998*
2355 Duncanville Road
PBK Architects (Houston); Aguirre
Color and massing are adeptly used to articu-

late the programmatic components of this visually compelling high school, in partial tribute to the work of Ricardo Legorreta.

50
Mountain View College, *1970*
4849 W. Illinois Avenue
Harrell & Hamilton; Chan & Rader
  (San Francisco)
This sprawling, Prairie-esque campus is arranged on both sides of a meandering ravine, with broad terraces and elevated walkways facing the interior of the site. The unassuming, neutral-colored buildings maintain a calm – but aloof – presence in this pastoral landscape.

51
Alamo Plaza Motel Courts, *c.1940*
712 Fort Worth Avenue
The Alamo Plaza was the state's first motel chain, owned and operated by E. L. Torrence of Waco. The Mission Revival style was a popular influence on the design of tourist courts throughout the 1930s and 1940s; Torence utilized the scalloped Alamo parapet as his chain's trademark in numerous locations across the southern United States. Nearby, the **(52) Mission Motel,** 514 W. Commerce Street, c.1935, displays similar mimetic influences.

53
Travel Inn Budget Motel, *1946*
815 Fort Worth Avenue
The most spectacular of the ten extant lodges and motels that line the old highway to Fort

Worth is this prominent compound occupying a bluff at Sylvan Avenue. The Spanish Colonial-style buildings also display late Moderne influences.

54
Texas Motel, *c.1940*
3816 Davis Street
Charles Dilbeck
The Texas Motel is organized around a rectangular motor court. The long front elevation is picturesquely treated in a rambling Ranch-style composition, anchored at the vehicular entrance by an elaborated office with a round turret. Throughout the 1940s, Dilbeck utilized this formula on numerous motel projects in Dallas and other north Texas towns.

55
Oak Cliff Christian Church, *1962*
1222 W. Kiest Boulevard
Fisher & Jarvis
In its functional organization and exterior form, Oak Cliff Christian Church is a thoroughly Modern building: rigorous and logical, without being trendy or self-indulgent. This compelling church complex marked the end of the fruitful partnership between Herschel Fisher and Donald Jarvis.

56

Kiest Park, *1932*

3080 S. Hampton Road

Wayne Woodruff, landscape architect

The bucolic, 250-acre tract for Kiest Park was donated to the City in the 1930s by Edwin Kiest, publisher of the *Dallas Times Herald*. With the exception of a stone recreation building designed by C.H. Griesenbeck and completed in 1932, few initial improvements were made in the new parksite, due to the City's financial woes. Landscape architect Wayne Woodruff completed a master plan in 1934 that gives the park its current rustic ambience.

58

Mountain Creek Branch Library, *1995*

6102 Mountain Creek Parkway

Milton Powell & Partners

In a largely undeveloped corner of southwest Dallas, this branch library is a campestral outpost of civic government. Native materials are used to clad simple geometric forms arranged around a central raised drum and lantern. Concentric circles form the outer edges of the lobby and reading room, which enjoys sweeping panoramic views to the north overlooking a spring-fed lake and rolling escarpment.

57

Redbird Airport Terminal, *1965*

5303 Challenger Drive

Jack M. Corgan

The small terminal building for the City-operated Redbird Airport features a pair of thinshell reinforced concrete "piltschaler" canopies at each entrance: a rare local use of technology that was popular in American architecture in the late 1950s. Corgan utilized a similar structural form for a picnic pavilion at Hamilton Park, in north Dallas.

59

Boude Storey Middle School, *1933*

3000 Maryland Avenue

Mark Lemmon

During the 1930s, Mark Lemmon was responsible for many of the finest institutional buildings in Dallas, including this junior high school in south Oak Cliff. The design is influenced by an earlier project, his Third Church of Christ Scientist in Oak Lawn. The school demonstrates Lemmon's mastery of masonry construction; the exquisite brick detailing imparts a richness of texture rarely encountered in Depression-era architecture.

60
Veteran's Administration Hospital, *1940*
4500 S. Lancaster Boulevard
V.A. Design Services Department
The original hospital facility for the Veteran's
Administration campus in south Dallas is an
awkwardly scaled building, further worsened
by the clumsy application of Georgian details
and ornamentation. Recent campus additions
by F&S Partners and Dahl Architects fastidi-
ously borrow only the color palette and a
single horizontal stripe from the original
to establish a new, graphically compelling
design vocabulary.

62
Rawlins Farmhouse, *1855*
850 S. Dallas Avenue
Lancaster, Texas
This dignified farmhouse was rebuilt after
the Civil War in a frontier Greek Revival
style. The modestly detailed square porch
is attached to the flat front facade, which
is made monumental by equally spaced
through-cornice dormers. Ground-level
windows of the house are paired symmetrically under the two outside dormer windows,
while the porch roof is truncated at the
middle dormer's window sill line.

61
W.A. Strain House, *1896*
400 S. Lancaster-Hutchins Road
Lancaster, Texas
Flanders & Moad
Following its introduction in the United
States in 1874, the Queen Anne style was
rapidly assimilated into American residential
architecture, later realizing its fullest,
unabashed fruition in Texas in this Lancaster
farmhouse. The architect was James Flanders,
who designed similar exotic houses in Dallas.
The steeply pitched hipped roof and lower
cross gables are trimmed with a distinctive
metal crest. In an exercise of mannerist aban-
don, Flanders removed the round tower from
its normal location at the front corner and
converted it to a slender vestigial element
jammed against one of the lower cross gables.
Solid brackets adorn the porches on both
floors and are also used in conjunction with
spindle-work on the first-floor porch railing.
The shingled planes and gable ornamentation
create a richly textured composition.

7 The Park Cities

The affluent independent municipalities of Highland Park and University Park, located three miles due north of downtown, feature the area's richest (if not most purely preserved) residential architecture from 1910 to 1940. Highland Park east of Preston Road developed first in 1907 as a typical suburban venture, but with special attention to fine planning and deed restrictions. Initial sections were laid out by Beverly Hills planner Wilbur David Cook. Turtle Creek, impounded as a series of small lakes, and its tributary Hackberry Creek, in its natural limestone channel, provide a picturesque topographic structure for the town plan and a lush setting. Cook (and later George Kessler in Highland Park West) used gently curving streets to create changing views, elegant streetscapes, and strategically located vest pocket parks.

University Park, the larger and more northerly of the two, began in 1915 as a cluster of residences along three streets west of newly formed Southern Methodist University. Founders and leaders of both Park Cities sought a quality of life better than that offered in Dallas. Two early slogans: "It's ten degrees cooler in Highland Park" and "Beyond the dust and smoke" typify the boosterism that led to separate incorporation of both cities.

In the cities' residential architecture is represented the best work of every period. From the teens and '20s are fine Italianate, English Renaissance and Tudor styles by Anton Korn and Hal Thomson and Spanish Colonial work by Fooshee & Cheek and J. Allen Boile. David Williams' work of 1926 to 1931 inspired that of O'Neil Ford from the '30s to '50s, and both mentor and student have houses here, as does regionalist eclectic architect Charles Stevens Dilbeck. The Park Cities are (and have always been) populated by residents of bold entrepreneurial spirit who have brought many "firsts" and "largests" to the cities: the first country club in Texas (Dallas County Club), the nation's first planned shopping center with its own off-street parking (Highland Park Village), the world's first drive-in bank (Hillcrest State Bank), and four of the largest churches of their denomination in the world. Because of high land values within the Highland Park Independent School District, perhaps 30% of the original housing stock has been demolished and replaced since 1975. In the 1980s, entire blocks of one-story cottages in less-pricey University Park were replaced by overscaled Georgian-style mansions. Unfortunately, in the '90s many fine older Highland Park homes have been lost as well.

The lasting appeal of the Park Cities has resulted in a powerful northward pull on quality development. The land along Preston Road and Dallas North Tollway has become "The Golden Corridor," threatening to extend pricey residential subdivisions and fine corporate addresses to the Oklahoma border.

7 The Park Cities

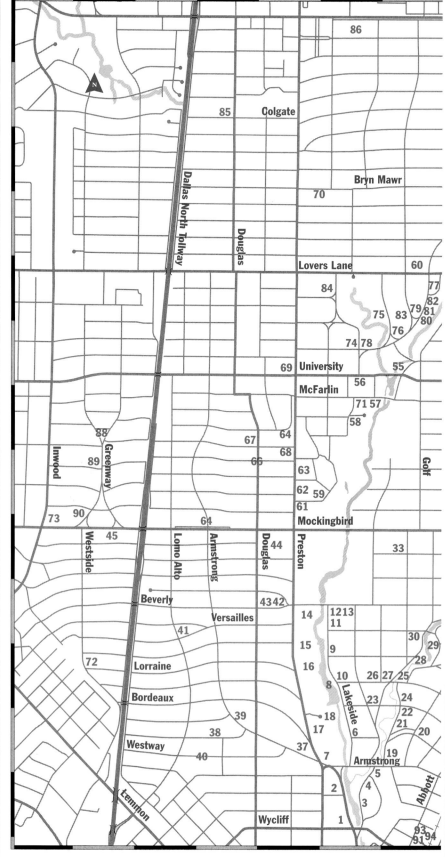

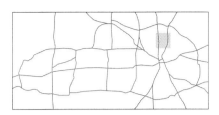

Northwest Highway Loop 12

Caruth

Southwestern

Turtle Creek

87

65

Hillcrest

Airline

Boedeker

Greenville

54

53

47

48 51

49
52
50

46

Bishop

Airline

SMU

Beverly 34

31
32

36

35

McCommas

Abbott

Euclid

Monticello

Knox

92

7 The Park Cities

If offered an opportunity to live anywhere in town, most Dallasites would choose this address. For a marriage of natural and architectural beauty, this street may have few peers in the United States. The manicured extension of the Turtle Creek greenbelt into the heart of Highland Park is bordered by estates designed by Korn, Thomson, Boile, Ford, Welch and Predock. Could this be heaven?

1
Private Residence, *1920*
4201 Lakeside Drive
Anton Korn
Bavarian-born Korn designed all of the homes in this block, and is credited with introducing the Tudor style to the Park Cities. He did so with great care to details such as divided lights, buttressing in corners and at eaves, slate roofs, and wonderfully Londonesque chimneys. At **(2) 4301 Lakeside,** Korn's expressive brick details enliven a more restrained gabled facade. Across Conner Lake **(3) 4324 St. Johns,** 1926, Hal Thomson's best Georgian enjoys sweeping views of the park and Korn's fine work.

5
Private Residence, *1954*
3756 Armstrong
O'Neil Ford (San Antonio)
A welcome Modernist gentility grants this home a hilltop serenity. Mexican brick gently sets off giant trees on all faces. Climbing ivy grounds the house into its lofty site. Delicate trellises and sunscreens protect sunny exposures and emphasize its demure appeal.

4
Private Residence, *1923*
4321 Overhill Drive
J. Allen Boile
Strong Spanish Colonial details, including a two-story leaded glass arched window and flanking sinewy columns beneath a stylized rose window seem to leap out from the smooth stucco walls of this home for the developer of Highland Park, Hugh Prather. Clay tile roof, wrought-iron screens and balcony rails, and a traditional mission door complete the mood of this stage-set design.

6
Private Residence, *c.1918*
4500 Lakeside Drive
Anton Korn
Korn's versatility is evident in this Italian Renaissance, replete with stone colonnade, wrought-iron screens and lanterns, decorative soffits and clay tile roof. Its public embrace contrasts with the seclusion of **(7) 4400 Preston Road,** 1929, also by Anton Korn, a limestone and stucco villa with extensive private gardens.

8
Exall Lake, *1890*
West side of Lakeside Drive at Euclid Street
Henry Exall dammed Turtle Creek to form
this lake as part of a 1326-acre development
that became Highland Park 15 years later.
By 1910, part of the lake was filled to build
Lakeside Drive and adjacent homesites. Stand
on the bridge opposite Lexington and look
north and south for a before and after.

9
Private Residence, *1989*
4800 Lakeside Drive
Frank Welch
This is a graceful Modernist interpretation
of neighboring historic homes, anchored by
pavilions at each end of its long facade. An
arched brick loggia supports second-floor terraces and screens generous windows set within
mahogany. Nearby **(10) 4700 Lakeside Drive,**
1913, is a cleanly stuccoed Italian Renaissance
house with softly arching windows and a green
tile roof. The elegant limestone chateaux at
(11) 4900 Lakeside Drive, 1916, Anton
Korn, centers symmetrically on a sculptured
segmental pediment. The Neo-Classical wedding cake **(12) 4908 Lakeside Drive,** 1915,
Thomson & Fooshee, has Corinthian columns
on a rich portico.

13
Private Residence, *1998*
4001 Beverly Drive
Richardson Robertson III (Los Angeles)
The interlocking volumes of this carefully
scaled Mediterranean villa have rich walls of
Texas shellstone. Detailed smooth limestone
sets off windows, balconies, and corners.

14
Private Residence, *1912*
4101 Beverly Drive
Herbert M. Greene
This prominently sited mansion in white
stucco and stone features Ionic columns
and Italianate balconies commanding a luxuriant tract of land and bend of Exall Lake.
Expressive carvings enliven each facade.

15
Private Residence, *1910*
4800 Preston Road
C.D. Hill
Chief among a parade of walled compounds
along Preston is this replica of Mount Vernon,
fronted by a double-height loggia. Time has
brought several remodelings. **(16) 4700**
Preston Road, 1917, by Anton Korn, is a
modestly scaled red brick compound, dressed
in light Georgian details and columns. **(17)**
4500 Preston Road, 1917, is a brick-and-
stucco Tudor design rendered in shades of gray.

18
Private Residence, *1993*
5 Willow Wood
Antoine Predock (Albuquerque)
From the street side, rough quarried limestone ledges anchor Predock's masterwork to
the earth. Yet on the Turtle Creek side, arcing
planes of glass and stainless steel open to tree-
tops and the sky. Rooftop terraces and a lacy
steel sky-ramp offer the owners multiple
venues for their bird-watching hobby.

19
Private Residence, *1930*
4408 St. Johns Drive
David R. Williams
Williams considered this his best work. A
simple four-bay scheme in soft creamy red
brick, with complementing gray shutters,
standing-seam copper roof, and shallow
wrought-iron wraparound porch blends in
with its sloping landscape. Ivy climbs to cover
part of the walls, accentuating the humble
nature of this early regionalist home. The
shutters, balconies, and screened sleeping
porch reflect a strong concern for natural
ventilation uncommon for the time. A patio,
mostly shielded from view, evokes Spanish
missions in its columns and arches.

20
Private Residence, *1967*
3616 Crescent
E.G. Hamilton
In quiet clarity, this flat-roofed two-story box
opens with a full expanse of windows to the
south and closes to the east and west with
brick walls that open only to allow a simple
bank of windows. The roof overhangs generously to shelter each face. A brick privacy wall
with encircling raised gardens provides a sense
of enclosure for the first floor and creates several intimate courts. There is much designed
into a such a seemingly small, quiet house.

21
Private Residence, *1925*
3712 Alice Circle
Fooshee & Cheek
Canted to the street to create a generous
lawn, this French country house adaptation
features a lively arched brick entryway in an
otherwise rough-hewn limestone facade.
Multicolor slate roof and massive detailing,
including simple gable brackets, complete
the effect. Landscaping terminates in a cozy,
semi-public corner park, complete with
bench under a stand of trees.

22
Private Residence, *1958*
3711 Lexington Avenue
Scott Lyons
The landscape swoops and swirls around
this simply detailed house. Its fingered, out-
spread plan reaches across the landscape
among oaks on a sloping site. Random fieldstone wall planes are topped by a blue fascia
treatment and flat roof. A two-story volume
projects out over the lowest part of the site,
its mass dissolved through full-height windows and doors to a shallow wraparound
balcony. The architect was an O'Neil Ford
collaborator, as evident from the spirit of
this fine contemporary home.

23

Private Residence, *1964*

3908 Lexington Avenue

O'Neil Ford (San Antonio)

A simple rectangular volume faces the street, with the unusual formality (for Ford) of matching bay windows flanking the entry steps. Soft Mexican brick is laid in Flemish bond courses to create a crisp tweedy pattern. Shallow arches over windows, shed roofs, and prominent, simple chimneys recall the time-honored ranch compound. In back, the house dissolves into a courtyard to accommodate numerous oaks.

24

Private Residence, *1964*

4606 St. Johns Drive

The Oglesby Group

Lionel Morrison, renovation and addition,
  1987

The reserved shed of the original "T"-plan stucco and fieldstone house was delicately expanded in the same materials. The stucco volume sits upon and overhangs an ivy-encrusted limestone base. A standing-seam metal roof dissolves to an open trellis. In back, fieldstone walls, pools, and fountains create both a more rigorously ordered land-scape and a series of usable outdoor spaces. The use of simple planes and the sound of flowing water bring peace and comfort.

25

Highland Park Town Hall, *1923*

4700 Drexel Drive

Otto Lang

Prinz & Brooks; Beran & Shelmire, additions
  and renovations, 1999

Designed in a Spanish Mediterranean style that preceded Highland Park Village, this town hall is a pleasantly small-scaled complex very much at home amid residences. Ornate limestone carvings frame major doorways and the sentinel tower. With its red clay-tile roof, creamy yellow stucco walls, simple fountain, and interesting details at every glance, it is an unusually inviting civic center.

James F. Wilson

26

Private Residence, *1994*

3908 Euclid Avenue

The Oglesby Group

A structural delight, this house reads as a creamy brick block with gray metal roof, which has been eroded to create windows, balconies, and passages. Steel beams and columns intrude into these openings to lend a constructivist edge. Set back on its site, this is a tall but respectful neighbor.

27
Private Residence, *1958*
4701 Drexel Drive
Scott Lyons
This well-scaled, simple tan-brick house consists of intersecting gabled sections. The two-story element projects forward to open up small balconies over windows below. Landscaping conceals remarkable features like a glass endwall framed by two brick columns.

28
Private Residence, *1919*
4726 Drexel Drive
Hal Thomson
Skillfully incised stucco details mark this two-story creamy house with gabled ends, red clay-tile tile roof, and exposed rafters. This is reported to be the first Dallas home designed in the Spanish Colonial style.

29
Private Residence, *1957*
4806 Drexel Drive
Enslie Oglesby and Jim Wiley
This diminutive glass-and-steel pavilion blurs the boundary between interiors and the outdoor landscape. The double-height plate-glass mullion grid receives doors and casement windows for ventilation. Stairs and other

details are stripped to their elemental nature. The effect is energetic contrast between the cool touch of concrete floors and open steel structure cradled in the relaxed, warm embrace of live oaks and other landscape. The Eames would be proud.

30
Private Residence, *1975*
3727 Miramar Avenue
The Oglesby Group
Tall hedges allow this razor-edged barn-like home to open its upper walls to cool north light. Forms are utterly without detail, turning the focus to the contemplative garden approach and a heavily wooded site. The facade is a symmetrical composition of doors and windows flanking a central fireplace.

31
Private Residence, *1926*
3628 Beverly Drive
Anton Korn
This immaculately crisp and balanced Tudor cottage commands a corner site. Double banks of upright-proportioned divided-light windows accentuate the verticality of gabled elements on either side of the entry. Cream and tan colors contrast with a blue-green slate roof, creating this colorful collage which was Korn's own residence. Across the street is Korn's **(32)** **3635 Beverly Drive,** 1925, a more masculine Tudor, with fieldstone base, steeply sloped slate roofs, and almost-black timber frame expressed to contrast with a cream background. Live oaks gnarl, twist, and turn to provide privacy and even a little mystery.

33
Private Residence, *1913*
3800 Maplewood Avenue
A gambrel roof delivers unusual character to this formal Colonial Revival house. Doric double columns structure a porch scheme of French doors and low balustrades to either side of the entry.

34
Private Residence, *1924*
3318 Beverly Drive
C.D. Hill
Seemingly a little brother to the Town Hall, this Spanish Mediterranean home includes an ornate corner entry portal, sinewy columns, and tri-arch windows. Its tan stucco exterior contrasts with a red clay tile roof.

35
Private Residence, *1994*
3311 Dartmouth
The Oglesby Group
An elegant linked trio of gabled white volumes has crisp details and standing-seam metal roofs. The series of small, middle, and large volumes telescopes across the site,

connected by semitransparent enclosed breezeways in perfect reinterpretation of the Texas farmhouse.

36
Private Residence, *1995*
3215 Princeton Avenue
Morrison-Seifert
A split two-story structure finished in stucco, this house has a pleasing veneer of stacked-bond limestone and windows above at the entry. Aggressively out of scale to its neighbors, it is a complement to the house across the street. The front entry includes storefront windows flanking an oversize door, with punctuating portal above. This is clean, cut-out Modernism, with simple linear volumes.

37
Private Residence, *1999*
4200 Armstrong Parkway
Tom Workman
Gaudi meets the Cotswolds! Dropped at the southern gateway to Highland Park, this copper-shingled fish of a house flouts convention with lavender-frame windows that seem to bubble up through the roof. White-stucco walls undulate and notch into the roof at curved junctures. Legend has it that Highland Park turned down the architect-owner's request to do a thatched roof.

38
Private Residence, *1948*
4400 Rheims Place
Howard Meyer
Meyer somehow married the sensitivities of both Wright and Mies van der Rohe in this finely executed Modern residence. Fieldstone carries much of the first floor and anchors the design, yet opens for banks of steel casement windows, especially on the second floor above a continuous balcony. The house extends beyond one chimney in an intimate day-room which terminates in the shady embrace of a mature live oak.

39
Private Residence, *1938*
4320 Armstrong
J.J. Patterson
The entry of this French Eclectic home skillfully juxtaposes Gothic-arched door, fieldstone gable, and round brick tower. Its shady site frames black timbers and contrasting tan stucco, beneath a steep slate roof.

41
Flippen Park (Versailles Park), *1929*
Lomo Alto between North and South Versailles
Fooshee & Cheek
A favorite of wedding photographers, this triangular park features a contemplative reflecting pool and fountain, azaleas, daffodils, and scenic live oaks. Its ornate Spanish Colonial Revival octagonal gazebo contrasts lacy wrought-iron and white stucco with a red clay-tile roof. Narrow paths invite romantic strolls. Pocket gardens and an open lawn allow for Frisbee tossing or quiet conversation.

40
Luxury Duplexes, *1930s*
4400 and 4500 blocks of Westway
Various architects, many by Fooshee & Cheek
This street of duplexes is a pleasing ensemble in multiple architectural styles. Balconies, porches, and details are added to simple forms to create pleasing variations on a theme.

42
Private Residence, *1929*
4200 Beverly Drive
Fooshee & Cheek
This rambling Mediterranean design thrusts forward an entry tower with an arched front door framed in fieldstone. Baby-blue window frames and red clay-tile roof contrast with beige stucco. Quieter is the pleasantly scaled Mediterranean **(43) 4208 Beverly Drive** also by Fooshee & Cheek.

44
Highland Park Village, *1931-1954*
Mockingbird Lane at Preston Road
Fooshee & Cheek
Selzer Associates, additions and renovations,
1979-present
Aging gracefully as the "first self-contained
shopping center in the U.S.," this complex
introduced off-street parking to retail. Its
seven phased stages allowed for construction
during the Depression. Spanish Colonial
Revival stone friezes and bas reliefs decorate
facades of beige stucco and myriad detail
materials. The tower of the Village Theater
and red-tile roofs tie together this beloved
town center. Not all additions have been sensitive, but the pavilions, balconies, arcades,
and colonnades are still predominant.

46
Highland Park United Methodist Church,
1926
3300 Mockingbird Lane
Mark Lemmon
On land donated by SMU, this church has
grown to be one of the largest Methodist congregations in the U.S. Its bell tower rises
above dense live oaks to announce a spirited
Gothic Revival design. Carved limestone
highlights arcades in tan brick throughout the
church campus. The buildings are a conservative but still warm backdrop to generous
gardens and courtyards. The Gothic theme is
carried through in leaded windows, buttressed
arcades, and stained glass.

45
Private Residence, *1938*
4637 Mockingbird Lane
John Astin Perkins
Landscape has mostly obscured this well-
preserved Streamline Moderne structure. Its
white stucco skin gets its breath from a blue
pipe-rail balcony, blue-framed windows, and
glass block. Modest and unassuming on its
busy street, it is a rare sample of its age.

Southern Methodist University

SMU was founded in 1911 on 100 acres donated by the widow of John Armstrong, developer of Highland Park. The University features a majestic central spine, Bishop Boulevard, and perhaps the most consistent Georgian architecture of any U.S. campus – a quality perhaps to be threatened by large new interventions by Ellerbe Becket and Hammond, Beeby and Babka.

47
Dallas Hall, *1915*
Hillcrest Avenue between Mockingbird Lane
  and Daniel Street
Shepley, Rutan & Coolidge (Boston)
This Classical Revival building with roots in the Pantheon and the University of Virginia set campus precedent in materials and organization. Heroic **(48) McFarlin Auditorium** shares Dallas Hall's Georgian brick and classical forms, and creates the campus cross-axis.

49
Greer Garson Theater, *1992*
Milton Powell & Partners
Its concave facade responds to the convex Hamon Library across a courtyard. The theater filters Georgian idiom through postmodern doctrine to create a design at home on campus but distinct from literal historicism.

50
Perkins School of Theology, Perkins Chapel,
  1951
Mark Lemmon
Good Fulton & Farrell, restoration, 1999
A focal point along the mall, the chapel includes Georgian brick and limestone, but classical details. Four Ionic columns and a pair of Doric pilasters line its portico and frame a trinity of doorways and windows.

51

Science Information Center, *1961*
O'Neil Ford; A.B. Swank
This Modernist brick box with limestone column grid and handsome arcade loosens up the campus theme. Floor plates are implied in rowlock brick courses. A suspended limestone and concrete stair fronts the campus facade.

52

Hamon Library, *1990*
Milton Powell & Partners
Reaching out toward the neighboring theater, this library completes a design of two halves. Its spare postmodernism creates a vocabulary with the theater that stands apart from the neighboring campus buildings. One particular reading room inside is a faithful rendition of the magical light that Kahn brought to the Yale Art Gallery.

53

Private Residence, *1915*
3444 University Boulevard
Early SMU leadership established the town of University Park on this block west of campus, including this Greek Revival home, fourth-oldest in the town. The house is prominently sited atop a small crown, with two-story portico and balcony supported by a pair of Ionic double columns. Its white siding and absolute symmetry heighten the formality.

54

Snider Plaza, *1927*
From Daniel Street to Lovers Lane
Various architects
Certain buildings along this shopping street approach architectural significance, but the overall atmosphere of these five blocks is their real gift. Awnings on every shop are de rigeur, as is an effort to be different, a cacophony the developer intended. Enjoy a 30-minute window-shopping break to take it all in, and pause at the central fountain, site of many street dances during the 1950s.

55

University Park City Hall and Fire Station, *1937*
3800 University Boulevard
Grayson Gill
The brickwork on this Williamsburg-style meeting house is especially well-handled, with a Flemish pattern of reddish-brown stretchers and black header units, all with pleasantly smeared white joints. A series of sentinel-like dormers protrudes from the shingle roof, which supports a shuttered cupola and weather vane. A 1973 addition is consistent with the original.

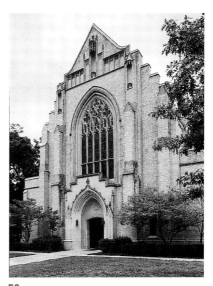

56

Highland Park Presbyterian Church, *1929*
Sanctuary, Mark Lemmon, 1941
Hunt Building, F&S Partners, 1980
A complement to Highland Park United Methodist in its Gothic Revival brick and carved limestone, this church offers a metal cupola and an encrusted metal spire instead of a bell tower. The sanctuary is central to the two-block campus with buildings that extend to either side and connect by a series of colonnades and intimate courtyards.

David Williams and O'Neil Ford

In 1926 mentor Williams and young pupil Ford took a legendary driving tour of central and south Texas to study and sketch vernacular buildings which would inspire a forthright regional architecture. The two collaborated in Williams' Dallas studio until the Depression forced Williams into public service in 1933. Ford moved to San Antonio in 1939, yet his brand of regional Modernism continued to have an impact on Dallas architecture until his death in 1982. Some of the best works of both are located in The Park Cities.

Richard Payne

57
Elbert Williams House, *1931*
3805 McFarlin Boulevard
David R. Williams
A pinnacle of Texas regionalism is this home for a former University Park mayor, inspired by the Joseph Carle House and Store in Castroville, Texas (1850s). All design, art and craft, inside and out, has indigenous sources.

59
Private Residence, *1924*
5929 St. Andrews Drive
David R. Williams
Williams presents a restrained Spanish Mediterranean design, in white-painted brick with red clay-tile roofs. Wings protrude from the main volume to catch breezes and to create an entry portal and balcony. Wrought-iron balcony rails and gate, and stylized light fixtures enhance the casual appeal of this design.

58
Private Residence, *1953*
3831 Windsor Parkway
O'Neil Ford (San Antonio); Scott Lyons
This house works hand in glove with its landscape, reaching out to embrace trees and gardens. Soft Mexican brick recedes behind ivy and into the shade of trees that surround and rise up through the design. Standing-seam metal roofs join brick, glassed-in, and open-air sections of this large but intimate house.

60
Private Residence, *1931*
3718 Lovers Lane
David R. Williams
This tiny-scaled house in the Texas ranch house form has a low-sitting second floor, with five simple dormers protruding from the shingled roof. Trees and neighboring houses dwarf this sugary exception to convention. The design opens in back to a tree-shaded patio, bordered by a narrow wing and garage.

63
Park Cities YMCA, *1951*
6000 Preston Road
George Dahl
Good Fulton & Farrell, additions, 1993
This is a Modernist delight in creamy brick and complementary fossilized limestone panels and window sills. Little things like recessing the first floor three feet below the second create shade and a feeling of enclosure.

61
Northern Trust Bank, *1991*
5440 Preston Road
The Oglesby Group
Difficult access, a tight site, and security were among the concerns this bank overcame. Its clock tower and simple hip-roofed rectangular volume with deep eaves and even trellises recalls traditional forms, but details are clean, with appealing limestone walls, cypress soffits, and a copper standing-seam roof.

64
Loma Linda Walls and Gates, *1924*
Mockingbird Lane at Armstrong Parkway and
Preston Road at Windsor Parkway
David R. Williams
Developers asked for these colorful follies and adjoining low walls to call attention to a new neighborhood. Moorish columns and arches play off painted brick, red clay-tile roofs, and colorful tile patterns and bas relief details.

62
First Unitarian Church, *1964*
4015 Normandy Avenue
Harwell Hamilton Harris; Beran & Shelmire
Harris readily acknowledged his debt to Wright's Unitarian Temple in Oak Park, Illinois, and even Sullivan's Wainwright Tomb in St. Louis, in conceiving this unusual worship space. Using a windowless stucco cube protected worshippers from summer heat and traffic noise on this busy street. Yet it also allowed for special lighting – daylight entering through prism glass blocks in a 12-ft.-wide band along the roof perimeter. Adorning the cube is a geometric motif in cast concrete. A diminutive plaza with abstracted colonnade provides a boulevard image that transitions smoothly from roadway to auditorium. The plaza is softened by trees along the street.

65
"Culture Gulch"
3600 block of Amherst Avenue
J. Frank Dobie so-named this pool, around which the Dallas intelligentsia built homes. The low-slung **3615 Amherst,** 1952, O'Neil Ford, cantilevers over the water next to **3625 Amherst,** 1949, O'Neil Ford. **3607 Amherst,** 1962, Arch Swank, completes the Modernist trio. Wonderfully layered **3620 Amherst,** c.1940, Charles Dilbeck, sits across the street, with irregularly set tan brick walls and ledges.

66
Private Residence, *1936*
4144 Shenandoah Street
Charles Stevens Dilbeck
This Norman French rustic farmhouse bears
craggy fieldstone walls and heavily detailed
windows with arched frames and orange-
brick surrounds. At adjacent corners are **(66a)**
4145 Shenandoah, a Tudor with brick laid
in an undulating pattern, and **(66b) 4200**
Shenandoah, with a gabled main volume,
deep-blue window frames and contrasting
orange brick trim. **(66c) 4201 Shenandoah** is
an ordered design of two intersecting swooping
gables in powdery fieldstone. Recently restored
(67) 4144 Stanhope is notable for the brick
pattern in its gable. **(68) 4101 Stanhope:** So
much gingerbread, it tastes good! A marriage
of fieldstone and brick details.

69
Private Residence, *1940*
4100 University Boulevard
Charles Stevens Dilbeck
This rambling assemblage is finished in
whitewashed irregular-set orange brick and
random limestone walls and orange clay-tile
roofs. Two-story wings create a walled courtyard, which is densely covered with shrub-
bery and small trees for privacy at a busy
intersection. Look for a different farmhouse-
inspired treatment at every window, whether
a projecting window seat, a small-screened
balcony, or gently arched double doors to
the street. Flairing brick chimneys anchor
the ends of the main volume.

70
Private Residences, *1936-1950*
4000 block of Bryn Mawr Drive
Charles Stevens Dilbeck
Dilbeck once made his own home and office
at 4085 (demolished 1999) on this block of
modest builder homes for which he provided
most of the designs. At 4012 are staggered
gables, balcony, and picture window. The
bay window at 4045 balances a second-story

balcony. A fanciful chimney and engaged
brick columns enliven 4041's entry.

71
Private Residence, *1934*
3819 McFarlin Boulevard
Charles Stevens Dilbeck
Restrained for Dilbeck, this simple rectangular form includes a second floor inserted into
the first at two junctures. Irregular-set brick
walls contrast with stucco. Interesting brick
details abound, including a massive arch at
the front door three soldier courses thick.
Windows in pairs with horizontal mullions
painted green complement and draw in a
softening landscape. A shake roof and exposed
rafters and a carriage driveway complete the
farmhouse feel.

72
Private Residence, *1941*
4676 Lorraine Avenue
Charles Stevens Dilbeck
The main facade of this exuberant – even for
Dilbeck – composition fronts Westside and
the expansive lawn of a church campus. The
house is finished in light fieldstone, with varied rectangular windows whose dense divided
lights are painted deep red and set in a black
frame. Gingerbread carpentry in red and
black frames two entries. Unmistakably audacious is the three-stage projecting chimney.
Soft-edged, orange brick provides the backdrop for **(73) 5301 Mockingbird,** c.1938. A
second-story cube has extruded brick diago-
nals and cornice details. The rounded smoke-
stack chimney is an indelible highlight.

Volk Estates

This subdivision of spectacular homes and pocket parks along curving streets was developed in the 1920s by shoe merchants Leonard Volk and son Harold, for whom real estate was only a sideline. Rich oilmen built here through the Depression to create the showplace of University Park.

76
Private Residence, *1928*
6701 Turtle Creek Boulevard
Greene, LaRoche & Dahl
Owner E.L. DeGolyer later built an estate on White Rock Lake that became the Dallas Arboretum. Soft-edged orange brick, with diagonal details, gives life to this Norman French mansion. Bay windows, a windowed drawing room, portico, exaggerated chimneys, and dormers add up to an intriguing design.

74
Private Residence, *1931*
6601 Hunters Glen Road
A semicircular portico with stripped-down Corinthian columns is the focus of a red-brick home heavily detailed in carved limestone.

77
Private Residence, *1994*
7028 Turtle Creek Boulevard
Landry + Landry
Calm self-assurance guided this design to fit into an established neighborhood without resorting to stylism. A pair of oversize green-gray casement windows with matching transoms punctuate the main facade, which is mostly obscured by handsome plantings.

Other Volk Estate houses of note include **(78) 6601 Turtle Creek Boulevard,** 1931, Anton Korn; **(79) 6801 Turtle Creek Boulevard,** 1929, John Scudder Adkins; Peter Marino, Bill Booziotis, renovations, 1993; **(80) 6810 Turtle Creek Boulevard,** 1950, John Staub; **(81) 6920 Turtle Creek,** 1926, Hal Thomson; **(82) 6930 Turtle Creek Boulevard,** 1933, George Dahl; **(83) 6801 Baltimore,** 1929, Hal Thomson, Richard Drummond Davis, renovation, 1998; and **(84) 6915 Hunters Glen,** 1936, Flint & Broad.

75
Private Residence, *1933*
6909 Vassar Avenue
Fooshee & Cheek
Built by oilman David Harold "Dry Hole" Byrd, this home was the site for oversized Texas–Oklahoma football game parties, serving up wild game. A double-height bay window, set in carved limestone, highlights the main facade. Whitewashed red brick creates a soft wall beneath a blue-green slate roof.

85
St. Michael and All Angels Episcopal Church,
1971; additions and renovations, 1994
8011 Douglas Avenue
HKS, Inc.
A transition between homes and commercial towers, this large campus maintains a proper scale. The sanctuary and bell tower remind one of Eliel Saarinen's compositions.

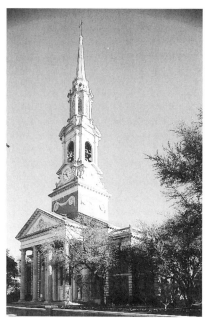

86
Park Cities Baptist Church, *1956*
3933 Northwest Parkway
Thomas, Jameson & Merrill
F&S Partners, addition, 1988
The campus plan centers on the sanctuary, flanked by mansard-roofed three-story buildings framing two formal lawns, lined by oaks.

Ornately carved limestone brings scale and texture to its tall steeple and bell tower.

87
Caruth Homestead (Caruth Hill), *1870*
8000 Cornerstone Parkway
A few blocks from the freeway, this plantation home of the pioneer family of north Dallas retains its setting amid formal gardens and a bois d'arc allee. Built from handmade brick, it was once a place of hospitality for travelers. Columns were added in 1938.

88
Greenway Parks, *1928*
Greenway Boulevard between Mockingbird
*   Lane and University Boulevard*
David R. Williams
Dallas' first pedestrian-oriented neighborhood was organized along a boulevard with triangular parks at each end. Tree-lined roadways and sidewalks welcome pedestrians, while homes front shared green-spaces.

89
Private Residence, *1951*
5381 Nakoma Drive
Howard Meyer
Here, Meyer uses a Neutra-esque composition rendered in materials that seem perfect for its Greenway Parks setting. The house is an AIA Dallas 25-Year Award Winner.

90
Private Residence, *1933*
5366 Montrose Drive
O'Neil Ford
This odd corner site allows for a design that opens to several greenway views. A gabled section faces east and meets a more articulated two-story volume facing south. A covered porch and courtyard bordered by a semitransparent brick wall combine views and privacy.

91
Private Duplex, *1995*
3509-3511 Springbrook Street
Lionel Morrison
Perhaps the cleanest, simplest statement of "house" possible, this is one of a collection of easily identified residences by Morrison and partners. Proportions and geometry are at once utterly reasoned and accessible. Three

subtle steps lead to the central, elongated front door, with steel canopy and transom. The celebrated steel-gridded glazed gable provides a sparkling signature. At Morrison's **(91a) 3501-3503 Springbrook,** 1988, a metal hip-roofed, tan brick main volume meets the street with a projecting two-story box, with two-car garage beneath a monumental nine-square opening. **(91b) 3510-3512 Springbrook,** 1990, by Morrison, is a striking departure; these beige stucco volumes unfold toward the back of the site, with green window and clay-tile roof above. **(91c) 4222 Abbott,** 1997, by Morrison-Seifert-Murphy, is a two-story metal-roofed brick volume with punched openings above a limestone stoop. **(92) 3510 Armstrong,** 1986, by Morrison-Seifert, features long, linear garden paths that lead beyond the extended steel beams to a linear interior of warm, cleanly detailed living spaces and an intimate pool and courtyard.

93
Private Duplex, *1987*
3508-3510 Edgewater Drive
McCall-Harris, Inc.
A concrete brick box is etched away for windows, balconies, and circulation. Masonry alternates between two flush-jointed gray courses and a single struck light-gray course. An exposed flue acts as a signature facade element between massive openings. Each unit has its own identity within a unified whole.

94
Private Duplex, *1987*
3504-3506 Edgewater Drive
Ron Wommack
Humbly scaled despite its linear two-story creamy brick main volume, the street facade centers on a column of doors, transom, glass awning, and second-floor window, all rendered into a single gridded composition. The side elevation is a play of extruded fireplace and exposed flue, placed in opposition to the negative space of a three-bay garage.

8 Preston Hollow/ North Dallas

Although "North Dallas" is frequently applied to a much larger area, this chapter focuses on a district four miles square, north of the Park Cities to the LBJ Freeway and centered on Preston Road, a frontier-era road that pre-dates Dallas. This sector developed from the 1930s through the 1960s as a well-heeled residential neighborhood structured by a disciplined one-mile grid of major thoroughfares and tidy rows of undistinguished post-World War II ranch-style houses. This development pattern overlays blackland prairie farmland occasionally punctuated by Bachman and White Rock Creeks and their tributaries, whose valleys support magnificent stands of oaks and pecans. These once-flowing waterways have been turned into scenic chains of small lakes for the benefit of private property owners, as in Preston Hollow (north of Northwest Highway between Inwood and Preston). Preston Hollow's most appealing quality (and that of neighboring Bluffview to the south and west) is the upper-class country suburban charm of the streetscapes, which feature soft road edges, wood rail or stone fences, irregular street planning, and natural thickets of native vegetation.

These neighborhoods host several of Dallas' finest landmarks of residential architecture – works of national acclaim by Frank Lloyd Wright, Richard Meier, Steven Holl, and Edward Larrabee Barnes, among others. Some of this work is quite visible, while several houses (such as Holl's Texas Stretto House) regrettably are most decidedly not visible from any public view.

Recently as many as 50 older houses of Preston Hollow, often with regional design themes and significant architectural merit, have been razed to make way for $10 million "personal monuments." The community has lost some of Charles Dilbeck's finest work and other great estates which could well have lasted another 100 years. Tour Strait Lane from Walnut Hill Lane north to Royal Lane to see the transition from a sensitivity to local climate and proper scale to European eclectic motifs.

Architectural biases aside, well-planned North Dallas is relatively free of strip commercial development, and instead features a number of appropriately spaced neighborhood shopping centers. And there is a startling absence of commercial development on several thoroughfares. Where one might expect to see intrusive non-residential uses, one instead finds institutional campuses of notable quality such as St. Marks School of Texas, The Hockaday School, and Temple Emanu-El.

8 Preston Hollow/ North Dallas

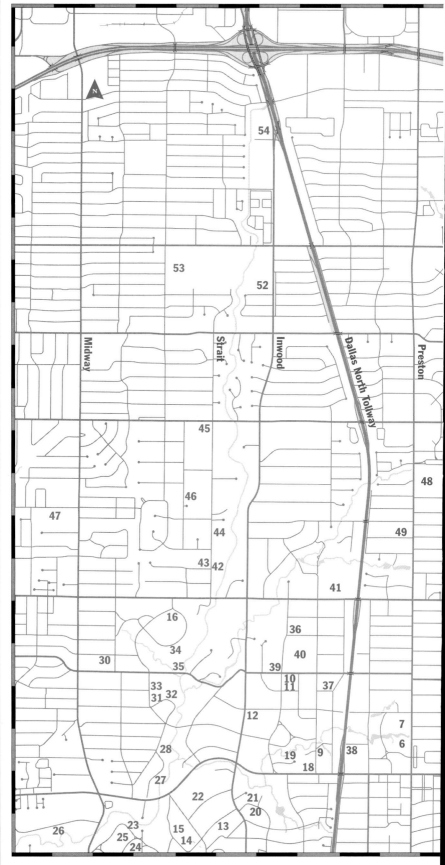

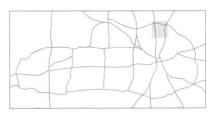

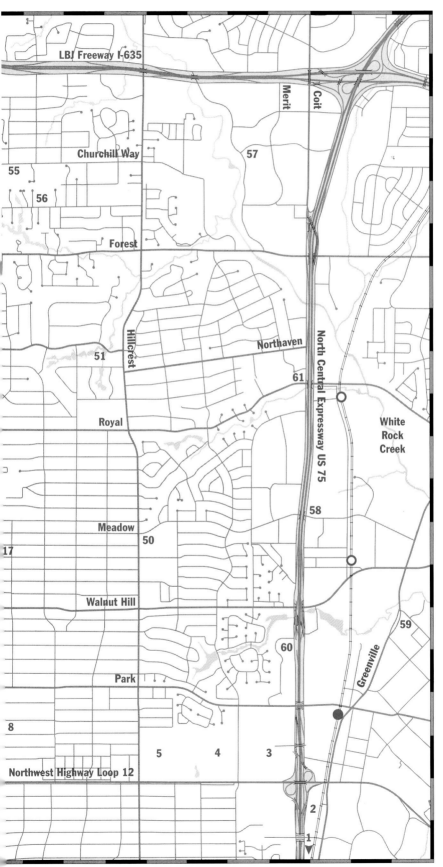

LBJ Freeway I-635

Merit

Coit

Churchill Way

57

55

56

Forest

Hillcrest

51

Northaven

North Central Expressway US 75

61

Royal

White
Rock
Creek

50

Meadow

17

58

Walnut Hill

59

60

Park

Greenville

8

5

4

3

Northwest Highway Loop 12

2

1

8 Preston Hollow/ North Dallas

1

Meadows Building, *1955*
5646 Milton Street
J.N. MacCammon

A favorite of local architects and an AIA
Dallas 25-Year Award winner, this office
building sports solar features popular in its
day that now lend a funky gentility. Long
walls face north and south to minimize glare
and heat. Ribbon windows welcome north
light; continuous balconies on the south cut
direct sunlight. Operable windows and exterior doors recall a time before central air. A
swooping entry canopy and classical penthouse frame the composition, topped off by
the distinctive rooftop signature. Rich colors
abound: aqua concrete ribs, tan marble end
walls, jasmine and snowy marbles at eye level,
and white terrazzo sidewalks. Later buildings
and the DART rail now hem in the site, but
generous oaks and a sculpture garden preserve
an urban oasis.

3

NorthPark Center, *1965*
North Central Expressway at Northwest
Highway
Harrell + Hamilton
Omniplan, Inc., additions, 1975
Neiman-Marcus Store, 1965
Eero Saarinen (Bloomfield, Michigan)

This is one of the country's first and best
regional malls, only getting better with age.
Spartan creamy brick columns and walls
with cast stone caps and sills, and simple
plate-glass openings, contrast with mature
oaks. Similarly hard-edged interiors, punctuated by fountains and atriums, carry a quiet
dignity. Sculpture from the Nasher Collection
and attentive retailers contribute to a singular
shopping environment.

2

Campbell Center, *1972*
8150 and 8350 North Central Expressway
Neuhaus & Taylor (Houston), first tower
HKS, Inc., second tower, 1980

A quaint reminder of disappearing gold-glass
commercial design, this quarter-mile-long
complex is a perfect foil to the DART rail
along its edge. The towers, angled 45 degrees
to the freeway for drama, rise above a parking
garage plinth. Visit at sunset for a visual spectacle that partly redeems this garish icon.

4

Hillcrest Mausoleum, *c.1938*
7403 Northwest Highway
Anton Korn

A rare venture for Korn into Beaux-Arts formality with Art Deco styling, this centerpiece
of a pastoral memorial park was probably
inspired during his work at Fair Park. It is
reported to be his favorite design.

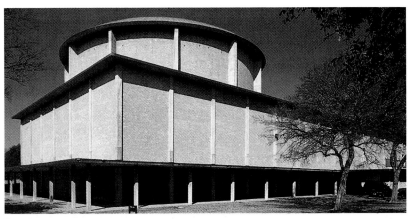

5

Temple Emanu-El, *1957*
8500 Hillcrest Road
Howard Meyer
Max Sandfield, associate architect
William Wurster (San Francisco), consulting architect

The pinnacle of Meyer's fine body of design work and winner of an AIA Dallas 25-Year Award, the temple is rendered cleanly in a tactile palette of concrete frame, orange brick, travertine, teak, bronze, slate and sand plaster. Its organizing element, an outdoor courtyard, rests contemplatively beneath anchoring oaks. Tree-lined parking further separates the campus from Hillcrest. The sanctuary interior is the project's heart, ornamented by Gyorgy Kepes' mosaic-encrusted brick joints, and Anni Albers' altar tapestry.

Scott Frances ESTO

6

Rachofsky House, *1997*
Preston Road
Richard Meier (New York)
Glimpsed through the entry gate, the public facade is a mostly opaque gridded Corbusian composition, floating above piloti and set behind a razor-smooth lawn and an auto court stained to a charcoal hue. The owner, an art collector, welcomes the characterization of the home as "an efficiency apartment above a museum." Hidden from view is the home's

primary facade, an open wall of glass and steel overlooking a reflecting pool. Meier's signature elements are clear: the exposed interior, transparency of structure, ceremonial stair leading to an outdoor landing, and unceasing white-on-white crispness.

7

Private Residence, *1999*
8831 Preston Road
Robert A.M. Stern (New York)
None among the series of "star-architect"-designed homes constructed in the 1990s in Dallas is as ebullient and emblematic of the age as this 22,000-sq.-ft. Neo-Georgian compound. The control Stern brings to such an oversized residence suggests a stray building from the similarly Georgian campus of Southern Methodist University located a few minutes to the south. Nouveau riche and old Dallas come together in this statement home that nevertheless seeks to be accepted as a sophisticated design. A central great hall links the two linear wings of the house, creating spacious front and rear courts. Brick and stone details and careful attention to fenestration and scale carry through the stylistic motif with aplomb.

Charles Stevens Dilbeck

The idiosyncratic houses of Charles Dilbeck (1907-1990) are quiet landmarks of Preston Hollow. He practiced a stylistically varied brand of regionalism born from self-education, working for his builder-father, and studying rural farmhouses. A typical "Dilbeck" is a complex composition that appears to have grown over time through a series of additions, taking off at odd angles to catch prevailing breezes or incorporating charming bays, turrets, or dormer rooms. Although his houses are always right for their sites and our Texas climate, they tend to transport us to another time and place. It is a sad commentary that we have lost four of these incomparable romantic homes during the brief span of preparing this guide for publication.

8
6122 Deloache, *c.1940*
A fantasy modeled on French Norman farmhouses, this home merges Arts & Crafts inspiration and Tudor elements. The home at **(9) 5500 Chatham Hill Road,** 1935, is a kindred spirit. A strong sense of materials is its unifying force – brick and uncoursed fieldstone, shingle roofs and leaded glass – while a colorful and sheltering landscape of gardens and a variety of trees complete a visually saturated ensemble.

10
5310 Park Lane, *1939*
Eclectic in forms rather than materials, this upright home includes signature balconies, bay windows, and an exposed-rafter shake

roof. The rather homely painted brick is enlivened by colorful gardens (like those of **(11) 9506 Meadowbrook,** 1939, and **(12) 5106 Deloache,** c.1946) and climbing ivy that nearly obscures the facade.

13
5030 Shadywood Lane, *1949*
Rustic stone walls and bunkhouse-style porch columns deliver the impression of a ranch house nestled into the city, here and at **(14) 4815 Shadywood,** 1943, **(15) 4803 Shadywood,** 1939, **(16) 9982 Rockbrook,** 1947, and **(17) 6315 Lakehurst,** 1942, in keeping with Preston Hollow's original relaxed feel. Oversized, handsomely expressed chimneys display Dilbeck's penchant for exaggerating key building elements.

18
Fifth Church of Christ Scientist, *1952*
5655 W. Northwest Highway
George Dahl
Religious symbolism, except for the implied
trinity of the main entry, is absent from this
AIA Dallas 25-Year Award design. Color is
reduced to the quiet interplay of buff brick,
a stone cap, and white mullions. Within this
austerity, however, subtle details like Flemish
bond, minimalist plinth-like stairs at the
entry, and integral planting beds gently sig-
nify human scale and presence.

19
Private Residence, *1957*
5455 Northbrook Drive
O'Neil Ford (San Antonio)
A sloping path of soft Mexican brick descends
from the roadway to this house through lush
gardens of roses, lantana, daisies, and holly. Its
standing-seam metal roof roughly matches the
road grade. Ford integrated the building into
a verdant landscape using materials and forms
inspired by the 19th-century Rio Grande
Valley architecture of Heinrich Portscheller.

20
Private Residence, *1995*
5400 Surrey Circle
Cunningham Architects
Stone for the front wall was salvaged from the
previous home on the site. Its placement back
from the street is another nod to the established neighborhood. Behind the wall two
concrete-block volumes connect at a wrought-
iron bridge and stairs created by artist David
Sines. Dense plantings reflect the neighborhood's mature character.

21
Private Residence, *1985*
9019 Broken Arrow Lane
Moore Andersson (Austin)
The standing seam metal roof of this home
continues the lines of neighboring houses in
earnest attention to "fitting in." Orange brick
and generous courtyards and the welcome
enclosure of a completely shaded lot imbue
this house with Moore's usual warmth.

22
Private Residence, *1981*
4929 Seneca Drive
Frank Welch
Simple forms, pared details, and the barest
hint of color in its walls give this house an
elegant, contemplative demeanor. In front is
an adaptation of the Southern porch. It connects the residence's two volumes, situated at
a clean right angle. In back a two-story balcony, like that of a 19th-century Texas ranch
house or hotel, overlooks a tree-lined pool.

23
Private Studio and Residence, *1929; 1930*
4715 Watauga Road
O'Neil Ford
Ford's first built work introduced unadorned,
simple shapes finished in humble, time-
honored materials. The home and studio form
an "L" that embraces a sheltering landscape.

24
Private Residence, *1994*
4712 Wildwood Road
Max Levy
Obscured by a dense stand of trees, this plain
beige house, divided into crisp rectilinear volumes, derives its character from structures
that respond to Texas weather. Canopies over
doorways, trellised balconies, and a sheltered
courtyard punctuate smooth stucco walls and
simple openings.

Bob Boettcher

25
Private Residence, *1994*
4711 Wildwood Road
Graham and Kathryn Greene
A Miesian calculated quality in this cubic
house joins with textures and hues among its
finish materials to create a taut but welcom-
ing composition. The classical base, building,
and cornice appear in limestone yet retain the
reserve of lines drawn on a page.

26
Private Residence, *1980*
4050 Cochran Chapel Road
David Webster George, FAIA
Sculpture, not architecture, comes to mind in
a design by seven knife-edged metal roof caps
over brick walls that at times alternate with
protruding chimney forms. The house's
familiar but spare elements march linearly

across the site to offer a series of views to a
creek in back. Abundant ivy and ample shade
trees shroud the home in an organic integra-
tion appropriate to the one-time Wright
apprentice's lack of concern for trends.

27
Private Residence, *1993*
9100 Guernsey Road
Taliesin Fellowship (Scottsdale, Arizona)
A block from the real thing, this Wright-
inspired house nestles into its site, centers
around a hearth, and sports deep overhangs
over ribbons of windows. Rustic random-
course limestone and low-sloping roofs with
stamped copper fascias evoke Wright's later
work. A lack of refined detailing, however,
reveals this to be the work of apprentices.

28
Private Residence, "Gillin House," *1958*
9400 Rockbrook Drive
Frank Lloyd Wright (Scottsdale, Arizona)
This residence recalls the pinwheel layout
of Taliesin East but overlays a grid of parallel-
ograms, rather than squares. The four-by-
four-foot grid governs the placement of walls
and the angle between the three wings. The
home sits low on its wooded site and remains
mostly hidden from public view. Limestone
walls carry the form of the building, laid in
random courses with an emphasis on stones
that naturally fit together to form 30-, 60-,
and 120-degree corners. Sheltered full-height
glass fills prominent openings off private living spaces. On the public facades, walls are
mostly stone, topped by ribbon windows snug
beneath overhangs. Rich wood details in the
ceiling give texture to interior spaces.

Paul Warchol

29
Private Residence, Stretto House, *1993*
Steven Holl (New York)
Max Levy, associate architect
Holl credited the stretto, or overlapping
musical segments, of Bartok's *Music for String,
Percussion and Celeste* as inspiration for this
open, sculptural residence. Its arcing roof sections and glassy private facade more clearly
echo the course of the spring-fed creek that
traverses the site. In fact, the meandering
linear floor plan seems to flow gently down
the sloping site, interrupted by four perpendicular concrete-block volumes, or "dams,"
that house service spaces. This metaphor
reaches its poetic climax in the open-sided
flooded room that edges into the creek.
Unfortunately, the house is completely concealed from view from the street.

30
Private Residence, *1995*
4330 Beechwood Lane
Morrison-Seifert
In honor of neighborhood convention, this
house is set back from the street behind a
simple entry court. Its facade, however, is
utterly unconventional – a strict rectangle of
beige stucco with a standing-seam metal roof
and symmetrical, minimal openings. Interior
spaces lead to a private courtyard. Though
hard-edged materials meet in flush connections, the house has a warm feel, thanks to
its single-story height and lush landscape.

31
Private Residence, *1956*
9612 Rockbrook Drive
Howard Meyer
Continuous north light and intimate courtyards sheltered by mature oaks enliven this
unassuming Modernist home. Soft brick,
exposed fir framing, and teakwood walls and
flooring make planar finishes sumptuous.
Expression of the design grid reinforces the
restrained aesthetic. See another Meyer house
and outdoor sculpture garden nearby at
(32) Private Residence, 4701 Miron, 1951.

33
Private Residence, *1958*
9624 Rockbrook Drive
Harwell Hamilton Harris
"Fingers" of this beautifully maintained home,
an AIA Dallas 25-Year Award recipient, extend
into its wooded, sloping site to create intimate
outdoor spaces. Rooms have at least two and
sometimes three exterior exposures. Harris
detailed stairways, balconies, and eaves with a
light touch that drew on structural expression
and organic abstraction in wood and brick.

34
Private Residence, *1983*
4608 Meadowood Road
Edward Larrabee Barnes (New York)
Looking from the street much like a ranch compound intersecting a Modernist art museum, a covered "dog run" breezeway links two white-stucco cubes. The home immediately descends its steep site, sloping from the entrance balcony to a central two-story living room overlooking a terrace. This house was designed for a Museum trustee while Barnes was working on the Dallas Museum of Art downtown.

35
Private Residence, *1939*
4717 Park Lane
O'Neil Ford & Arch Swank
Ford and Swank replied to a client who wanted a Louisiana plantation home with this design. In its massing and symmetry it recalls the plantation, but the resemblance mostly ends there. The wooded natural landscape shelters the "back" side of the home, rather than the usual highly ordered plantings that would frame a formal public facade. Materials are brick and wood, too, rather than stone or other precious finishes. The rear walls also notably dissolve into banks of windows, further opening the imposing structure to its site. Time has allowed climbing ivy to encroach on the building, further softening the formality intended by the client. Other Ford houses from the same period include **(36) 5311 Falls Road, (37) 5535 Kemper Court,** and **(38) 5722 Chatham Hill Road.**

39
Private Residence, *1957*
5243 Park Lane
Edward Durell Stone (New York)
This is renowned as the house with an island dining area surrounded by water (a 40-by-100-foot white-marble-floored great hall in which the dining table and an indoor swimming pool are housed). Though the urban Modernist feel of the home is at odds with its more casual wooded site, the masonry screen, shielding glass-walled spaces from direct sun and view, turned up in subsequent designs by other architects.

40
Private Residence, *1994*
5323 Park Lane
Smith-Ekblad
Not all residential architecture in the popular eclectic stylistic veins is deplorable. Designed with great attention to detail, this English Gothic Revival house is respectfully reminiscent of its precedents. Carried out with exacting craftsmanship in limestone and slate, the home's construction includes many refinements such as casement window hardware designed by the architect. See also **9707 Meadowbrook,** 1999, Richard Drummond Davis.

41
Private Residence, *c.1940*
5535 Walnut Hill Lane
Maurice Fatio (Palm Beach)
Beyond the gatehouse, down a winding path through an allee of trees and sculptured gardens, is this stately villa, with finely detailed cut limestone veneer and steep, hipped slate roofs. Its symmetrical facade, with shallow-arched pediment and intricate frieze carvings, stands in refined grandeur amid lush gardens and open lawns, protected by dense perimeter hedges along busy Walnut Hill Lane. This 20-acre estate is a rare work by Fatio outside of his usual South Florida turf.

Strait Lane

42
Private Residence, *1964*
10210 Strait Lane
Philip Johnson (New York)
Johnson adapted the precast concrete arches
that he used on the pond of his New Canaan
home to act as a "slip cover" over this house's
plan. The plan was by another architect and
given to Johnson as the client's wish. The
arched colonnade motif appears again on
the Johnson-designed Amon Carter Museum
in Fort Worth. The open loggias and balconies are pleasant as a vaguely Old World
form, but infilled arches are startling in a
residential setting.

43
Private Residence, *1998*
10235 Strait Lane
Larry Boerder
Residences like this beautifully detailed
Mediterranean exemplify the creeping transi-
tion of Preston Hollow from its casual, rural
feel to stage set for the nouveau riche chateau.

44
Private Residence, *1998*
10330 Strait Lane
Fusch-Serold
Nothing short of "castle" describes this
Gothic- and Renaissance-inspired 46,000-sq.-
ft. chateau. The list of living space, amenities,
and fine materials culminates with the telling
modern feature: parking for 14 and an indoor
car wash.

45
Private Residence, *1998*
10777 Strait Lane
Fusch-Serold
Imagine a reproduction of the White House –
in red! Not clear is whether, as in occasional
Texas custom, it is also over-scale to the
Washington, D.C., original.

46
Private Residence, *1988*
10434 Lennox Lane
Max Levy
Consider this a "high regional" house, incorporating simple, plainly connected forms of
the ranch, used to express functional groups
and gesture to landscape and natural lighting
opportunities. Glass ribbons in the wall of
one pavilion admit light between shelves in a
small library. Crisp detailing lends elegance to
these humble forms.

47
Episcopal School of Dallas Gill Library, *1984*
4100 Merrell Road
Lohan Associates
This is the most satisfying building on a
private school campus begun by Beran &
Shelmire in 1980 and most recently expanded
with Graham Greene's elegant Cook Building,
1996. Mies' influence on these "successor"
firms is subtle here, and the best views are
from the old quarry pond in back.

St. Marks School of Texas

48
St. Marks School of Texas
10600 Preston Road
Chapel and Classroom Building, 1988
Tapley/Lunow (Houston)
Dining Hall and Alumni Commons, 1993
Corgan Associates

Recent additions and renovations to the handsome regional Modernist buildings first built for this school did more than extend the tan brick, concrete, and shed-roof vocabulary across a generous site. Architects instilled a master plan that connected new and old buildings through a series of pleasant walkways and informal courtyards. A bell tower, banding in a new brown brick and other restrained but colorful details enrich the plan.

48a
Science and Mathematics Quadrangle, *1961*
O'Neil Ford (San Antonio) with Richard
*   Colley, Sam Zisman; Duane Landry*
Tan brick and metal shed roofs established a simple, regional Modernist corner to what would soon become a much larger campus. The narrow buildings open to natural light on both sides, implying gentle, informal courtyards with their "L"-shaped footprints.

48b
Green Library, *1963*
O'Neil Ford (San Antonio)
Added to establish a central campus focus, this hall rises up an understated two stories, with its slot windows disappearing into the roof soffit. It adopts a Beaux-Arts "U"-shaped academic plan, then brings in soft tan brick and Modernist exposed-concrete colonnades around an intimate central courtyard.

48c
Decherd Performing Arts Center, *1974*
The Oglesby Group
This arresting barn-like form recalls pioneer Texas ranch buildings that charm with their simplicity.

James F. Wilson

49
Private Residences, *1998*
5911 and 5917 Glendora
Morrison-Seifert-Murphy
Flouting nostalgic trends, these homes, designed together as "siblings" for separate clients on narrow, deep lots reflect an unabashed Modernist approach. What may have been restrained window and cornice details in another architect's design are here eliminated. Volumes are pristine, seamless cubes, whose windows are incised into them. Only limestone, concrete, and ceremonial wood-plank entry and red-steel balcony violate the snowy exteriors. And yet spacious interiors with ample connection to outdoor courts and pool mitigate any harsh effect.

50
Benjamin Franklin Middle School, *1956*
6920 Meadow Road
Broad & Nelson; Mark Lemmon; Caudill
*   Rowlett Scott (Houston)*
Clear expression of poured concrete structure combines with warm brick and windows oriented toward sunlight opportunities to give this planar building a strong sense of place. In this design, a long-established Dallas school architect and an emerging Houston-based firm, challenging conventions in school design, came together to make a gesture toward the familiar materials of the day and a bold glimpse into the Modernist structural expression that would dominate the next two decades.

James F. Wilson

51
Private Residence, *1985*
6730 Northaven Road
Cunningham Architects
Remarkable when seen from the air, the parti
for this compound came from Mies' unbuilt
"scheme for a country house." Its curving
entry drive picks up a long orange-brick wall
that bisects the house as it provides a privacy
screen roughly parallel to a creek along the
rear of the site. Main living spaces, faced in
white brick, snuggle up to a matching brick
wall and proceed in linear fashion down the
sloping site to terminate in a pavilion cantilevered over the creek bank. A third, tan
brick faces a volume just behind the orange
wall at the entry, creating a tripartite elevation, coolly rendered in brick.

52
Lamplighter School
11611 Inwood Road
Jonsson Library and Fine Arts Wing, 1985
Frank Welch
Original Buildings, 1966
Ford, Powell & Carson
In its original incarnation, the school had a
strong residential scale, with deeply sloping
roofs over spaces that extended into the
simple landscape to take advantage of light
on three sides. The few two-story spaces were
softened through generous openings and ivy
that climbed to cover much of the white-
stucco exterior. Signature to later additions
is an earnestly formal central structure with
a square plan, anchored at each corner by
exaggerated "chimneys." Its metal roof slopes
from each corner to a cupola.

53
The Hockaday School, *1963*
11600 Welch Road
Harwood K. Smith & Partners
Expression of its poured-concrete structural
frame sets the tone for this sprawling campus
of mostly two-story buildings. Changes in
grade are reflected in lower levels that emerge
to keep floor plates unbroken. This effect is
most notable at **(53a) Rita Crocker Clements**
Lecture Hall and Crow Science Building,
1983, Beran & Shelmire, where the drop-off
canopy nestles beneath classrooms above that
extend back into the site and eventually meet
ground level. Infill is travertine and tan brick.
Additions have maintained the 1960s feel of
the campus except for **(53b) Hoak Portico,**
1996, Beran & Shelmire, and Corgan
Associates, which offers a distinctly postmodern rotunda as a counterpoint to the cohesive
structural expressionism.

54
St. Rita Catholic Church, *1987*
12521 Inwood Road
Tapley-Lunow (Houston)
One of Dallas' best-executed examples of
postmodern historicism, this church campus
is dominated by its steep copper roofs and
a campanile abstracted from the tower in
Piazza San Marco. The sanctuary interior
reflects the central altar placement of Vatican
II. Rich, exposed-wood-structure ceilings soar
upward, punctuated by a series of gable windows. The stained-glass art of Lyle Novinski
makes the sanctuary one of Dallas' most complete and inspiring spaces. The sanctuary
cupola and campanile, faced in dark tan
brick, are highly visible and inviting from
the adjacent thoroughfare.

55

St. Alcuin Montessori School, North Wing,
1995
6144 Churchill Way
Frank Welch & Associates
The circular performing arts center serves as
the new campus center for this K-8 school.
Its gently sloping red roof sets it apart from
the flat-roofed single-story classrooms added
across a creek and to the west of the existing
school. The center's cupola, however, is
reflected in a central light monitor on each
new classroom building. Buildings adjoin at
connective walkways, creating an open-feeling
circulation, which neatly frames several intimate courtyards and gardens. Great care went
into creating spaces conducive to learning in
simple buildings.

James F. Wilson

57

Park Central XII (Former Steak & Ale
Headquarters), *1986*
12404 Park Central Drive
Cunningham Architects
Turning to structural expression amid postmodern's highest excesses, this corporate headquarters is interesting in the spaces subtracted
from its frame. Symmetrical wings border a
full-height garden at the pedestrian entry. A
pool in black granite naturalistically traverses
the lobby interior in symbolic connection to
White Rock Creek. Two office blocks meet
off-center at a ceremonial escalator bank.

56

Church of Jesus Christ of Latter Day Saints
Dallas Temple, *1984*
6363 Willow Lane
Church Architectural Staff; West &
Humphreys
Nowhere else will one find such soaring
and piercing steeple forms. Five towers in
all, one at each corner and a fifth between
flanking entries to this temple, ensure that
no passerby will miss it. Exteriors are faced
entirely in stone, a remarkable upgrade to
the brick one might expect. Extensive, color-
fully landscaped grounds, gated and walled
from the street, reinforce the formality of its
elegant appearance.

58

Office Building, *1986*
10440 North Central Expressway
Skidmore Owings & Merrill (Houston)
SOM's discipline to the grid is evident.
Expressed base and cornice stay within an
overriding reliance on revealing floor plates
and column alignments in the gridded fenestration. Its restrained details and the mirror-
like effect created by flush-mounted glazing
give the tower a distinctiveness that has worn
well since its completion. More audacious
downtown towers from the same office would
later rise up, but without the serenity of this
moderately scaled sibling.

59
American Heart Association National Headquarters, *1977*
7320 Greenville Avenue
The Oglesby Group
Remarkable for its strong solar orientation, with minimal openings to the east and west, shelter to the south, and a broad expanse of curtain wall to the north, this is an energy-efficient yet pleasing design. Its concrete-"T" roof supports reach out over the entry to create a sheltered approach. A jutting light scoop runs counter to the broad standing-seam metal roof to admit sunlight into the lobby.

60
NorthPark Presbyterian Church, *1991*
9555 North Central Expressway
The Oglesby Group
A church given the opportunity to rebuild its campus on a new site built with organizational clarity and cohesion that the typical decades-long build-out does not allow. A central cloister garden serves as a transition from parking to classrooms and offices, as well as the sanctuary situated to one side. The congregation returned to a more traditional nave form with its sanctuary, although the central aisle divides an asymmetrical layout of straight pews to the left and angled pews to the right, which terminate in choir seating next to the altar. At first jarring, the arrangement sensibly provides natural seating. Continuing the asymmetry are clerestory windows cut into one side of the steeply sloped roof. Louvers in these windows ensure that direct sunlight strikes only the cross and stone wall behind the altar. Limestone walls adorn the exterior, contrasting with a dark gray metal roof that rises up to an abstracted steeple.

61
North Central Expressway, *1999*
US 75 from Downtown to I-635
HOK
In a departure from its usual procedures, the Texas Department of Transportation hired an architect to design amenities for a $500-million expansion of North Central Expressway. The architects designed all visible components of the project, including retaining walls, bridges, and light fixtures, as well as landscaping and decorative elements at major intersections. Architectural interventions ensured that the mostly depressed freeway remains pleasant to travel, with retaining walls that are broken up into segments and given more natural colors. Trees and planting beds line the roadway where possible. Highway structures are streamlined and pleasingly simplified. TxDoT even adopted parts of the design work for future construction department-wide. Ten miles long and ten years in construction, the new North Central fulfills its role as primary traffic artery, and now with beauty and grace.

9 Far North Dallas/Plano/ Northern Suburbs

A rule of thumb regarding the growth of cities is that the farther you get beyond some invisible core (often symbolized by a loop) the further you get away from the city's unique soul. The outer, highway-dominated edge of one city is no different than the outer, highway-dominated edge of another. Or so it seems to the traveler, eyeing through the windshield the same selection of motel chains and franchise restaurants just left behind.

Such a generalization might be made of Dallas and the small towns – Plano, Richardson, Addison, Parker, Farmers Branch, and others – that comprise its northern suburbs. In the last 20 years, the Dallas North Tollway, Interstate 35, and US Highway 75 have encouraged seemingly endless growth northward.

And yet, within this context, where office buildings and strip shopping centers play to the highway and large, expensive builder homes hunker down beneath exaggerated roofs of cedar shingles, talent and imagination have survived. To find them, it is often necessary to do the impossible (drive slowly), or the unexpected (exit). Either action yields rewards for those who value the individual architectural problem well-solved and appropriate.

In this landscape "appropriate" can mean buildings as diverse as Morris-Aubry's Providence Towers with its 120-foot central arch that turns the heads of passersby, or St. Joseph Catholic Church where stripes of brick and masonry recall the Italian Gothic churches of the priest's background. Here, in North Dallas, it has never been inappropriate for an office building to stand as an isolated icon, aloof from its neighbors, but gradually the impulse for some sort of fellowship with other structures has taken hold. The Legacy Business Park, home to several major international companies of electronic manufacturers, is one attempt to create such a connection and, by extension, a sense of place. Another is Addison Circle, where the developer let the popularity of high-density, apartment living in downtown Dallas influence a mixed-use community of apartments in the small town of Addison.

Ironically, South Fork Ranch, the building that most says Dallas to the international, television-watching community, is located in this northern region of the city. If there is something to be said for it, it is that it sits squarely and honestly in the prairie that defines Dallas' topography. This same prairie has lately been on the minds of some of Dallas' most talented architects as they make inroads into the banal, inward-turning neighborhoods of expensive builder homes. Dallas, these architects seem to be saying, is not just about fast-paced business, it's about carving out a lifestyle in the prairie. It is, in the deepest sense, about being at home on the range.

Far North Dallas/Plano/Northern Suburbs

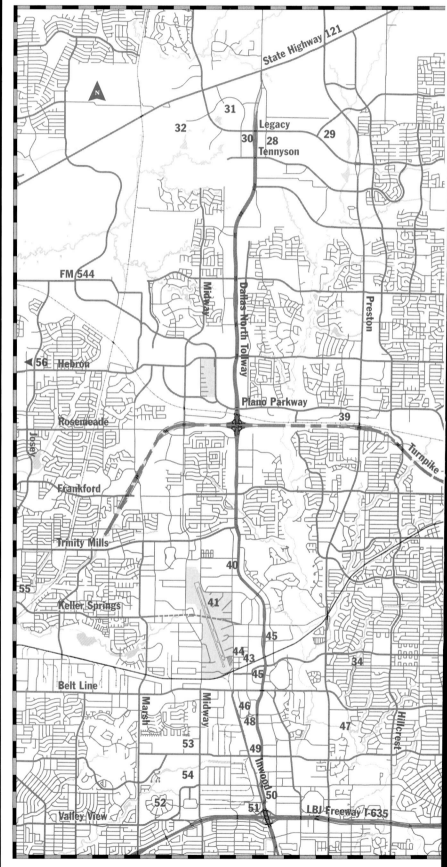

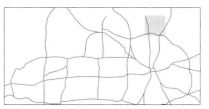

9 Far North Dallas/Plano/ Northern Suburbs

Richard Payne

1
Texas Instruments Semiconductor Building,
1959
13500 North Central Expressway
O'Neil Ford (San Antonio); Richard Colley
(Corpus Christi)
Arch Swank, associate architect
Sam Zisman, planning consultant
A groundbreaking building for a revolutionary industry in its infancy. Among the innovations introduced or expanded by Ford in
this building were the use of long-span, thin-
shell-concrete hyperbolic paraboloid roof
modules; a precast concrete tetrapod intersti-
tial floor system; and the combination of
research and manufacturing facilities in one
building. Equally important to Ford, however,
was the inclusion of lushly planted courtyards
and richly detailed interior spaces.

grow. The buildings' exposed concrete structural frames with brick in-fill facades effectively suggest the early work of renowned
British architect James Stirling – and also
respect the budgetary concerns of the public
institution. In order to make the best of an
otherwise nondescript site, the architects
developed a plan that placed buildings on
both sides of an existing lake – helping to
integrate structures with the water.

3
St. Joseph Catholic Church, *1986*
600 S. Jupiter Road, Richardson, Texas
F&S Partners
This sanctuary of this church utilizes the
wide floor-plan and fanned-out pew arrangement popular in contemporary churches,
but also includes the prominent center aisle
– reinforced by a bold ceiling pattern – that
is commonly found in more traditional
churches. The bold striping of the brick and
masonry exterior gives the church high visibil-
ity in the community, and also suggests building styles common in the Italian cities where
the church's pastor was educated.

2
Richland College, *1972*
12800 Abrams Road
The Oglesby Group; The Perkins & Will
Partnership (Chicago)
Part of the Dallas County Community
College District, Richland College was
conceived as a two-year, commuter-oriented
institution, with provisions for expansion of
facilities as the area's population continued to

4
Sonic Drive-In 2000 Prototype, *1998*
520 Centennial Boulevard, Richardson, Texas
Machado & Silvetti Associates (Boston)
Asked by the nation's largest drive-in chain to
develop a prototypical restaurant for the 21st
Century, the architects tip their hats to the
golden era of automobiles with a space-age
chrome oval and brightly colored neon lights.

5
Blue Cross–Blue Shield Building, *1981*
901 S. Central Expressway, Richardson, Texas
Omniplan, Inc.
A collaboration between the architect and
Datum Engineering, the building used an
innovative precast column-and-beam unit
that allowed for the long spans needed to
house thousands of modular workstations.

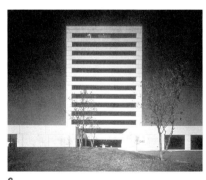

6
Chase Bank Building, *1975*
100 North Central Expressway, Richardson,
Texas
Omniplan, Inc.
Another Omniplan-Datum collaboration
resulting in "structure as architecture." Here,
the length of the structural beam – which is
also the spandrel – was determined by the

maximum length that could be legally carried
by truck on the Texas highways.

7
Richardson City Hall, *1980*
411 Arapaho Road, Richardson, Texas
F&S Partners
The organizing element for this two-story
brick city hall is a bold vaulted extrusion
roofed in copper and sliced to form a north-
light clerestory. Next door is the fussier
(7a) Richardson Public Library, 1970,
900 Civic Center, Richardson, Texas,
JPJ Architects.

8
Ericsson Office Building, *1986*
740 E. Campbell Road, Richardson, Texas
Skidmore Owings & Merrill (Houston)
This 10-story tower is notable mainly for its
illustration of the "disciplined" SOM style –
here manifested as a "symphony of squares"
that is easy to read, and at the same time rich
and enduring.

9
Nortel Complex, *1993*
2201 Lakeside Boulevard, Richardson, Texas
Hardy McCullough MLM
This regional headquarters is a sprawling
brown-brick concoction obedient to Greenway
Park's stringent design guidelines, set on a
parking garage base and topped by a linear
vaulted "galleria." Its scale and dramatic form
demand a second look. If Nortel ever vacates,
the Telecom Corridor will have a ready-made
shopping mall.

University of Texas at Dallas

The University of Texas has steadily expanded its presence in Dallas since the 1970s, particularly at its Richardson campus. Based on a master plan by The Oglesby Group, the institution has used work by a variety of excellent architects to enhance the prestige of the relatively young campus.

10
McDermott Library, *1975*
2601 N. Floyd Road, Richardson, Texas
The Oglesby Group
Housing both undergraduate and graduate libraries – with technical services occupying a space in between the two – the McDermott Library manages to moderate the scale of its symmetrical exterior with diverse massing and an interesting assortment of shading methods.

10a
Cecil and Ida Green Center for the Study of
Science and Society, *1993*
F&S Partners
Along with the McDermott Library, the Cecil and Ida Green Center is probably the most distinguished example of the many University of Texas at Dallas facilities designed by talented local architects. Other significant campus projects include **(10b) Founders Building,** 1963, O'Neil Ford (San Antonio); **(10c) Fine Arts Studio Facilities,** 1979, F&S Partners; **(10d) Engineering Building,** 1992, Omniplan; and **(10e) Multi-Purpose Administration Building,** 1992, F&S Partners.

11
MCI Headquarters, *1991*
Campbell Creek Campus
2400 N. Glenville Drive, Richardson, Texas
HOK
This home to MCI's 1,000-person engineering group is one of the most recognized symbols of Richardson's status as a telecommunications hotbed. The buildings were designed and constructed on a very fast track (12 months), yet still manage to creatively address the need to protect a stand of trees along a creek that runs through the site.

12
Private Residence, *1989*
2412 Canyon Creek Drive, Richardson, Texas
Stacy Architects
The architect added a collection of engaging forms and a strikingly geometric window wall to make room for a spa and exercise area – and in the process added interest to an otherwise pedestrian exterior.

13

Fujitsu Networking Transmission Systems,
1991
2800 Telecom Parkway, Richardson, Texas
Omniplan, Inc.
Fujitsu's first research and manufacturing
facility built outside of Japan, this project was
another important milestone in the development of the Richardson "Telecom Corridor."
The building is designed with a restraint that
reflects the conservative culture of its owner.

14

House with a Sky View, *1996*
2601 Dublin Road, Parker, Texas
Max Levy
On seven acres north of Dallas, Max Levy
has created a remarkable house that makes
maximum use of the surrounding prairie and
beautiful North Texas sky. Three primary skylight elements illuminate interior spaces and
also animate the otherwise low-key exterior.

15

Southfork, *c.1970*
3700 Hogge Road, Parker, Texas
What can you say? No matter how many
talented Dallas designers create thoughtful,
innovative buildings both in and out of the
city, millions of television viewers around the
world will still think that this represents the
best the city has to offer. And thanks to syn-
dication, this situation may be permanent.

16

CCCCD Spring Creek Campus, *1989*
2800 E. Spring Creek Drive, Plano, Texas
HOK; Corgan Associates
Spring Creek was the Collin County
Community College District's second campus, and its sophisticated design helped to
enhance the prestige of the fledgling institution. The architects used warm, natural materials and thoughtful detailing to create spaces
that are both grand and comfortable – without resorting to the "mall-isms" that spoiled
so many public projects of the late 1980s.

Craig Kuhner

17

Allen Doctors Building, *1984*
515 W. Main Street, Allen, Texas
Good Haas & Fulton
In order to maximize the rentable space in
this three-building complex, the architects
organized the buildings along an exterior
gallery. This gallery, covered with a shed-
roofed light monitor, provides both filtered
natural light and access to individual offices
– eliminating the need for interior corridors.
The use of glossy white tile in the gallery suggests the project's function as a clinic, and
varying sill heights and high-contrast white
downspouts establish a rhythm on the facade.

18
Masonic Lodge, *1925*
1414 Avenue J, Plano, Texas
This "Small-town Romanesque" structure
in downtown Plano was restored in preparation for the celebration of the Texas
Sesquicentennial in 1986, and declared a
Plano historic landmark in 1987. Among
the building's notable features are the arched
lintels and horizontal bands of rugged cut
stone that animate its brick facade.

23
Private Residence, *1898*
1813 Avenue K, Plano, Texas
Located on the northern edge of historic
Plano, this is a nice example of a single-story
Queen Anne Victorian home, including
period details such as fish-scale shingles in
the gable ends and stained glass accents.

24
Private Residence, *1890*
901 18th Street, Plano, Texas
In the early 1900s, it was common for Plano
property owners to modify their homes to
incorporate the latest architectural trends. This
house is an example of the subtle combination
of styles that was often the result. In 1905, an
ornate three-story tower and Victorian porch
were removed to make way for the veranda
with classical pillars and trim that exists today.
Plano also includes some nice examples of
early farm houses that have survived as neighborhoods have grown up around them,
including **(25) Private Residence,** 1894,
1900 W. 15th Street; and **(26) Private
Residence,** c.1910, 1601 Alma Drive.

19
Private Residence, *1898*
1211 E. 16th Street, Plano, Texas
Proof that there was life in Plano before the
arrival of Legacy and acre after acre of Builder
Vernacular homes. The Queen Anne-style
Carpenter-Edwards house was one Plano's
most well-known residences in the early 20th
century, and – with its ornamental tower,
stained glass windows, and three-quarters
porch – it continues to serve as a neighborhood landmark. Other notable homes in the
area include **(20) Private Residence,** 1901,
1413 15th Street; **(21) Private Residence,**
c.1910, 1301 14th Street; and **(22) Private
Residence,** c.1910, 1615 Avenue H.

27
Fire Station No. 1, *1997*
1901 Avenue K, Plano, Texas
Phillips Swager Associates
This building, which houses both the logis-
tical and administrative arms of the Plano
Fire Department, is largely residential in scale
and character – a reflection of nearby neighborhoods and its role as a home to on-duty
firefighters. At the same time, however, it
manages to hold its own amidst a strip of
down-on-their-luck retail buildings – establishing a strong identity with cantilevered
awnings, angled downspouts, and strikingly
gabled forms.

Legacy

If suburban business parks are, as some people believe, replacing downtowns as the centers of American commerce, then Legacy may be on its way to becoming the next Manhattan. This master-planned development boasts nearly 25,000 employees, the headquarters of several multinational corporations, $4 billion worth of technical infrastructure, and a growing network of support services along its perimeter – all contributing to Plano's position as the state's fastest growing city.

28
EDS Corporate Headquarters, *1994*
5400 Legacy Drive, Plano, Texas
HKS, Inc.
Dallas-based HKS has played a major role in forming Legacy's architectural character – taking advantage of the park's loose design guidelines to create facilities that express the corporate cultures of their occupants. One of their earliest projects in the park is this mammoth, multi-building headquarters facility for Electronic Data Systems (which has actually owned Legacy since 1983). The firm's more recent Legacy projects include the low-budget, fast-track **(29) Dr. Pepper/7-Up Corporate Headquarters,** 5300 Hedgcoxe Road, and the more luxurious **(30) Fina Corporate Headquarters,** 6100 Legacy Drive.

31
J.C. Penney Corporate Headquarters, *1994*
6501 Legacy Drive, Plano, Texas
HKS, Inc.
Another early HKS contribution to the Legacy landscape, this serviceable headquarters facility contains 1.9 million square feet of space in eight low-rise buildings. The buildings are connected by a 1,250-ft.-long, tree-filled atrium intended to serve as a setting for impromptu employee interaction.

32
Frito-Lay Corporate Headquarters, *1986*
7701 Legacy Drive, Plano, Texas
FCL Associates (Chicago)
This headquarters facility is decidedly modern, yet clearly attuned to the needs of its human inhabitants. The buildings are thoughtfully sited – responding to the existing hills and lake – the materials are warm and inviting, and the floor plan maximizes natural light and mobility.

33
Hendrick Middle School, *1987*
7400 Red River Drive, Plano, Texas
JPJ Architects
This school's use of flexible, modular, open-space classrooms – clustered around a central atrium – reflected the new teaching concepts that were taking hold in Texas in the mid-1980s. And at a cost of just $55 per square foot, the project also reflected a response to the financial challenges faced by growing school districts. Other area projects by JPJ include **(34) Prestonwood Elementary,** 1972, 6525 La Cosa Drive, Richardson, Texas; and **(35) Plano Senior High School,** 1976, at 2000 Independence Parkway, Plano, Texas.

36
Claude Curtsinger Elementary School, *1996*
12450 Jereme Trail, Frisco, Texas
Corgan Associates
The growth of Dallas' northern suburbs has created a boom in the construction of new schools to educate the children of these bedroom communities. Many of these new schools – like this one in Frisco – are utilizing new planning and design strategies in hopes of minimizing cost and maximizing learning. Here the architects placed small classrooms in clusters around shared activity rooms, which are in turn arranged around a large, triangular multipurpose room. Another noteworthy new school in the area is **(37) Bethany Elementary School,** 1992, at 2418 Micarta, Plano, Texas, Corgan Associates.

38
Haggard Library, *1989*
2500 Coit Road, Plano, Texas
Hidell Architects
Plano residents take great pride in the high priority they place on education and learning. As a result, the city is liberally sprinkled with neighborhood libraries like this one. Here, north-facing, saw-tooth clerestory windows create a light-filled environment that includes community meeting spaces and a very thorough collection of reading materials to supplement school programs.

James F. Wilson

39
Prince of Peace Catholic Community Sanctuary, *1995*
5100 W. Plano Parkway, Plano, Texas
Cunningham Architects
Second phase, Corgan Associates
Probably the most remarkable contemporary place of worship in Texas, and possibly one of the best in the country, Prince of Peace makes dramatic use of natural materials to create a series of supremely reverent spaces.

40
Triangle Pacific Corporation, *1978*
16803 Dallas Parkway
Gwathmey-Siegel (New York)
This headquarters for a kitchen cabinet manufacturer uses a rich travertine marble exterior to muster an upscale corporate image – even as it sits in the middle of a perfectly flat five-acre lot sandwiched between two access roads.

41
Addison Airport Terminal, *1984*
4584 Claire Chennault Drive, Addison, Texas
Townscape Architects
This small private jet terminal uses limestone-like ceramic tile and liberal doses of glass block to create an environment that appeals to corporate jet passengers and pilots, while still offering low cost and high durability.

42
Tollway Plaza Office Buildings, *1999*
15950 and 16000 Dallas Parkway
Omniplan, Inc.
Reminiscent of the early office-building
designs of Skidmore Owings and Merrill,
these twin nine-story office towers feature
sophisticated stone-and-glass curtain-walls
with Mondrianesque mullion patterns.

43
Addison Circle, *1997*
4949 Addison Circle, Addison, Texas
RTKL Associates
In response to the growing popularity of
high-density apartment living in downtown
Dallas neighborhoods, Addison town officials
and developer Post Properties have created a
new pedestrian-friendly, mixed-use urban center in historically un-urban Addison.

44
Addison Theatre and Conference Centre,
  1992
15650 Addison Road, Addison, Texas
Cunningham Architects
The architect took a diverse program and
undistinguished site and created a dynamic
community focal point – one that conveys
quite a bit of sophistication in a town previously known primarily for office parks, strip
shopping centers, and chain restaurants.

45
Colonnade Office Buildings, *1984-1998*
15303 Dallas Parkway, Addison, Texas
Haldeman Powell & Associates
This massive, three-building, high-rise office
complex is noteworthy for the large barrel-
vaulted atrium that unifies the various phases
of the development.

46
Landmark Office Building, *1984*
14840 Landmark Boulevard, Addison, Texas
Cunningham Architects
An incredibly simple three-story brick box
that manages to turn an absolute lack of
adornment into a virtue. The only projection
from the facade is a small awning at the main
entry, and the space within is equally straightforward – one level of parking under two
floors of understatedly elegant office space.

James F. Wilson

47
Private Residence, *1998*
6511 Westgate Drive
Cunningham Architects
In a typical North Dallas neighborhood, the
architect created a very atypical suburban
home. The simple exterior – animated by
integrally colored plaster – freed more of the
construction budget for spatial complexity
and better detailing on the interior. A flood
plain at the rear of the lot, which provides
privacy and unusually expansive views, sug-
gested that most interior-exterior interaction
be directed to the rear of the house.

48
Office Buildings, *1982*
5000 and 5050 Quorum Drive, Addison, Texas
HOK
With their long black metal-and-glass facades
and street-hugging site plan, the buildings
of this multi-phase office development have
occasionally been described as a "black snake"
curving along Quorum Drive.

49
Providence Towers, *1987*
5001 Spring Valley Road, Farmers Branch, Texas
Morris-Aubry (Houston)
Thanks to its 120-foot arch, this may be the
city's most recognizable suburban office building. Up close, the arch means less – it isn't
utilized in any grand fashion – but the building still stands out among its 1980s rivals.

50
Dallas Galleria, *1983*
LBJ Freeway at Dallas Parkway
HOK
Gerald Hines' successor to his immensely
popular Galleria project in Houston, the
Dallas Galleria is just as large, sanitized, and
lucrative as its Houston counterpart. The

facade of former Galleria tenant **(50a)**
Marshall Field was designed by Philip
Johnson (New York).

51
Occidental Tower, *1986*
5005 LBJ Freeway, Farmers Branch, Texas
HKS, Inc.
By hugging the street, this slick vertical extrusion of a very distinctive site works with the
nearby Galleria to create a high-density urban
feel for the significant Tollway-LBJ intersection. A notable design element is the semi-
detached "feather" on the building's prow.

52
Brookhaven College, *1978*
3939 Valley View Lane, Farmers Branch, Texas
Pratt Box Henderson & Partners
This campus – the last of the commissions
awarded by the Dallas County Community
College District during their initial campus-
development program – creates some intriguing outdoor spaces with its sloping roofs and
sheltered courtyards.

Greenhill School

53
Greenhill Lower School, *1984*
4141 Spring Valley Road, Addison, Texas
Gwathmey-Siegel (New York)

53a
Greenhill Administration Building, Middle
School and Fine Arts Complex, *1996*
Lake/Flato Architects (San Antonio);
William Hidell
The facilities at North Dallas' exclusive
Greenhill School include the work of some
of Texas' – and the nation's – most talented
architects. What's most amazing, however,
is not the expressions of style in individual
buildings, but the remarkable degree to which
the campus as a whole hangs together. The
most likely explanation for this cohesion is
the respect that each new architect has shown
for the work of their predecessors. This respect
is probably most clearly illustrated in the pro-
gression from O'Neil Ford to Enslie Oglesby
to Lake/Flato Architects that is manifested in
the following projects: **(53b) Science Building**
and Dining Hall, 1963, O'Neil Ford; A.B.
Swank; **(53c) Preschool Facility,** 1974, The
Oglesby Group; and **(53d) Greenhill School**
Gymnasium, 1999, Lake/Flato Architects (San
Antonio); William Hidell.

Balthazar Korab

54
Mobil Exploration and Production Research
Laboratory, *1983*
13777 Midway Road, Farmers Branch, Texas
Pei Cobb Freed & Partners (New York)
A thoughtful combination of a four-story
cylindrical office tower and a two-story laboratory building – both distinguished by their
extensive use of natural light. A large mobile
by Calder sits on the roof.

55
Carrollton City Hall, *1987*
1945 Jackson Road, Carrollton, Texas
The Oglesby Group
The final phase of a three-building government complex, this project is Enslie Oglesby's
salute to his mentor, Alvar Aalto, complete
with a Council Chamber roof structure bor-
rowed from Säynätsalo Municipal Center.

56
Grace Lutheran Church, *1988*
1200 E. Hebron Parkway, Carrollton, Texas
Cunningham Architects
Gary Cunningham's stripped-down style and
innovative use of low-cost materials delivered
this small church for just $65 per square foot
– while still conveying a lyricism and rever-
ence missing from most Modern churches.

10 Irving/Las Colinas/ Mid-Cities

Although the 30 miles that separate the downtowns of Dallas and Fort Worth have now grown into an uninterrupted metropolitan landscape, there is nothing cohesive about the Mid-Cities. It is a vast area of roughly 16 miles east-west by 30 miles north-south composed of more than 20 municipalities laced together by an auto dominated freeway-scape that could be Anywhere, USA.

Starting over 30 years ago, the area became a repository for things regional. Six Flags Over Texas was here first, then Texas Stadium, and The Ballpark in Arlington, and now Lone Star Park, but most significantly, the Mid-Cities area was chosen as the site for DFW International Airport. By design, DFW Airport lies in the geographic center of the region, and since 1973 has been the economic engine fueling its growth. Some of the Mid-Cities (Irving, Grand Prairie, Arlington, and Grapevine for instance) date from the last quarter of the 19th century, as market centers serving farming settlements strung along the West Fork of the Trinity River. Little evidence of this history remains, and these have now grown into large cities in their own right, of almost 200,000 (Irving) to more than 250,000 (Arlington) population.

The success of DFW Airport led directly to Ben Carpenter's dream of developing the family ranch into Las Colinas, a planned community of 12,000 acres to the east in an undeveloped part of Irving. By 1985, the mesquite covered hills had become the premier corporate address in Texas, with much to offer the architectural tourist both in the way of elegant headquarters in verdant settings and an Urban Center built around a 125-acre man-made lake and canals. With the recent expansion of mid-density housing to go with bell towers, water taxis and a fixed guideway people-mover, this corporate Disneyland is starting to exude a real sense of place.

The natural Mid-Cities landscape was generally open prairie but a portion is bisected from north to south by the Eastern Cross Timbers – a handsome but narrow belt of oak woodlands in a more scenically hilly and sandy topography. Solana is here, with its colorful village of stunning corporate buildings by Legorreta and Mitchell-Giurgola, as is Ross Perot's Circle T Ranch, which portends an environment of excellence. The affluent northern Mid-Cities of Southlake, Colleyville and Flower Mound are a handsome environment taken collectively, but unfortunately offer few noteworthy individual works, residential or public, and like many modern suburbs, have no historic "downtown." Of particular interest is Southlake's initiative to create one. Southlake Town Square (planned and designed by David Schwarz) will be carefully watched locally to see if a City Hall and public square can in fact successfully anchor a "Main Street" retailing environment.

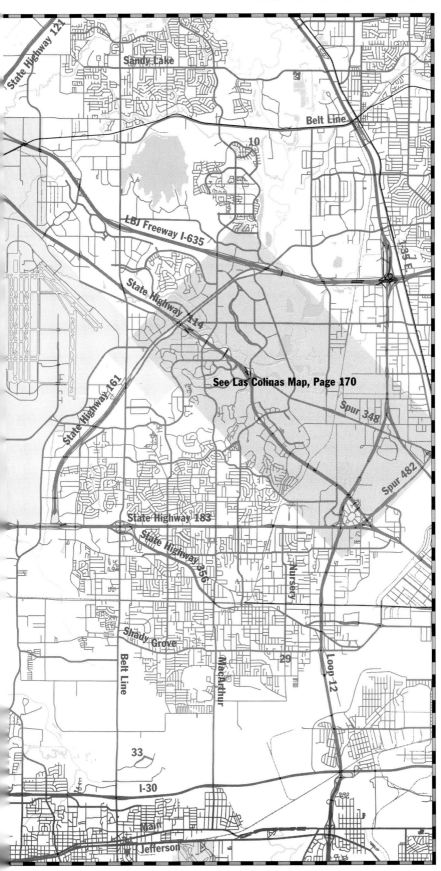

Sandy Lake

Belt Line

10

LBJ Freeway I-635

State Highway 114

State Highway 161

I-35 E.

See Las Colinas Map, Page 170

Spur 348

Spur 482

State Highway 183

State Highway 356

Nursery

Shady Grove

29

Loop 12

Belt Line

MacArthur

33

I-30

Main

Jefferson

10 Irving/Las Colinas/ Mid-Cities

Solana

1
IBM Westlake, *1989*
5 W. Kirkwood Boulevard, Westlake, Texas
Mitchell/Giurgola (New York)
Peter Walker, Martha Schwartz (San Francisco),
*   landscape architecture*

The 1,600-acre Solana development, constructed originally for IBM, owes its genesis
in part to the success of Las Colinas, a suburban center tied to airport proximity and its
utopian isolation from the usual social and
economic urban fabric. Solana transcends Las
Colinas, however, as a community united
through its elemental architectural and landscape vision, overlaid with bold clarity from
the beginning. IBM Westlake is organized
into six interconnected cubic reddish-brown-
stucco buildings and two long and low parking structures that frame an arrival sequence
through a highly sculptured and integrated
landscape. Solana's strongest imagery is found
in **(2) Solana Village Center,** 1989, Village
Circle at W. Kirkwood Boulevard, Legorreta
Arquitectos (Mexico City); Leason Pomeroy
Associates (Irvine, California). These are
intensely colored buildings in punched planes

of stucco, connected in the figure-ground
relationships of a Mexican hacienda or
ancient Mayan cities. **(3) Marriott Hotel,**
1990, 5 Village Circle, Legorreta Arquitectos;
Skidmore Owings & Merrill (Los Angeles);
Leason Pomeroy Associates, opens the inward
hotel form with bold geometry and ties to the
landscape and other buildings. **(4) IBM
Southlake,** 1989, SH114 at Kirkwood
Boulevard, Southlake, Texas, by Legorreta
Arquitectos (pictured above), is the low-scale
sand-colored counterpart to IBM Westlake,
its sloping walls hugging the land and rein-
forcing primary sculptural axes.

5
Southlake Town Square, *1999*
F.M. 1709 at Carroll Road, Southlake, Texas
David M. Schwarz Architectural Services
*   (Washington D.C.); Urban Architecture*
Schwarz fabricated a historic town center
for a new community that wanted one in
the worst way. Fine retailers endorsed the
concept, but officing above the store has
yet to prove up.

6
Grapevine City Hall, *1996*
413 Main Street, Grapevine, Texas
ArchiTexas
The popular need for a sense of history amid
the suburban clutter is embodied here. Its
clock tower and lantern-toting cowboy are
visible around town. Its loggia, side courtyard,
and historical park make this nostalgic red-
brick and limestone design a public favorite.

7
Grapevine Mills, *1997*
3000 Grapevine Mills Parkway, Grapevine,
Texas
RTKL Associates
Shopping energy inspires super-graphic,
Mondrian-patterned walls and spills out in
power-center-like entries and giant sculptural
icons: North Texas flanked by U.S. and Texas
flags, a football (of course), clever bluebonnets,
and a stylized yellow Eiffel Tower. Exuberant,
useful steel-cutout signage in Old West motifs
carries the imagery to the street.

George Silk

8
D/FW Airport, *1973*
Irving, Texas
HOK (St. Louis); Brodsky, Hopf & Adler
(New York); with Omniplan Architects
Harrell & Hamilton and Preston M. Geren
& Associates (Fort Worth)
Its easily expanded destination-travel design
has been superseded by the compact needs of
hub-and-spoke flying, but D/FW remains an
aerial prairie icon and business catalyst, draw-
ing major corporations to the area. Take a
50¢ ride down the "main drag" to see the
vastness of one of the world's busiest hubs.

9
D/FW Airport Delta Remote Support Facility,
1992
East side of International Parkway south of
main terminal buildings
Haldeman Powell + Partners
Scored precast concrete panels in subtle
earth tones are assembled in Constructivist
intersections of building planes to break up
and enliven vast spaces. Steel canopies and
colonnades bring human scale and shelter.

10
Dallas Cowboys Center, *1982*
9800 Cowboys Parkway, Irving, Texas
Ford Powell & Carson (San Antonio)
A low-key headquarters building gets its verve
from the play of fossilized limestone panels
and steely dark-tinted storefront fenestration,
which opens to the south and at corners in this
gently sawtooth exterior. Sculptural pieces,
including a Cowboy star fountain and minimalist spiral-stair coaching towers are the only
clues to the football empire.

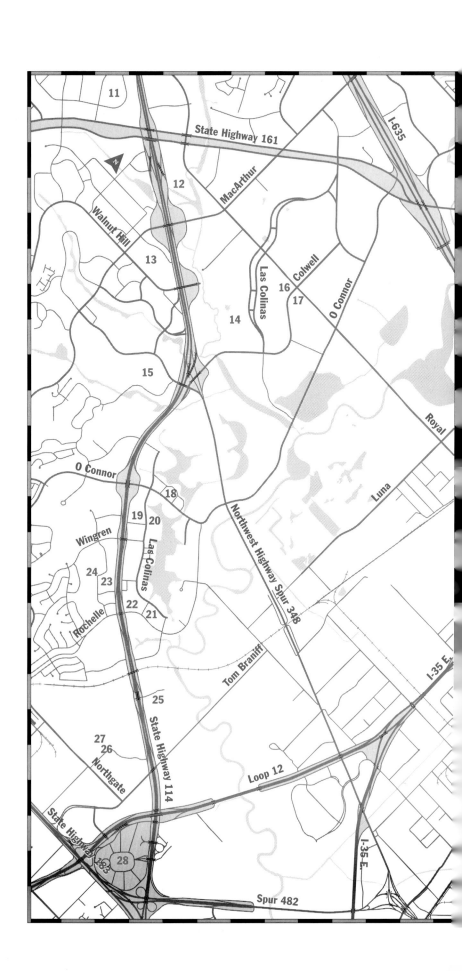

Las Colinas

As the 12,000-acre Las Colinas (Spanish for "The Hills") urban development has evolved in concert with its founder's vision, the architectural standards established by Skidmore Owings & Merrill/San Francisco (Charles Bassett) in the 1984 three-building centerpiece and plaza – Williams Square – have remained unsurpassed. While the housing for some 25,000 full-time residents is architecturally insignificant, a number of office buildings – serving some 70,000 workday residents – are notable. In particular, these include those built for Exxon, and for hi-tech companies such as Nokia, GTE, and Hitachi.

11
Hitachi Manufacturing Center, *1987*
6431 Longhorn Drive, Irving, Texas
Kajima (Dallas)
The high-tech nature of this building is revealed in the crisp pairing of two shades of gray stone pulled out as panels away from an implied black box of tinted curtain-wall. The low-scale building nevertheless makes a striking image from the freeway, with its skyline array of tanks and towers.

13
Zale Corporation Headquarters, *1984*
901 Walnut Hill Lane, Irving, Texas
HOK
Humble concrete tilt-wall provides a sublime solar screen that shelters and energizes the facades of simple office blocks. An endwall of glass block sparkles in the sun like the diamonds the company markets. Parking terraces and landscaping settle building into site.

12
Nokia Americas Headquarters, *1998*
6000 Connection Drive, Irving, Texas
Good Fulton & Farrell
This highly articulated complex is shorter and more pleasingly proportioned than similar corporate offices along the freeway. Its mass is broken into bays with extruded curtain-wall stair towers. The top floor peels back to form a Modernist cornice beneath metal trellises.

14
Exxon Corporate Headquarters, *1996*
5959 Las Colinas Boulevard, Irving, Texas
HOK
One of many recent corporate relocations, this compound's broad, low-sloping roofs extend out to shade continuous clerestories at the top floor of each building with soothing Prairie Style appeal. Fenestration is grouped in elongated central banks and shorter end banks, set back beneath rich stone spandrels.

Las Colinas

15
GTE Telephone Operations World Headquarters, *1991*
600 Hidden Ridge Drive, Irving, Texas
HKS, Inc.
A simple vocabulary of metal panels and clad columns, curtain-wall, and smooth and rusticated sandstone encloses office buildings flanking a connecting spine.

16
SBC Center for Learning, *1988*
6301 Colwell Boulevard, Irving, Texas
Good Haas & Fulton
The structural frame for a corner entry emerges skeleton-like from this flush-skinned training center. An engaged rotunda leads to the building's signature, a wavy wall of tan brick with punched openings and a grid of shallow inset brick squares.

17
Office Building, *1995*
100 E. Royal Lane, Irving, Texas
3 Architects
A long, linear facade breaks to accept a concave central curtain-wall entry, its doorway set in an extruded shaft of glass and metal. Elsewhere, airplane-flap awnings and ordered, exaggerated downspouts slice up wall planes.

18
The Towers at Williams Square, *1984*
5215 N. O'Connor Boulevard
Skidmore Owings & Merrill (San Francisco)
A standard for other towers in the Urban Center to emulate, this complex has also captured the entrepreneurial spirit of Las Colinas in the granite expanse of the plaza (by the SWA Group), through which gallop **(18a) The Mustangs of Las Colinas,** Robert Glen. Bristling with energy and ornery individuality, these larger-than-life bronzes traverse an abstract creek-bed, complete with fountain spray from the mustangs' hooves. The granite and glass towers have balconies tucked beneath their roofs, a gesture of civility in this utterly civil urban center.

19
Mandalay Canal, *1981*
201 E. Carpenter Freeway, Irving, Texas
HKS, Inc.
Inspired by Venice, and the San Antonio Riverwalk closer to home, this canal provides useful passage by water taxis or the more

casual stroll along its banks. The waterway and bordering trees, as well as Lake Carolyn, relieve the sparse urban feel among the towers and parking garages. Its campanile, bridges, and European village flavor make this one successful postmodern people place.

20
Mandalay Hotel, *1981*
221 E. Las Colinas Boulevard, Irving, Texas
WZMH
Distinctive for extruded cylinders of corner balconies, this hotel recesses windows on each floor beneath spandrels of precast concrete. Its circular drive cordons off outside traffic through landscaping and privacy walls. Red-tile roofs, too, relieve the precast sameness.

21
Cigna Tower, *1982*
600 E. Las Colinas Boulevard, Irving, Texas
HOK
Serving as an anchor of the Urban Center loop, this curving tower is skinned in tripartite bands of brushed metal panels and bands and green tinted glass. Its first two floors recede at street level to create a double-height entry with black granite columns.

22
Chase Bank/Las Colinas, *1984*
545 E. Carpenter Freeway, Irving, Texas
Skidmore Owings & Merrill (Houston)
Designed as an intersection of one granite-and-glass block with a taller, hip-roofed tower, this restrained abstraction also introduced

grazing cattle sculptures to complement the mustangs in Williams Square.

23
Industrial Properties Company, *1996*
400 E. Carpenter Freeway, Irving, Texas
Good Fulton & Farrell
This two-story precast-concrete box nestles into its sloping site to create an intimate one-story entrance with reinforced planes that imply a classical portico and colonnade, repeated at the opposite end in two stories.

24
Hickok Center, *1979*
451 S. Decker Drive, Irving, Texas
Ralph Kelman
Concrete columns and "T" panels form a crisp structural framework, with first-floor brick infill and a deep entry loggia, above which perimeter balconies sit with metal handrails echoed in louvered sunscreens above (reminiscent of Saarinen's John Deere Headquarters).

25
Cistercian Chapel, *1992*
1 Cistercian Road, Irving, Texas
Cunningham Architects
In deference to the brick and concrete-frame
(25a) Cistercian Monastery School, 1965,
O'Neil Ford (San Antonio); Duane Landry,
Cunningham inserted a narrow breezeway
that, inside the abbey, completes an intimate
cloister. The public is welcome to this spartan
chapel, which rises in walls of quarry-split
2 1/2-ton limestone blocks. Steel brackets
inserted into the wall support the cantilevered
fir roof a foot away from each wall to allow
sunlight through a ribbon of cast glass and
onto the craggy rock walls. Spindly cables
hold the roof system in delicate tension.
Banding in the facade comes from weathered
surface blocks.

James F. Wilson

25b
Cistercian Library, *1998*
1 Cistercian Road, Irving, Texas
Cunningham Architects
Continuing the use of orange brick and concrete in the existing school, Cunningham
opened the library to north light through a
bank of tall vertical windows. Elegant concrete cantilevers contribute to the network of
walkways on the campus.

26
University of Dallas Campanile (Braniff
Memorial Tower), *1968*
1845 E. Northgate Drive, Irving, Texas
O'Neil Ford (San Antonio); Duane Landry
Like Trinity University's tower in San
Antonio, Ford here flares the base and capital
to give it an organic feel as a beacon along
Carpenter Freeway and on campus. The
nearby **(27) University of Dallas Chapel of**
the Incarnation, 1985, Landry & Landry, is
built in the humble form of a single story,
with concrete columns, soft brick walls, and a
deep entry. The roof steps up above the altar,
clad in copper with clerestories that admit
sunlight to create a diffuse central light over
the shallow, wide and shadowy worship space.

28
Texas Stadium, *1966*
SH183 at SH114, Irving, Texas
A. Warren Morey
Resting like some stalled primordial giant
armadillo at the confluence of three primary
arteries, the Cowboys' playing home remains
an "unfinished" icon. The hole in its roof, left
that way, some say, so that God could watch
his favorite team, keeps weather elements in
the game. Exposed around the exterior, too,
are columns, seating supports, circulation
ramps, and elevator towers in a messy but
structurally fascinating spaghetti of concrete.
The intrusion of a ring of slick luxury boxes
has tempered the structuralist clarity, but
still clear is the open-air slot of engineering
bravado at the juncture of the seating bowl
and the roof.

29
Islamic Mosque, *1998*
1320 S. Nursery Road, Irving, Texas
Oglesby-Greene
Its forms are quite apart from usual Dallas
architecture, but this mosque nevertheless
reflects a strong Modernist hand, able to meet
the needs of sacred spaces without importing
some stylistic copy. Ornament is minimal and
abstract. The mosque's banded concrete-block
walls are its organizing image, sweeping radi-
ally and dissolving into a delicate colonnade.

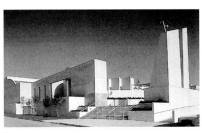

31
C.R. Smith Museum, *1992*
4601 FAA Drive, Fort Worth, Texas
Corgan Associates
Breaking out of the stale box that a corporate
museum can be, American Airlines' showplace
is a rigorously planned set of galleries, theater,
and plaza, with elements that slice, fracture,
and fold sculpturally according to functional
needs. Its knife-edged limestone veneer above
a granite base gives it a cool elegance, offset
by the traffic-stopping stylized airplane wing
that caps a tilted glass gallery wall.

30
Euless Public Library, *1996*
201 N. Ector Drive, Euless, Texas
Phillips-Swager Associates
An asymmetrical barrel-vault extends the
length of this library and is finished in a glis-
tening standing-seam metal roof that is its
lasting image. The rectangular space below,
faced in tan brick, is its basic organizing element. Notched into it are a series of highly
articulated banded-brick silos. Bright green
columns, triangular bay window, entry portal,
and signage suggest active use of the building.
This is a welcome civic building in the often
nondescript retail and commercial lands
between Dallas and Fort Worth.

32
AMR/The Sabre Group Headquarters, *1979*
4200 SH360, Fort Worth, Texas
William Pereira Associates (Los Angeles)
A campus of three adjoining three-story
wings that hover lightly above the sloping,
wooded site, this headquarters' human activity metaphorically spills out into view as open
metal stairways on two buildings and as a
white space-frame for the glazed entry canopy.
This space-frame runs the length of this primary building, visible through first-floor glazing. Bands of tinted black glass sit within
light-gray spandrel frames. Terraced parking
steps down from the building through a dense
natural landscape.

33
Lone Star Park, *1997*
2200 N. Belt Line Road, Grand Prairie, TX
HKS, Inc.
The mixed Spanish Colonial and Early Texana
theme of this horse racetrack is more an enter-
taining pastiche than historicism. Its thin
details act as a stage-set for the warmup track
that occupies the spot that a mission would
reserve for the grand plaza. And why not? The
horses are the main event, as evidenced by the
shimmering high-tech back elevation, with
expansive views to the racetrack below.

34
Avion Village, *1942*
Belt Line Road at Avion Parkway, Grand
Prairie, Texas
DeWitt & Swank; Richard Neutra (Los Angeles);
David Williams
An urgent need to house World War II aviation workers spawned this 216-dwelling community. Similar to Williams' Greenway Parks
(see Chapter 7), Avion Village centered on a
large central green-space. Fingers of the green-
space extended between housing clusters. Cars
followed a looping perimeter roadway with
cul-de-sacs to the backs of houses 10 to 20 at
a time. Williams designed two-story units,
with indigenous gallery porches and masonry.
Neutra's one-story units and community
buildings were planar Modernist structures
with prefab roof modules shifted to overhang
a home's south side for solar control. Chain-
link fences and changes to make street facades
work as the fronts of homes have spoiled the
purity of Avion Village's planning, although
the housing stock is largely intact.

35
Siemens Entry Canopy, *1957*
2910 Avenue F East, Arlington, Texas
O'Neil Ford (San Antonio); Richard Colley;
Arch Swank; S.B. Zisman
Ultrathin hyperbolic paraboloid concrete
shells front this low-scaled Modernist build-
ing. I.M. Pei and Mexican engineer Felix
Candela were consultants.

36
Six Flags Over Texas, *1961*
SH360 at Interstate 30, Arlington, Texas
Randall Duell & Co. (Los Angeles)
Isolated on the loosely populated prairie
between Dallas and Fort Worth when it was
opened, Six Flags has become a venerable
landmark at the epicenter of the development
merging the fabric of the two cities. Later
entertainment and sports venues have built
on its pioneering success.

37

The Ballpark in Arlington, *1994*
1000 Ballpark Way
David Schwarz (Washington D.C.); HKS, Inc.
The product of a flawed design competition,
The Ballpark has nevertheless become a
smashing public success. Italian Renaissance
arcades, loggias, and campaniles have been
adapted as the superstructure for a pleasantly
irregular ball field inside. Texana imagery grips
every facade, from plentiful metal stars in the
outfield to cast-stone stars on the exterior, and
from longhorns and medallions between
arches to heroic friezes just above eye level.

39

River Legacy Living Science Center, *1996*
703 Green Oaks Boulevard NW, Arlington,
*   Texas*
Jones Studio; Gideon Toal
Built with sustainable materials and systems
to serve as the education center for a 625-acre
riparian preserve on the West Fork of the
Trinity River, this center recalls the Bavinger
House by Bruce Goff in its expressive design,
especially its flaring and swirling roof. Its rusticated fieldstone walls mirror nature as they
emerge from the water like rock outcrops. An
observation deck and teaching patio reach out
into and over the Trinity.

Craig Kuhner

38

University of Texas at Arlington Architecture
**   Building,** *1984*
601 W. Nedderman Drive, Arlington, Texas
Pratt Box Henderson & Partners
An orange brick exoskeleton with vertical louvers protect this large rectilinear box from
damaging sunlight. A first-floor loggia borrows from classic academic building designs.
A grand interior stair connects to each floor
and opens up a vertical common space. A
shallow pin-up review gallery runs along one
interior facade. Landscaping creates a generous formal commons and softens the planar
edge of this tall classroom building.

40

Most Blessed Sacrament Church, *1982*
2100 N. Davis, Arlington, Texas
Selzer Associates
The simple shed is elevated to a grand scale in
the interlocking complementary volumes of
this church. Finished in tan brick with reveals
to emphasize important horizontals and verti-
cals in the facade, each shed is topped by a
standing-seam metal roof that steps up at its
peak to create a large clerestory to admit
modulated natural light. The entry carries a
traditional trinity of portals with rich wood
doors beneath shady brick recesses.
Traditional in its plan, the church is a sturdy
graduate of the postmodern heyday.

11 Downtown Fort Worth

Fort Worth holds up easily under the romance attached to its cattle drives and oil wells. All the Texas clichés, in fact, cease to be clichés here because what they get at is somehow too real, too much an accepted part of life. To have been the place "where the West begins" for well over a hundred years is to have grown accustomed to all things western.

It is easy to forget that Fort Worth began life as a cavalry outpost. Having found a suitable site at the top of a bluff overlooking the Trinity River, Major Ripley Arnold's scouting party established a fort in 1849. Arnold named the post after his former commander, William Jenkins Worth, who had died of cholera in San Antonio.

Fort Worth's mission was to protect the towns and cities to its east, primarily Dallas, from Indian attacks. That's a fact that stands out in the history of the age-old feud between the cities. Now that the D/FW Airport has joined them together in the eyes of the world, their rivalry may have disappeared for good. But in 1873, when Dallas had the railroad and Fort Worth didn't and a Dallas newspaper charged that Fort Worth was such a sleepy little town that a panther could sleep undisturbed in its streets, it was meant as a dig. Unfazed, Fort Worth citizens seized upon the idea and began to call their hometown "Panther City." (Be sure and note the panther heads carved into the string course of the Flatiron building here.)

The soldiers moved on in 1853, and their barracks quickly became the new homes of settlers. By 1890, their lofty location above the river would become the home of the grand Tarrant County Courthouse, built of Burnet granite like the Texas Capitol.

The hilly topography of Fort Worth added its drama to the architecture of downtown just as the coming of the railroad created the beginnings of a city plan. The great wealth of cattlemen, (from the days of drives up the Chisholm Trail to the period of stockyards and railroads) influenced architecture. And most of the city's understated skyscrapers from the '20s and '30s – the W.T. Waggoner Building, for instance, and the Sinclair – were underwritten by oil money.

Fortunately, some of that oil money is still at work improving downtown Fort Worth. Members of the Bass family have made it their cause to enrich their hometown on every architectural front. Homes for low-income families are built into the hillsides of downtown; cutting-edge office buildings like First City Bank Tower and City Center II rise next to the restored, 19th-century buildings of Sundance Square; and the Bass Performance Hall adds a Baroque-tinged spirit to the role of culture in the city. All this attention and Fort Worth still projects the quiet charm of a small town in Texas. It just doesn't want to be Dallas.

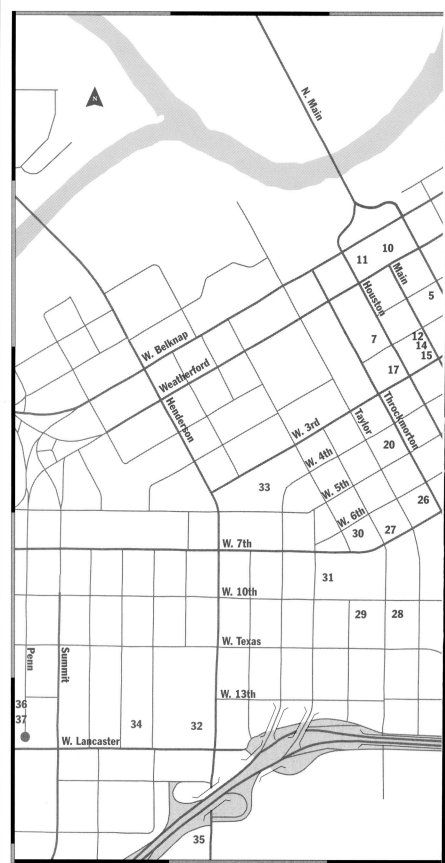

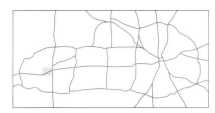

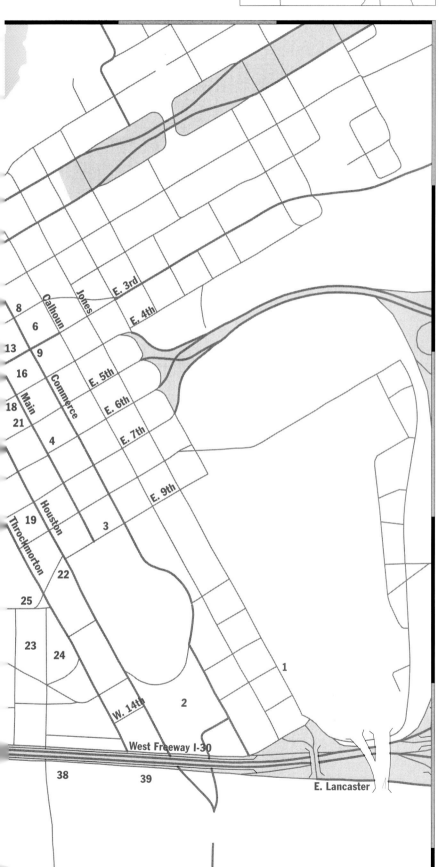

11 Downtown Fort Worth

1
Santa Fe Depot (Union Passenger Station), *1899*
1601 Jones Street
The "Fort Worth Union Depot" offered early resolution for a single passenger terminal downtown. But the building's awkward interpretation of Beaux-Arts vocabulary revealed both its great distance from Chicago and a moment just before southwestern railroads commissioned great architects. Remodeling in 1938 removed a brick entry portico and art-glass windows.

Richard Payne

2
Fort Worth Water Gardens, *1974*
14th Street at Houston Street
Johnson/Burgee (New York)
Responding to uncivil treatment of downtown in the '50s and '60s, the Amon Carter Foundation sought out Johnson/Burgee to fulfill a grander vision of renewal. Inverted elevations of the sunken garden establish an urban retreat greater than the sum of its blocks, isolated within a timeless demonstration of water and gravity.

3
Radisson Plaza Hotel (Hotel Texas), *1921*
815 Main Street
Sanguinet & Staats; Mauran, Russell & Crowell (Kansas City)
"The Texas," as first named, combined highrise experience of the local firm with hotel expertise of Mauran, Russell & Crowell. Alterations to floor plan and name began in the 1960s, but the hotel remains vibrant in revenue and memory, particularly as the last overnight stop for John Fitzgerald Kennedy on November 21, 1963.

4
Blackstone Hotel, *1929*
601 Main Street
*Elmer Withers; Mauran, Russell & Crowell
  (Kansas City)*
The city's then-tallest building and first venture into Art Deco styling opened one month before the October 1929 stock market crash. The 22-story hotel currently prepares for its place in local Deco Revival.

5
First City Bank Tower, *1982*
201 Main Street
Paul Rudolph (New York); 3D/I (Houston)
Such picturesque adaptations of the modern box bristle as fortresses for the Bass interests. Their downtown investments soared with this 33-story tower, then Rudolph's 38-story **(6) City Center II,** 1984, anchored by his **(7) Worthington Hotel,** 1981.

8
Fire Station No. 1, *1907*
Commerce Street at 2nd Street
The City Beautiful Movement in Fort Worth's early 20th-century years resulted in low-scale individual acts rather than comprehensive planning. This Beaux-Arts firehouse, which once housed city government as well, is a showcase for period brickwork, a survivor of the low-rise downtown of yesteryear, and now a museum.

9
Bass Performance Hall, *1998*
4th Street at Commerce Street
David Schwarz Architectural Services
(Washington D.C.); HKS
The city's newest landmark is a $67 million revival of la Belle Epoch, financed largely by the Bass family and associated foundations. Its 2,056 seats witness multi-venue technology.

10
Tarrant County Courthouse, *1893-95*
100 W. Weatherford Street
Gunn & Curtiss (Kansas City)
In 1849 frontier troops established Camp Worth at this bluff. During the 1890s boom, county officials approved this design, inspired by the new Capitol in Austin, sharing Burnet granite and Second Empire details. Much splendor returned with a 1980s rehab, followed by trompe l'oeil "granite" skin on the 1958 **(11) Civil Courts Building.**

12
Sundance Square, *1981*
300 block of Main Street
Thomas E. Woodward & Associates
An eclectic collection of fronts, built between the 1880s and early 1900s along several block faces centered on Main Street, presents a mixed-use revitalization effort of the Bass family. Inspired by the 1970s movie about the West in transition, this complex includes **(12a) Caravan of Dreams,** four 1880s facades on Houston Street as shells for a 1983 performing arts center by architects Margret Augustine and James Wooten.

13
Knights of Pythias Hall, *1901*
313 Main Street
Sanguinet & Staats
Fraternal Pythians, once boasting 30,000 Texas members, commissioned a medieval guild hall for their chivalrous image. Street-level revenue supported charitable works, a formula continued by Haltom's Jewelers and its trademark clock. The Bass family restored this picturesque pile by 1983 as an anchor for Sundance Square.

14
Western Union, *1931*
314-16 Main Street
James Davies, Sr.
While most buildings now part of Sundance Square fell on hard times, this relatively large three-story corner of brick and terra-cotta retained its original occupant until 1983. Few exterior alterations had been made to sidewalk windows and entries, and its fine zigzag details.

15
Land Title Block, *1889*
111 E. 4th Street
Haggart & Sanguinet
Billed as "perhaps the finest Victorian commercial building remaining," this monument
to brick craft confirms the early talents of
architect Marshall Robert Sanguinet. The
builder's Land Mortgage Bank safe survives,
and rehabilitations after 1983 rescued this
corner from skid row.

16
Chisholm Trail Mural, *1985*
400 block of Main Street
Richard Haas (New York)
Residents are not ashamed of their "Cowtown"
nickname, magnified to this blockface of a
thundering herd on the post-Civil War, pre-
railroad path to northerly markets. Through
such virtual imagery, also at **(17) 300 block
of Houston Street** and the Civil Courts
Building, Haas blurs any line between art
and architecture.

18
Burk Burnett Building, *1914*
500 Main Street
Sanguinet & Staats
Samuel Burk Burnett established reputation
and fortune on cattle, first on the Chisholm
Trail then at his 6666 Ranch. In 1915 he
further proved business sense upon adding
his two-part last name to this exuberant
skyscraper, rehabilitated in the 1980s by
Bass Brothers Enterprises.

19
W.T. Waggoner Building, *1919*
810 Houston Street
Sanguinet & Staats
Ella Halsell Waggoner owned the building
named for husband William Thomas, symbol
of their ranching and oil empire northwest of
Fort Worth. Marble-clad street fronts, two-
story banking lobby, and classic Chicago-style
terra-cotta regained notoriety following
restoration in 1985.

20
Bank One Tower, *1974*
Fifth Street at Throckmorton Street
John Portman (Atlanta); Preston Geren
From a decade when "environmental glass"
meant reflecting its surroundings, the former
Fort Worth National Bank startled close-in
downtown with its first modernist highrise.
Alexander Calder's red stabile **(20a) Eagle**
sculpture punctuates its surrounding plaza.

21
Sinclair Building, *1930*
512 Main Street
Wiley G. Clarkson
Oilman Richard Otto Dulaney learned from
his cattle-king predecessors to invest in real
estate, and survived the depression by secur-
ing a major oil company as his tenant. Zigzag
details reemerged through a 1990 restoration
of the exterior and elevator lobby.

22
Flatiron Building, *1907*
1000 Houston Street
Sanguinet & Staats
Farsighted builders not only maximized square
footage on this odd-shaped lot, they created a
remarkable landmark. Sharing characteristics
with its 1902 inspiration in New York,
Sullivanesque details here are outstanding.

23
Fort Worth City Hall, *1971*
1000 Throckmorton Street
Edward Durell Stone (New York); Preston Geren
Ten years after commencement of Boston
City Hall, this city moved offices into one
of the most popular – and discontextual –
motifs of the '60s and '70s. Civic offices have
occupied this area, including **(25) Old City
Hall,** since 1893.

24
St. Patrick Cathedral, *1888-92*
1206 Throckmorton Street
James J. Kane
This complex became a cathedral in 1969,
evolving from a local center of Roman
Catholic instruction beginning in 1889 with
Kane's **(24a) St. Ignatius Academy,** now
School of Religion. Twin spires never rose as

planned, and remodelings resulted in a 1940s
Baroque interior and 1950s white paint on all
exterior masonry.

25
**Public Safety and Courts Building
  (Old City Hall),** *1938*
Throckmorton Street at 10th Street
*Wyatt C. Hedrick; Elmer G. Withers
  Architectural Company*
In the late 1930s federal funds helped city
officials construct modern offices and a new
library, both at old adjacent addresses. City
hall stripped the classical temple to a flat
hexastyle portico in polished granite, surrounded by limestone and infilled with metal
grills and windows. Elected officials moved
in 1971, and subsequent bungling caused
demolition of the library in 1990.

26
Fort Worth Club Building, *1925*
306 W. 7th Street
Wyatt C. Hedrick
Club members moved from decade-old
Arts-and-Crafts digs at 106 W. 6th, placing a
tenant furniture store in this building's first
five floors and regional companies in upper
wings. The sprawling Spanish Renaissance
13th floor remains home to club enterprises,
augmented in 1975 by a 14-story office tower
west addition.

27
Electric Building, *1930*
410 W. 7th Street
Wyatt C. Hedrick
Once part of the real estate empire of
Houston banker Jesse Holman Jones, this
19-story tower housed the Texas Electric
Service Company. Its seven-story north annex
included the Hollywood Theater, designed
by Houston architect Alfred Charles Finn.
Surviving Deco details, inside and out, are
subjects of recent rehabilitation.

28
St. Andrews Episcopal Church, *1912*
817 Lamar Street
Sanguinet & Staats
The premier local architects could design
anything, including an English Gothic parish
church of Missouri dolomite for one of the
city's oldest congregations. Work began in
1908, incorporating the altar from its 1877
predecessor, art glass from England and St.
Louis, and sumptuous wood interior. The
adjacent sympathetic parish house of brick
and cast stone was designed in 1949 by the
firm of Preston M. Geren.

29
U.S. Courthouse, *1933*
501 W. 10th
Paul Cret (Philadelphia); Wiley G. Clarkson
This block and **(38) U.S. Post Office** replaced
an 1890s Romanesque facility at Jennings
and 11th. Cret gained a foothold in Texas at
Austin's university campus, then this and
other major projects for the U.S. Treasury.
A stripped-down Beaux-Arts temple, the
courthouse embraces regional imagery of
Native Americans, western outlaws, and Texas
Rangers through metal screens and interior
courtroom murals.

30
NationsBank Texas, *1960*
500 W. 7th Street
Skidmore Owings & Merrill (New York);
  Preston Geren
Modernism developed by Le Corbusier and
others, and ascendancy of banker developers,
brought the column-and-beam geometric cage
early to Fort Worth. Horizontal members
allegedly shade the modernist Texas sun. Original
tenant First National Bank commissioned Isamu
Noguchi to produce **(30a) The Texas Sculpture**
for its adjacent plaza, since remodeled.

31
Burnett Plaza (Comerica Bank Texas), *1983*
801 Cherry Street
Sikes Jennings Kelly; Preston Geren
The 1980s boom rivaled the 1920s in Texas,
and deregulated banks eagerly provided symbols of their wild ride on the wave's crest.
Interfirst Bank's name disappeared in the
ensuing bust, but its headquarters tower survives along with the 1983 landscape of adjacent **(31a) Burnett Park,** by Peter Walker and
Martha Schwartz, displaying four Henri
Matisse sculptures **(31b) Backs.**

32
Masonic Temple, *1930-32*
1100 Henderson Street
Wiley G. Clarkson
Masonic temples of the 1920s surpassed
nearby government or business edifices. And
since their functions changed little, as with
this four-square-block landmark, exterior and
interior embellishments survive in remarkable
condition. Here an internal program credited
to Paul M. Heerwagen features a Gothic-truss
grand hall and other picturesque spaces.

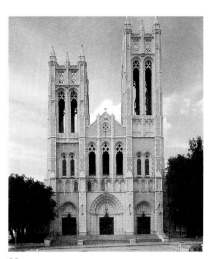

33
First United Methodist Church, *1931*
800 W. 5th Street
Wiley G. Clarkson
A soaring example of Gothic Revival, with no competing elevations nearby, this brick and terra-cotta sanctuary anchors a large church complex. Adjacent buildings and landscapes from 1954-56 and 1969-70 establish a cloister atmosphere.

34
Health South Rehabilitation Center, *1927-29*
1212 W. Lancaster Avenue
Wiley G. Clarkson
The architect developed a Renaissance villa for this 30-bed infirmary for women and children, with additions in 1958. Conversion to a rehabilitation hospital added a three-story wing in 1990.

35
Public Market Building, *1930*
1400 Henderson Street
B. Gaylord Noftsga (Oklahoma City)
This private venture offered modern accommodations for permanent food vendors and stalls for farm products. The Spanish Renaissance landmark has housed many tenants, and recently was saved from new freeway construction.

36
Eddleman-McFarland House, *1899*
1110 Penn Street
Howard Messer
Survivors of optimism at the last turn of a century, this brick, stone and metal fantasy, and **(37) Pollack-Capps House** credited to Messer in 1898, crowned the premiere residential area known as Quality Hill. Both are now offices.

38
U.S. Post Office, *1933*
251 W. Lancaster Avenue
Wyatt C. Hedrick
Federal planners expressed confidence through such depression projects. The 1950s overhead freeway cut this area from downtown, and railroads no longer carry most mail, but this temple of communication survives for redevelopment.

39
Texas & Pacific Passenger Terminal and
  Warehouse, *1931*
1600 Throckmorton Street
Wyatt C. Hedrick
A colossal development consisting of the passenger terminal and office tower, plus warehouse west of the Post Office, revealed the importance of rail transport – and this particular railroad – to Fort Worth.

12 Fort Worth Beyond Downtown

Just west of downtown Fort Worth, something of the city's true soul begins to emerge. It is here, out on the land and beneath the big Texas sky that Fort Worth reveals its deepest passions. Louis Kahn's exquisite Kimbell Art Museum faces Philip Johnson's Amon Carter Museum across a museum-size stretch of prairie. Nearby towers the Will Rogers Coliseum where the annual Fort Worth Livestock Exposition and rodeo are held. Its presence, in what has become the cultural district, is a subtle reminder that Fort Worth is a city where one can study a 14th-century predella panel by Duccio and a Santa Gertrudis bull in the space of an hour. The yearly International Van Cliburn Competition offers still another cultural possibility.

The Coliseum, the Will Rogers Memorial Auditorium, the Pioneer Memorial Tower, the Casa Mañana theater and a handful of other buildings owe their existence to Amon Carter's frustration that Dallas was chosen as the site of the Texas Centennial celebration. Carter, a businessman who owned the local newspaper, decided that Fort Worth should partake of the Centennial festivities, too, and he requested and received federal funds from President Franklin Roosevelt to build a fair grounds for Fort Worth. Although the centennial was over by the time construction was finished, the buildings remained to enhance the social and cultural life of the city.

Even before the 1908 Trinity River flood that prompted Dallasites to hire Kansas City planner George Kessler to design a city plan, Fort Worth had already enlisted his services for the development of a park system. The resulting beauty of The Botanic Garden, which was not constructed until 1933, still communicates Kessler's skill. His rose garden is now complemented by the nearby 1970 Japanese Garden, created in an old rock quarry on the grounds of the park.

Only in residential design does one encounter an element of pretense in Fort Worth. For instance, in neighborhoods like Westover Hills, grand estates that conjure up British manor houses or French villas continue to define the domestic architectural aesthetic. And yet, those who are willing to explore will discover fine houses by Edward Larrabee Barnes, I.M. Pei, Paul Rudolph, Harwell Hamilton Harris, Lake/Flato, and Fort Worth's own very talented firm of Sanguinet & Staats.

12 Fort Worth Beyond Downtown

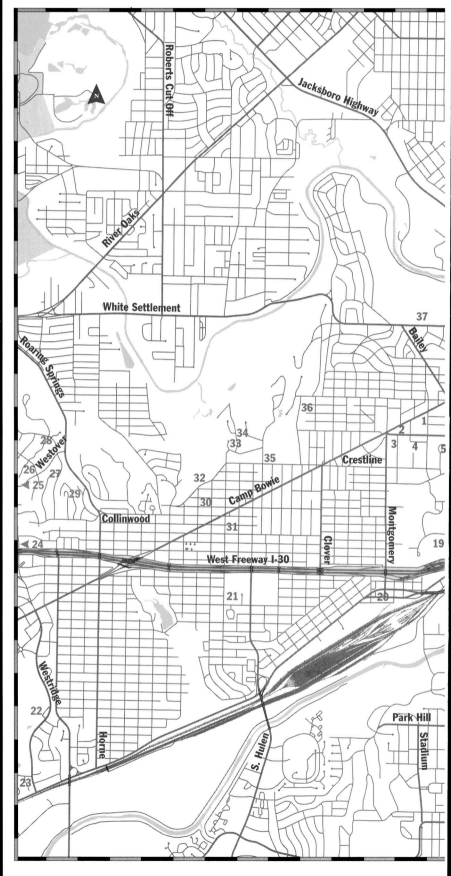

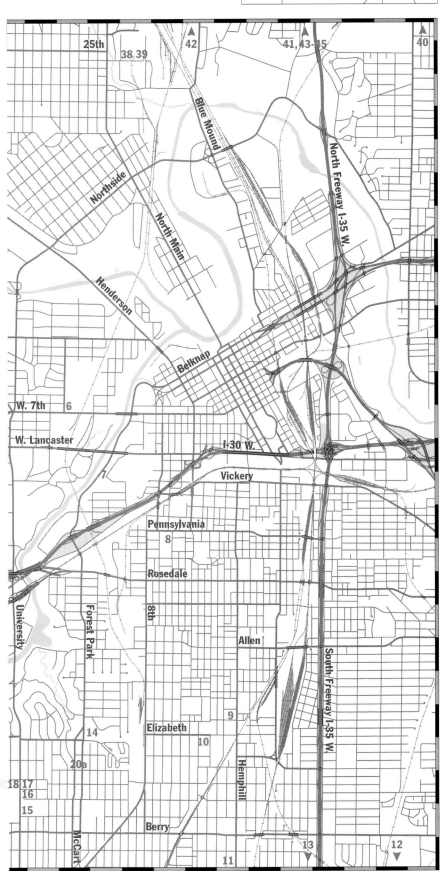

12 Fort Worth Beyond Downtown

1
Kimbell Art Museum, *1972*
3333 Camp Bowie Boulevard
Louis Kahn (Philadelphia); Preston M. Geren
    & Associates, associate architects
Kay and Velma Kimbell emerged from small-town Texas in the early 1900s to build an empire on foodstuffs. Their art collecting commenced in 1931, climaxing in 1966 with selection of Kahn for what would be his last personally supervised design. Engineer August Komendant and local contractor Thomas S. Byrne Inc. facilitated a brilliant series of rein-forced concrete cycloidal vaults. Each bay over the interior accepts sunlight through a 2.5-ft. aperture along its apex; light is diffused beau-tifully inside by aluminum reflectors.

Richard Payne

2
Amon Carter Museum, *1961*
3501 Camp Bowie Boulevard
Joseph Pelich, addition, 1964
Johnson/Burgee (New York), addition, 1977
During a 1950s circuit through elite Texas society, Johnson met Ruth Carter, daughter of Fort Worth newspaper icon Amon Carter and steward of his extensive collection of American Western art. Johnson's collaboration with Carter placed a temple on an acropolis,

in Johnson's view. Subsequent extensions were supervised by Johnson. Early expansion of the museum's scope is exemplified by the outdoor display of **(2a) Upright Motives #1, #2, #7** by English sculptor Henry Moore.

3
Museum of Modern Art of Fort Worth, *1954*
1309 Montgomery Street
Herbert Bayer (New York)
Ford, Powell & Carson (San Antonio),
    additions, 1974
The Museum of Modern Art was the first of the museum district's facilities to be designed in the International Style and established the standard of excellence reflected in the designs of the Kimbell and Amon Carter. The Museum of Modern Art is currently building a new museum designed by Tadao Ando (Japan) across Arch Adams Street from the Kimbell. It contains a high quality of contemporary art that complements the collections of the other museums.

4

Will Rogers Memorial Auditorium, Coliseum, and Tower, *1936*
3301 W. Lancaster Avenue
Wyatt C. Hedrick; Elmer G. Withers
Amon Carter's determination to make his town the center of Texas during its 1936 centennial celebration of independence from Mexico led to this complex dedicated to his friend Rogers, who died in 1935. New Deal funds subsidized the chief design work of Herman Paul Koeppe and coliseum engineering by Herbert M. Hinckley Sr. The adjacent **(4a) Live Stock Exhibit Halls** constructed between 1935 and 1955, plus recent expansions, sustain Western roots and diversity within the surrounding cultural district.

5

Casa Mañana, *1958*
3101 W. Lancaster Avenue
A. George King & Associates
Reviving the original 1936 "house of tomorrow," a hastily built open-air coliseum with revolving stage, this facility's clear-span aluminum geodesic dome sprang from the mind of R. Buckminster Fuller and the rolling mills of Henry Kaiser. Contractors completed the dome in 114 days.

6

Montgomery Ward Warehouse & Store,
    1928; 1937; 1963
2600 W. 7th Street
Since Dallas had the regional catalog distribution center for Sears, then Fort Worth naturally coaxed Montgomery Ward into the traditional intercity rivalry. The company outgrew its 1911 warehouse and moved to this Trinity River flood plain location in an enormous warehouse adaptation of Mission Revival. Remodeling in 1963 unfortunately removed its Alamo-esque entry pavilion.

7

North Holly Water Treatment Plant, *1917-54*
1500 11th Street
Joseph R. Pelich and others
City promoters in the early 1900s pursued a misplaced image rivalry with San Antonio, appropriating Mission Revival for a number of odd but well-executed designs. This complex of utilities, engineered by Hawley, Freese & Nichols and highlighted by Pelich's 1932 mission parapets, occupies a manicured setting below the central business district, just above the Trinity River near magnificent 1939 Lancaster Avenue Bridge.

8

Thistle Hill, *1904; 1910*
1509 Pennsylvania Avenue
Sanguinet & Staats
Cattle baron W.T. Waggoner celebrated the marriage of daughter Electra to A.B. Wharton with this 11,000-square-foot gift, originally a "world's fair classic" design with wraparound portico. Its purchase in 1910 by cattleman Winfield Scott resulted in more recognizable Colonial Revival styling and the upgrading of exterior materials. The restored house, large carriage house, and grounds now host occasional public functions.

9
Reeves-Walker House, *1908*
2200 Hemphill Street
Neither Italianate nor Queen Anne styling
had gone out of fashion for those who could
afford them in the early 20th century, though
the porte cochere and paired columns on
these pedestals hint at early Prairie influence.
Stockbroker William Reeves commissioned
the house, bought by grain merchant John L.
Walker in 1917.

10
Dulaney House, *1923*
1001 Elizabeth Boulevard
Wyatt C. Hedrick (attributed)
Elizabeth Boulevard features a collection
of the largest and best-preserved early 20th-
century houses in Fort Worth. Oilman
Richard Otto Dulaney commissioned this
Italian Renaissance villa of tawny brick and
green-tile roof on a prominent corner in this
still-fashionable neighborhood. Dulaney later
built the Sinclair Building downtown (see
Chapter 11) with similar flourishes.

11
Our Lady of Victory Academy, *1910*
3300 Hemphill Street
Sanguinet & Staats
This Collegiate Gothic edifice marked a
regional zenith in Catholic boarding schools,
housing an auditorium, chapel, classrooms,
and dormitories under one roof. The large
surrounding tract sustained dairy cattle and
other means of independence until new educational and religious buildings had emerged
by 1988. Historic Landmarks Inc. saved the
building in 1993.

12
Harris Residence, *1913*
4621 Foard Street
Julian and Vila Harris came from New
England to work with Julian's relatives, owners of nearby Cobb Brick Co. and the Cobbs
Orchard Addition development. The Harrises
owned a copy of Gustav Stickley's 1912 *More
Craftsman Homes* and built their two-story
cottage from one of its featured designs, using
Cobb's rustic clinker bricks. The subdivision
blossomed a decade later, and the Harris family lived here for 72 years.

13
**Alcon Laboratories, R.D. Alexander
    Administration Center,** *1987*
6201 South Freeway
Omniplan, Inc. (Dallas)
This three-building complex serves as an
elegant focal point for a one-hundred-acre
corporate campus. It organizes the campus
into stratified layers of masonry bases and
superbly articulated glazed upper floors. The
curvilinear facade fits comfortably within the
myriad angular and rectilinear buildings on
this campus of the world's largest manufacturer of ophthalmic products.

14
Charles M. Davis House, *1937*
2055 Ward Parkway
Robert P. Woltz, Jr.
Experimental houses with streamlined finishes
at the 1936 Centennial Exposition in Dallas
strongly influenced a handful of Moderne
proponents across the state. Davis had engineered one such house of concrete at Fair
Park, and Woltz worked with George Dahl
on the exposition, which was the likely origin
of this standout in an otherwise traditional
Berkeley Addition.

15
Sid W. Richardson Physical Science
  Building, *1971*
S. University Drive at Bowie Street
Paul Rudolph (New York); Preston M. Geren &
  Associates, associate architects

TCU began as a private school in Fort Worth
in 1869, growing steadily after affiliation in
1889 with the Disciples of Christ denomination and adopting the current name in 1902.
The city donated the beginnings of this campus in 1911 and local architects, including
Van Slyke & Woodruff, established a theme
of understated classical designs clad in blonde
brick. Beginning in 1971 with Paul Rudolph's
Sid W. Richardson Physical Science Building,
designers of national reputation brought bold
and modern facilities to University Drive. In
1982 the Chicago office of SOM designed
an award-winning addition to the 1924 **(16)**
Mary Couts Burnett Library, South University
Drive at Princeton Street, following the 1981
introduction of Kevin Roche – John Dinkeloo's
(17) J.M. Moody Building for Fine Arts
Communication. This 130,000-square-foot
facility houses decorative arts in its north
wing, which is connected by an octagonal
entry court to the south wing for speech and
broadcast media labs. Ventilation and haz-
ardous waste disposal add to the facility's
cutting-edge design. Most recently, Hardy
Holzman Pfeiffer designed the $12 million
(18) Walsh Center for the Performing Arts,
1998, with Pepsico Recital Hall's dramatic
geodesic-dome-like wooden acoustical shell
engineered by Jaffe Scarborough. Contextual
fidelity is manifested in the use of blonde
exterior brick and metal trim, as found in
other buildings on campus.

17
J.M. Moody Building for Fine Arts
  Communication, *1981*
S. University Drive at Cantey Street
Kevin Roche – John Dinkeloo (Hamden,
  Connecticut)

18
Walsh Center for the Performing Arts, *1998*
S. University Drive at Cantey Street
Hardy Holzman Pfeiffer (New York)

19
Fort Worth Botanic Garden, *1933-34*
3220 Botanic Garden Drive
S. Herbert Hare/Raymond Morrison
The garden's stunning axial cut through dense woods emerged from the city's 1912 purchase for parkland, and a 1930 landscape design by Hare. City Forester Morrison supervised 750 federally funded relief workers, including skilled stonemasons, who completed the bulk of work in 15 months. A number of recent additions augment this first-class natural preserve, including Kingley Wu's **(19a) Japanese Gardens,** 1970.

20
Round House Office Building, *1982*
3519 Vickery Boulevard
Moore Ruble Yudell (Santa Monica)
Named for long-vanished railroad services nearby, the Roundhouse Cafe occupied a sturdy building that survived its own origins. Conversion of the concrete-block structure to serve office functions brought an axial series of towers, each detailed in themes that announce the public entry, staircase, conference area, and mechanical systems. Moore Ruble Yudell also designed the 1982 **(20a) Townhouses** at 2600 McCart Avenue.

R. Greg Hursley

21
Marty Leonard Community Chapel at Lena Pope Home, *1990*
4701 W. Rosedale Street
Fay Jones + Maurice Jennings (Fayetteville)
Lena Pope's shelter for homeless children began in 1930 and is now a center for disturbed, abused and neglected adolescents.

The Leonard family, local department store founders and entrepreneurs, cajoled Fay Jones to emulate his 1980 Thorncrown Chapel on the property's open plain near a freeway. Jones responded with a resplendent landmark, his first cruciform plan and first use of brick piers, causing a self-contained experience of lofty trusses and indirect light.

22
Private Residence, *1952*
4808 Westridge Avenue
Edward Larrabee Barnes (New York)
Frank Sherwood, renovation
A number of Texas architects, particularly those exposed to Richard Neutra in the 1930s, utilized a system of load-bearing masonry walls supporting clear-span beams for orderly, open plans. Barnes specified local stone for a regional touch, in contrast with Hood Chatham's 1954 **(23) Private Residence,** 5102 Sealands Lane, a more universal reflection of another pioneer Modernist.

24
St. Peter the Apostle Catholic Church, *1997*
1201 S. Cherry Lane, White Settlement, Texas
Landry & Landry (Dallas)
Outside, this purely functional design delivers interior light through clerestories, and opens only onto the congregation's own parish plaza and school. Inside, the wife-husband firm evoked a number of historical references, including the octagonal baptistry plan, Southwestern mission illumination, and Romanesque banded brick patterns.

25
Westover Square Townhouses, *1986*
6400 Westover Drive, Westover Hills, Texas
Tod Williams & Associates (New York); Taft
   Architects (Houston); Duany Plater-Zyberk
   (Miami); Cass & Pinnell
David Schwarz (Washington D.C.), site
   planning
Since the 1920s the rough terrain of Westover Hills attracted affluent clients to its well-ventilated bluffs. For a few remaining difficult

lots, Schwarz developed guidelines appropriate to the picturesque neighborhood, with results ranging from temple forms to Prairie School elevations.

26
Private Residence, *1974*
1801 Deepdale Drive, Westover Hills, Texas
Paul Rudolph (New Haven)
Rudolph created a structural tour-de-force for this private estate that maintains scrupulous privacy. Massive cantilevers create dramatic points of interaction within this assemblage of rectilinear blocks that overlap and extend visual sight lines. Other notable projects nearby are **(27) Private Residence,** 1901 Canterbury Drive, Westover Hills, Texas, Emery O. Young, 1986, and **(27a) Private Residence,** 1900 Canterbury Drive, Westover Hills, Texas, FLW Foundation (Phoenix), 1985.

28
Private Residence, *1969*
1900 Shady Oaks Lane, Westover Hills, Texas
I.M. Pei & Partners (New York)
Triangular shapes dominate this 18,750-sq.-ft. residence that is sited on a prominent location within Westover Hills, a town surrounded by Fort Worth and containing many of the most prestigious residences in the area. The glazed sky-roof identifying the public living spaces of the residence was an early experiment that served as a precursor to the Louvre Pyramid and the Meyerson Symphony Center in Dallas.

29
Hall-Windfohr House, *1938; c.1952*
1900 Spanish Trail
John Staub (Houston)
Staub's adaptation of the Monterrey style, here on a rambling estate with native and imported vegetation, proved its popularity with quintessential Texan clients. Anne Burnett, granddaughter of Samuel Burk Burnett, was first married to a Mr. Hall and later to a Mr. Windfohr.

30
Bryce House, *1893*
4900 Bryce Avenue
Messer, Sanguinet & Messer
William J. Bryce came to Fort Worth as a bricklayer, eventually owning the Denton Press Brick Company and collaborating with Marshall Sanguinet on a number of developments. Bryce's Richardsonian Romanesque home also served as a stately mansion during his term as mayor, 1927-35.

31
Private Residence, *1890; 1894; 1906*
4729 Collinwood Avenue
Marshall R. Sanguinet
The architect built his own house as one of the first in this Arlington Heights plat, originally in Shingle style but altered after an 1893 fire and expanded with porte cochere and other changes in 1906.

32
Williams-Penn House, *1907-09*
4936 Crestline Road
Sanguinet & Staats (attributed)
This late "world's fair classic" mansion reveals the enormous popularity of such styling 15 years after its Chicago debut, and the reluctance of Sanguinet's firm to move his client into the 20th century. Henry Williams amassed a fortune in banking and pharmaceuticals, and sold his house in 1926 to oil executive John Roby Penn.

33
Private Residence, *1996*
1301 Humble Court
Lake-Flato (San Antonio)
Japanese influence in the form of decentral-
ized plan and harmony with the landscape is
unmistakable and, in fact, is based on travel
with the client in Nippon. However, through
clever use of steel framing, native stone walls,
and sheet-metal roofs, this oriental ensemble
becomes occidental hacienda.

34
Private Residence, *1956*
1200 Broad Street
Harris & Sherwood
Harwell Hamilton Harris had just left Austin
and the office of architecture dean at UT
when he met Amon Carter's daughter Ruth,
then married to Mr. Johnson and later to
Mr. Stevenson. For their palatial compound,
Harris drew heavily upon California's 1920s
Hollyhock House, and thus upon Frank
Lloyd Wright's curious amalgam of Japanese
and meso-American massing and landscapes.

35
River Crest Country Club Clubhouse, *1986*
1500 Western Avenue
Taft Architects (Houston)
Taft's monumental and rigidly symmetrical
epicenter of a sprawling golf course serves as
anchor and visual gateway to this exclusive
subdivision. Remnants of its 1911 predecessor
survive in a number of rustic stone walls and
bungalow shelters scattered across the system
of fairways.

36
Gartner House, *1930*
935 Hillcrest Street
John Staub (Houston)
Staub attached the functional areas of this
house, built for insurance executive Herman
Gartner and wife Elizabeth, behind a huge
Flemish gable acting as entry portico and red
brick mass against the lofty ceramic-tile roof.
Staub later designed the porte cochere wing.

37
Greenwood Mausoleum, *1957; 1971*
3100 White Settlement Road
Harwell Hamilton Harris (Dallas)
Harris' growing practice in 1956 included
respectful remodeling of one of Louis
Sullivan's ingenious banks in Minnesota.
Appropriating its broad, textured archway
motifs, he developed this massive, center-
court crypt to the specifications of morti-
cian John Bailey and made provision for
expansion through repetitive pavilions.
The second was added in 1971.

38
The Coliseum, *1908*
123 E. Exchange Avenue
Berkley Brandt (Chicago)
Ward Bogard, rehabilitation, 1986
By the end of the 19th century, this enormous
open-span building became an American
icon, where communities witnessed performing arts, speeches, and spectacles such as,
in 1918, the world's first indoor rodeo. Its
Mission-Revival details attracted hoards to
the annual Fat Stock Show through 1942,
and a $3 million rehabilitation ensured a
place in the stockyards' newer role as family
entertainment venue.

39
Livestock Exchange Building, *1903*
131 E. Exchange Avenue
Thomas E. Woodward & Associates (Dallas),
*   renovation, 1978*
Fort Worth first appeared where the Trinity
River entered a line of frontier outposts, but
by the 1890s it boomed where meat-packing
met the railroads. This elegant building held
offices of stockyard patrons, and remains an
instantly recognized symbol of Cowtown,
with its California mission details and Molly,
the cast-metal longhorn steer in its parapet.

40
Motorola Paging Infrastructure
**   Headquarters,** *1997*
IH 820 at N. Beach Street
HOK (Dallas)
If the downtown Post Office was once a temple of communication for the 20th century,
this sprawling complex is a pantheon for mil-
lennial wavelengths. Here the custom design
and manufacturing of paging hardware and
software extends across 360,000 square feet,
insulated from busy roadways by a lake and
its geyser fountain.

41
Burlington Northern & Santa Fe Railway
**   Operations Facility,** *1996*
2400 Westport Parkway West
KVG/Gideon Toal; Lake-Flato (San Antonio)
Huge company mergers, changing technolo-
gies, and dynamic markets brought two old
Fort Worth railway servers from colder cli-
mates to build their new partnership near
Alliance Airport and regional intermodal
operations there. This facility, reminiscent

of depots past, controls trains across two-
thirds of the United States.

42
U.S. Bureau of Printing and Engraving
**   Western Facility,** *1992*
9000 Blue Mound Road
Kirk Voich Gist
Complementing a new Federal Reserve
regional office in Dallas, the symbiotic
manufacturing of currency takes place in
this $66-million fortress, which includes a
19,000-sq.-ft. vault. Employees and visitors
enter a pyramidal skylit lobby paved with
the bureau's heroic seal.

Jim Winn

43
Alliance Airport Control Tower, *1992*
Alliance Boulevard
Aubry Architects/PGAL Architects (Houston)
Just as the Bass family has recently lavished
development upon downtown, the Ross Perot
family has cast a vast new commercial empire
across north Tarrant County. Heart of air
operations is the FAA tower, an eye-holding
geometric-formula solution recalling Wright's
Romeo and Juliet windmill at Taliesin. Its
conical nerve center serves as a teflon-clad
radar device. Nearby are examples of free-
trade technology at immense scale: **(44)**
American Airlines Maintenance Facility,
designed by Corgan Associates/LA Fuess
(Dallas), 1991, and **(45) Alliance Gateway**
Warehouses, designed by Gromatsky-Dupree
(Dallas), 1994-1999.

13 The Hinterlands

Within an hour's drive from downtown Dallas or Fort Worth lie North Texas' most remarkable architectural landmarks, the county courthouses of the single decade of the 1890s. Getting there is half the fun. The architectural tourist should eschew the Interstates for the back roads that course the variety of rolling prairies and post oak woodlands to the county seats. These market towns tend to be found on 35-mile spacings – about as far as the farmers of that day could travel by horse and wagon to conduct Saturday business.

Town organizers of the mid-1800's frequently set aside public squares, not for open space, but (in keeping with Anglo-American tradition) as prominent sites for preeminent civic buildings. These often were situated at the highest point in the county, lending great symbolic prominence to the importance of county government. Similarly, the typical gridiron plan of streets was often positioned so that the courthouse terminated the vista of a main street in one or both orientations. The public squares became a focus for community life – cotton grading, cattle auctions, political rallies, and legal business – and mercantile establishments saw the business potential of being on the square. Some of the squares are still thriving; buildings are lovingly restored and occupied by antique shops, cafes, and coffee houses. But because the new highways tend to bypass the old downtowns of the county seats, other squares are declining, their businesses succumbing to new Wal-Marts on the edge of town.

The courthouses themselves are magnificent polychrome masonry temples "rising above the town like a cathedral in France," according to an early *Harper's* article. All those featured in this Guide were constructed between 1885 and 1913. Some are Second Empire, others are Richardsonian Romanesque. In the latter style, James Riely Gordon was perhaps the most accomplished architect. His cruciform-plan Ellis and Wise County Courthouses challenge even the exuberance of Richardson's Trinity Church, and borrow much in form and detail from the masterpiece. The palette of materials is native – pink granite from Burnet, red sandstone from Pecos, creamy limestone from north of Austin -- and the carved ornamentation is a delight.

The booming courthouse town of Denton is home to a concentration of work by O'Neil Ford, who lived in Denton during his childhood and college years before moving to Dallas. One of his very best works, the simple and crafty Little Chapel in the Woods (with Arch Swank, 1939) is on the campus of Texas Women's University. First Christian Church, although later, is in a similar straightforward spirit. It and Ford's Denton Civic Center combine his knack for structural invention with his usual regional warmth.

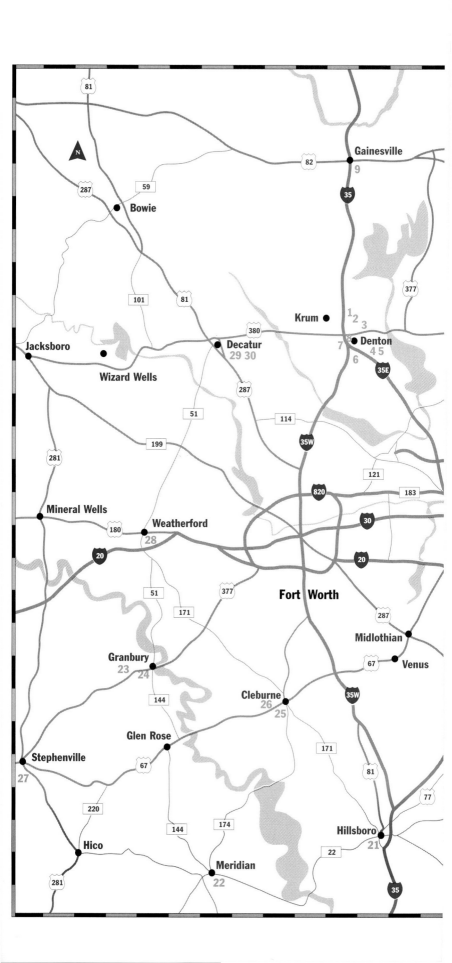

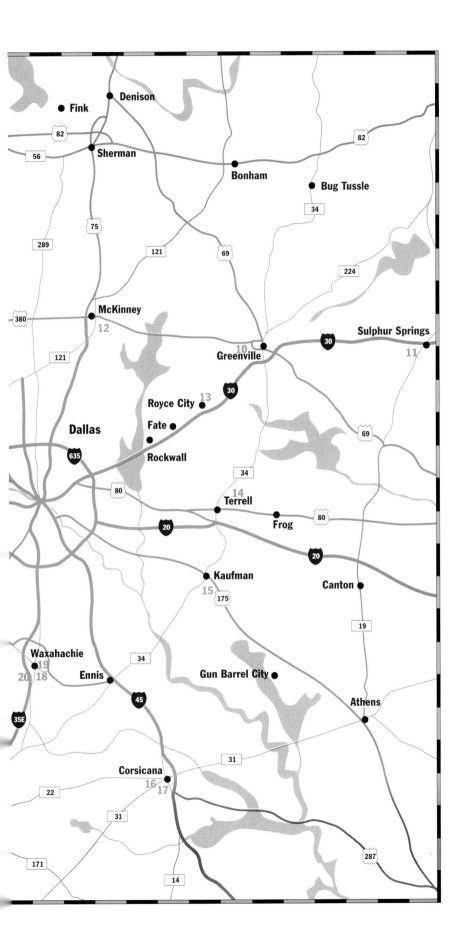

13 The Hinterlands

Willis Winters

1
Little Chapel in the Woods, *1939*
Texas Woman's University, Denton, Texas
O'Neil Ford & Arch Swank
This much-admired jewel by Texas regional-
ists Ford and Swank is an exercise in noble
simplicity employing beautifully laid exterior
fieldstone and great interior parabolic arches
in variegated brick. The chapel was built
through a collaboration of National Youth
Administration construction trainees and art
students at the college who produced carved
and stenciled woodwork, wrought-metal fixtures, and stunning large-scale, stained-glass
windows. In the **(2) First Christian Church,**
1203 N. Fulton, 1959, Ford stretched the
simplicity of his early design ideals. Brickwork
supports a hyperbolic paraboloid concrete
roof, a technique engineered by Felix Candela
of Mexico City and also used in Ford's manufacturing facility for Texas Instruments.

3
Emily Fowler Public Library, *1949*
502 Oakland Street
Wyatt C. Hedrick (Fort Worth)
O'Neil Ford, addition, 1969
Ford, Powell & Carson (San Antonio),
    addition, 1980
In 1969 Ford added a wing, with his arid-
climate touches, to Hedrick's original building. Then his firm designed an addition with
a landscaped atrium. Of note is the stacked
tile wall at the front of the building.

4
Denton Civic Center, *1966*
321 E. McKinney Street
O'Neil Ford (San Antonio)
Wire-spoked bicycle wheels inspired Ford's
roof engineering here, a suspension system
of pipes and prestressed cables radiating outward from the center and leaving the large
interior space free of internal supports. In
Ford's nearby **(5) Municipal Building,** 1967,
he took the concrete, steel and glass common
to Modern buildings and wove them into a
delicate geometry around a tranquil sunken
courtyard. Denton's city hall features his
additional palate of tile pavers, wood lattices,
and doors carved by brother Lynn Ford. Also
part of the city hall complex for Denton, the
(6) Municipal Swimming Pool, 1965, combines diffused sunlight with an encompassing
berm to define an oasis in the city center.

7

Denton County Courthouse, *1896*
Town Square (Dallas Drive at Oak Street)
Denton, Texas
W.C. Dodson (Waco)
Dodson's Denton commission demonstrates
a reluctant but robust transition from his
typical Second Empire mode toward
Romanesque styling. Despite Denton's recent
urban growth, it remains centered on the old
courthouse, restored in 1985 by Ward Bogard
& Associates of Fort Worth.

8

**Lucille "Lupe" Murchison Performing Arts
Center,** *1999*
University of North Texas, Denton, Texas
Hardy Holzman Pfeiffer (New York), KVG
Gideon Toal (Fort Worth)
Reorientation from city to freeway for this
established campus is at least partially accom-
plished through the faceted zinc-clad roof of
UNT's 1,000-seat concert hall and 400-seat
lyric theater. Flanking service wings accom-
modate offices and rehearsal rooms.

9

Cooke County Courthouse, *1911*
Town Square (Main Street at Commerce Street),
Gainesville, Texas
Lang & Witchell
This firm that excelled in steel frame skyscrapers developed a courthouse model beginning in 1910 at Harris County and culminat-
ing with Cleburne's **(26) Johnson County
Courthouse,** 1912. The Gainesville version
presents a Beaux-Arts exterior, but dazzles
with its elaborate Prairie School interior.

10

Hunt County Courthouse, *1929*
Town Square, Greenville, Texas
Charles H. Page (Austin)
Hunt County celebrated its heyday of cotton
production with this transitional Neo-Classical
temple clad in brick and terra-cotta, by a prolific public-building architect. Stepped-back
massing dominates its block-sized real estate,
just leaving room for a grand stairway.

11

Hopkins County Courthouse, *1894*
Town Square, Sulphur Springs, Texas
James Riely Gordon (San Antonio)
Gordon found great success by importing
H.H. Richardson and Boston's Trinity Church
to the blackland prairies of Texas. Here one of
his smallest designs typifies a formula of Texas
granite and sandstone, re-entrant entries, and
a massive tower as airshaft.

12

Heard-Craig House, *1900*
205 W. Hunt, McKinney, Texas
James Flanders (Dallas)
Flanders typically danced on the edge of
transition from one popular mode to another,
in this case Queen Anne to Prairie four-
square. Symmetry is a hint rather than a rule
in this lofty residence built for merchant
Stephen Heard.

13
First United Methodist Church, *1904*
701 Church Street, Royce City, Texas
James Flanders (Dallas)
As with many architects of his generation,
Flanders developed successful formulas for
institutional buildings, most notably with
Methodist congregations. His signature three-
tower church joined progressively taller spires
with Gothic-arched windows and a lace of
decorative shingles or plaster work.

14
Matthew Cartwright House, *1883, 1894*
505 Griffith Avenue, Terrell, Texas
C.A. Gill
Local rancher and banker Cartwright updated
Gill's initial work in 1894 through "World's
Fair Classic" details popularized by the
Chicago exhibition. One- and two-story
columns, wraparound galleries, and
balustrades are topped by a bristling tower.

Willis Winters

15
Church of the Merciful Savior, *1909*
South Jackson Street, Kaufman, Texas
Walter H. Slack (New Bedford, Massachusetts)
This storybook Episcopal sanctuary, combining New England church proportions with
Norwegian medieval *stavkirche* woodcraft,
presents a stained cedar exterior and sumptuous natural oak interior. The architect pur-
portedly issued the plans in 1902 to a
congregation at nearby Forney .

16
Navarro County Courthouse, *1905*
W. 3rd Avenue at 13th Street, Corsicana, Texas
James Flanders (Dallas)
Corsicana separated business and government
by placing the courthouse on a hill several
blocks from Main Street and railroad tracks.
Here Flanders followed his own Beaux-Arts
muse, reserving the interior for a fantasy of
Art Nouveau glass and Sullivanesque plaster.

17
Mills Place Addition, *1924-1930s*
Mills Place Drive and West Park Avenue,
Corsicana, Texas
David Williams (Dallas) and others
Developed upon the 19th-century estate
of Congressman and U.S. Senator Roger
Quarles Mills, its subdivision in 1924 offered
large exclusive lots for 38 impressive residences.
Outstanding architectural results include
works by flamboyant designer Williams: the
(17a) Francis B. McKie House, a rambling
1930 masonry villa at 613 Mills Place, and
the **(17b) William and Bessie Stroube**
House, his clever 1927 adaptation of
Monterrey Style at 1115 West Park, brim-
ming inside with handcrafted detail. Also in
Corsicana (west end of Park Avenue West) is
the **(17c) F.N. Drane House,** 1931, Williams'
remarkable collaboration with O'Neil Ford,
a low-slung villa of stone and tile, with
wood carvings by Ford's brother, Lynn.

Texas stones supports an astonishing level of
detail, from a Salamanca-influenced Spanish
Romanesque tower to the carved faces of
local citizens on red sandstone capitals.

19
"Rosemont" Residence, *1894*
701 South Rogers, Waxahachie, Texas
James Riely Gordon (San Antonio)
Credited to Gordon during his local courthouse commission, this Queen Anne monument of woodcraft, accented with exotic
Moorish domes and curves, anchors the
town's Bullard Heights southside district.
Mill owner Burt Ringo Moffitt built the
landmark and multiple outbuildings as a
tribute to his rose-cultivating wife, Eliza.

Willis Winters

18
Ellis County Courthouse, *1895*
Town Square, Waxahachie, Texas
James Riely Gordon (San Antonio)
Beloved backdrop for Texas-grown movies
and cover model for Southwestern Bell
Telephone books, Gordon's masterpiece is
perhaps the most recognized courthouse in
the state. His Richardsonian palette of earthy

Willis Winters

20
Waxahachie Abstract Company
(Citizens National Bank), *c.1896*
Rogers Street at Main Street
Messer, Sanguinet & Messer (Fort Worth)
Marshall Sanguinet had just finished working
for courthouse architect James Riely Gordon
when he joined the Messers for this bank
design. Its Richardsonian presentation mirrors
the courthouse, but in different materials of
contrasting white limestone and red brick.

21
Hill County Courthouse, *1892*
Town Square, Hillsboro, Texas
Wesley Clark Dodson (Waco)
ArchiTexas, reconstruction, 1999
Dodson's multiple courthouse commissions of
this period centered a large courtroom under
the wood-frame, pressed-metal-clad clock
tower. His finest example, at Hillsboro, burned
in 1992, but reemerged within and upon its
surviving limestone walls through careful
reconstruction by ArchiTexas, of Dallas.

22
Bosque County Courthouse, *1886, c.1935*
Town Square, Meridian, Texas
James J. Kane (Fort Worth)
Like many of the courthouses built in the
boom that followed 1881 legislation allowing
bond financing, Meridian's temple of justice
utilized abundant local stone. Unfortunate
strip-down remodeling in the 1930s removed
the Second Empire roofs and clock tower.

24
Hood County Courthouse, *1892*
Town Square, Granbury, Texas
W.C. Dodson (Waco)
A compact version of Dodson's highly
successful model, this landmark is surrounded
by one of the state's best 19th century
squares. Preservation in the 1970s of
Granbury's city center helped inspire the
national Main Street revitalization program.

25
Layland Museum (Carnegie Library), *1905*
201 North Caddo, Cleburne, Texas
Smith & Moore
Steel-magnate Andrew Carnegie supplied
$20,000 and a list of requirements, resulting
in a temple of learning remarkably similar to
other such libraries nationwide. The town, in
turn, agreed to sustain its new facility,
although this example is now a museum. The
Beaux-Arts classical interior, including second-
level auditorium and stage, remains unaltered.

Willis Winters

23
Granbury Opera House, *1886*
116 East Pearl Street, Granbury, Texas
A seven-bay shop front of local limestone
with imported pressed-metal highlights
demonstrated the expandability of Italianate
styling during Granbury's business heyday.
Restoration in the 1970s ensured continued
bookings of live entertainment.

Willis Winters

26
Johnson County Courthouse, *1913*
Town Square, Cleburne, Texas
Lang & Witchell (Dallas)
Early in the 20th century, a county seat
needed a landmark edifice, and a railroad
town needed a clock tower, both supplied
here with drama and sophistication.
Abstraction of classical details, along with
Sullivanesque plaster and geometric art glass
inside proved this firm's awareness of the
Prairie School, but the domed tower exposed
intimate knowledge of Finnish architects
Eliel Saarinen and Lars Sonck.

27
Erath County Courthouse, *1892*
Town Square, Stephenville, Texas
Gordon & Laub (San Antonio)
James Riely Gordon's early partnership
with D. Ernest Laub resulted in several
Romanesque courthouses, and perfection in
this case of the central masonry tower as ven-
tilation shaft. Rehabilitation in 1987 reflected
public affection for a grand civic monument.

28
Parker County Courthouse, *1885*
Town Square, Weatherford, Texas
Dodson & Dudley (Waco)
W.C. Dodson developed his Second Empire
model, with large second-floor courtroom
and tiered central tower, through this commission in an early partnership. Although
the interior is heavily altered, its majestic
limestone elevations dominate a major
crossroads and traffic roundabout.

Willis Winters

29
Wise County Courthouse, *1896*
Town Square, Decatur, Texas
James Riely Gordon (San Antonio)
Gordon's design closely resembles his better-
known work in Waxahachie, but the Decatur
temple features a predominance of pink
granite, topped by red tile shingles and, with
a hint of the coming Beaux-Arts tidal wave,
circle-motif balustrades above corner entries.

Willis Winters

30
Daniel Waggoner Mansion, *1883*
1003 E. Main Street, Decatur, Texas
Headquarters for Waggoner's million-acre
Three-D Ranch brought an Italianate villa
to the West Texas frontier, on a hillside just
outside of town. Waggoner's son William
Thomas later discovered oil on the ranch and
provided, along with their 16-room, six-bath
crested mansion, a stereotype for Texans as
depicted in the 1955 movie *Giant*.

Index/Selected References

Selected References

"A Texas Fifty." *Texas Architect* 39 (Nov-Dec 1989).

Barna, Joel Warren. *The See-Through Years: Creation and Destruction in Texas Architecture and Real Estate 1981-1991.* Houston: Rice University Press, 1992.

Caswell, Jon, Ed. *A Guide to Older Neighborhoods of Dallas.* Dallas: Historic Preservation League, 1986.

Cohen, Judith Singer. *Cowtown Moderne.* College Station: Texas A&M University Press, 1988.

Dallas Chapter/American Institute of Architects. *Dallasights.* Dallas, 1978.

_____. *The Prairie's Yield.* New York: Reinhold Publishing Corp., 1962.

Dillon, David. *Dallas Architecture 1936-1986.* Austin: Texas Monthly Press, 1985.

Galloway, Diane and Kathy Matthews. *The Park Cities: A Walker's Guide and Brief History.* Dallas: SMU Press, 1988.

George, Mary Carolyn. *O'Neil Ford, Architect.* College Station: Texas A&M University Press, 1992.

Greene, A.C. *Dallas: The Deciding Years – A Historical Portrait.* Austin: The Encino Press, 1973.

Henry, Jay C. *Architecture in Texas 1895-1945.* Austin: University of Texas Press, 1993.

Holmes, Maxine, Ed. and Gerald Saxon. *The WPA Dallas Guide and History.* Dallas: University of North Texas Press, 1992.

Kelsey, Sr., Maris P. and Donald H. Dyal. *The Courthouses of Texas.* College Station: Texas A&M University Press, 1993.

Little, Carol Morris. *A Comprehensive Guide to Outdoor Sculpture in Texas.* Austin: University of Texas Press, 1986.

McAlester, Virginia and Lee. *A Field Guide to America's Historic Neighborhoods and Museum Houses, The Western States.* New York: Alfred A. Knopf, 1998.

McCarthy, Muriel Quest. *David R. Williams, Pioneer Architect.* Dallas: SMU Press, 1984.

McDonald, William L. *Dallas Rediscovered.* Dallas: The Dallas Historical Society, 1978.

Roark, Carol. *Fort Worth's Legendary Landmarks.* Fort Worth: TCU Press, 1995.

Robinson, Will. *Reflections of Faith: Houses of Worship in the Lone Star State.* Waco: Baylor University Press, 1994.

_____. *Texas Public Buildings of the 19th Century.* Austin: University of Texas Press, 1974.

_____. *The People's Architecture.* Austin: Texas State Historical Association, 1983.

Tarrant County Historic Resources Survey: Near North Side and West Side, Westover Hills. Fort Worth: Historic Preservation Council for Tarrant County, Texas, 1988.

Tyler, Ron, Ed. *The New Handbook of Texas.* Austin: The Texas State Historical Association, 1996.

Winters, Willis C. *The Lakewood Houses of Clifford D. Hutsell.* Dallas: Preservation Dallas, 1996.

Photography Credits

Cover	Craig Blackmon
page ii	Craig Blackmon
page 10	Richard Payne
page 36	Willis Winters
page 56	Craig Blackmon
page 72	Craig Blackmon
page 84	Craig Blackmon
page 100	Willis Winters
page 114	Craig Blackmon
page 134	Scott Frances ESTO
page 150	James F. Wilson
page 164	Jim Hedrich
page 178	Craig Blackmon
page 188	Craig Blackmon
page 200	Willis Winters